M000214543

ENDOR~~~~~~~~ ~~~

RELIGIOUS REFUGEES

"Religious wounds can be deep, hard and painful wounds to heal. To recover, it's help-ful to know it's not just that we hurt, but why and where we're hurting. What I love about *Religious Refugees* is the balanced approached Mark Karris takes toward spiri-tual recovery by respecting both domains of theology and psychology. Well-studied in each field, Karris professionally and compassionately helps readers make peace with their faith without losing their minds or sacrificing dignity. Whether you're nurtur-ing your own religious journey or guiding someone who is, this book is a must-read!"
— **Jennifer Knapp**, singer/songwriter, author of *Facing the Music*

"Austrian theologian Frederick von Hugel (1852-1925) compared the church as an organization to the bark on a tree. Bark is dead wood, but it protects the dynamic life surging within the tree from disease, dehydration, death. Mark Karris has gifted all of us with a valuable resource on how to deal with the crusty bark while tapping into the sap and living off the fruit of the tree."
— **Leonard Sweet**, bestselling author of *Rings of Fire* and distinguished professor at Drew University, Tabor College, George Fox University, and Evangelical Seminary

"If you're in the middle of what Mark Karris calls the D/R Process (deconstruction and reconstruction of your faith), you absolutely need Mark's new book. With the wisdom of a philosopher, the skill of a counselor, the tenderness of a gentle parent, and the accessibility of an old friend, Mark meets you where you are, walks with you, and points to a beautiful way forward, what he (and Mother Teresa) call "the simple path." This is a powerfully helpful book and needed now more than ever!"
— **Brian D. McLaren**, author of *The Great Spiritual Migration*

"To all who have had their faith shaken to the core—and these days, their number is swelling—Mark Karris' *Religious Refugees* is a precious gift! With refreshing hon-estly, unconventional insight and tender grace, Mark helps struggling and former Christians discern a path forward to a more wholistic, fulfilling, and compelling kind of faith in Christ. How I wish I'd had a guide like *Religious Refugees* when I went through my painful faith crisis as a young person! If you or someone you care about is facing a faith crisis, this is the book you're looking for!"
— **Dr. Greg Boyd**, Senior Pastor, Woodland Hills Church, author of *Inspired Imperfection: How The Bible's Problems Enhance Its Divine Authority*

"Coming from a background that held the biblical text as a rigid rulebook, providing scripted answers to all life's messy concerns, to seeing Scripture as an ancient, ambiguous, and diverse text bursting at the seams with wisdom for the unscripted journey called life is often a lonely, exhausting, and deeply unsettling process. Mark Karris's *Religious Refugees* is a compelling guidebook for religious refugees seeking the wisdom and tools to move beyond unhealthy views of God and walk this sacred path toward spiritual and emotional maturity."

— **Pete Enns**, Professor of Biblical Studies at Eastern University and the author of *How the Bible Actually Works, The Sin of Certainty,* and *The Bible Tells Me So*

"A person could read five different books on the deconstruction and reconstruction process of leaving religion, or they could read, *Religious Refugees: (De)Constructing Toward Spiritual and Emotional Healing* by Mark Karris. As someone who has spent twenty years counseling people in religion recovery and life after religion, I recommend you read Mark's book. Not only has he walked this journey himself, he brings a depth of insight and wisdom as a theologian, philosopher, and psychologist. Making peace with your religious past, healing from spiritual abuse, detoxing from harmful religious indoctrination, navigating spiritual crisis, new ways of approaching life's existential questions, cultivating new tools and mindsets for personal liberation, and exploring non-religious spirituality are some of the critical areas that Mark skillfully addresses in *Religious Refugees*. I consider this book an invaluable and comprehensive resource for any person who is in the process of deconstruction and reconstruction."

— **Jim Palmer**, author of *Notes from (Over) the Edge,* and *Inner Anarchy*

"If you are interested in truly understanding what is going on with Christianity in America today so that you can build something new for yourself or others, then *Religious Refugees* is for you. With an eye toward productive, reconstructive actions from the beginning, Mark Karris deftly lays out what is so unsatisfying about modern, institutional religious expressions and how they can be re-imagined and rebuilt."

— **Josh Packard**, co-author of *Church Refugees: Sociologists Reveal Why People Are Done With Church but Not Their Faith*

"Mark Karris explores the journey many of us have taken through the winding and treacherous road of faith deconstruction. The experiences he shares will either be familiar to you, or I guarantee are familiar to someone you love. Karris offers a wise and practical way forward through a compelling integration of psychology and spiritual formation that will undoubtedly instill hope for religious refugees on the journey of reconstruction. Some of the stories in this book will be challenging to hear and some will certainly give you the knowledge you aren't alone. I highly recommend this book!"

— **Stephanie Williams O'Brien**, author of *Stay Curious: How Questions and Doubts Can Save Your Faith*

"Using hard fought wisdom combined with astute study and cheeky humor, Mark Karris crafts a framework for making meaning of the disorienting season of deconstruction. He not only offers insights for understanding the unique deeper journey, he also offers clinical insights and practices to reconstruct after deconstruction, to move from old bound ways into new spaces of freedom. Engaging with this book is like having a wise and loving friend accompany you, validating your experience and encouraging you to take steps toward wholeness and love. Karris uses descriptive, creative, imaginative language that helps to hold what has been previously hard to grasp. *Religious Refugees* should be required reading for all spiritual directors, therapists, pastors, indeed all who are walking with others in the deeper journey."

– **Lacy Finn Borgo**, DMin, spiritual director, teacher, and author of
Spiritual Conversations with Children: Listening to God, Together

"If you feel that you are standing on the ground of yesterday's temple feeling forlorn and covered by ash, Mark Karris has written this book for you. In *Religious Refugees,* Mark provides a map and invaluable practices to aid your journey across the vast religious wasteland to a new and healthy spiritual horizon. This book is as timely as it is useful"

– **Alexander John Shaia**, author of *Radical Transformation:*
The Four-Gospel Journey of Heart and Mind

"When leaving authoritarian Christianity, you need three things: a book of sacred depth and compassionate wisdom that describes something close to your experience, a spiritual director who listens without judgment, and a therapist trained in trauma relief. *Religious Refugees* will be that book for many of you who are "done" with repressive Christianity and the one you will want to take with you to spiritual direction and therapy!"

– **Rev. Teresa Blythe,** founder of the Phoenix Center for Spiritual Direction
and author of *Spiritual Direction 101: The Basics of Spiritual Guidance*

"Many of us have seen our original foundation for faith in God crumble in the face of reason, experience, science, or personal crises. Mark Karris knows what that's like personally. He also knows reconstruction and transformation is possible after faith has been deconstructed. Using personal experience, scripture, neuroscience, and common sense, Karris blazes a life and God-affirming path for those seeking an authentic life of love."

– **Thomas Jay Oord**, author of *The Uncontrolling Love of God* and *God Can't:*
How to Believe in God and Love After Tragedy, Abuse, and Other Evils

"Mark Karris writes with authority about a subject every person with "Post-Traumatic Church Syndrome" needs—the deconstruction and reconstruction of faith. Both personally and professionally informed, this book is sure to be a resource for individuals struggling with matters of spiritual health and healing."

– **Rebecca Riley Moyer,** author of *Post-Traumatic Church Syndrome: One Woman's Desperate, Funny, and Healing Journey to Explore 30 Religions by Her 30th Birthday*

"Many today are on a necessary spiritual journey of deconstruction that leads to the inevitable question: What now? Karris responds to that essential question with wisdom, compassion and vision as he invites those on the journey to keep going, find healing, discover wholeness and move toward the reconstruction of a fresh spirituality worth living."

> – **Michael Hidalgo**, Lead Pastor of Denver Community Church and author
> of *Changing Faith: Questions, Doubts and Choices About an Unchanging God*

"The oft-misused term "deconstruction" has become popular among spiritual refugees to the point of overplay. It's like a second conversion we may not even choose. It's more like a disorientation we undergo—for some liberating and others traumatic (literally). And there's not really a travel guide through the wilderness that follows. Until now. Mark Karris has traversed the D/R journey and in this book, traces an exceptional way forward that combines cutting-edge psychological research, sound theology, and wise practical lessons from his own life experience. Honestly, he had me at "self-compassion is the key." From that point, I knew I could trust him. I will be recommending Karris' incredible work broadly."

> – **Brad Jersak**, PhD, author of *A More Christlike Way*

"Mark Karris' *Religious Refugees* does an unbelievable job in bringing the dechurched into a profound understanding and love for the God that Jesus reveals. Mark courageously clears away the religious brush so we can get at the core of Jesus' words and ultimately the heart of God. What a compassionate guide describing the journey to know God more fully and love God more deeply."

> – **James P. Danaher**, Professor Emeritus of Philosophy, Nyack College, and
> author of *Jesus' Copernican Revolution: The Revelation of Divine Mercy*

"The Church is a place of great beauty and healing. It can also be a place that traumatizes, excludes, and abuses. Mark Karris recognizes the tragic beauty of the church and seeks to bring God's healing touch to those whose faith has been deconstructed and are looking for a credible and healthy way to follow Jesus, a pathway of theological, spiritual, and relational reconstruction. I am grateful for Mark Karris' gentle, yet firm and direct, approach to the church and acceptance and affirmation of those who are seeking new visions of Christianity. Thank you, Mark, for this inspirational and healing text!"

> – **Bruce Epperly**, author/co-author of over forty books, including
> *The Mystic in You: Discovering a God-filled World*

"Mark has written an engaging and helpful book detailing the many stages and frustrations of deconstructing your Christian beliefs amidst disillusionment and offers tentative ways of reconstructing your beliefs by questioning your assumptions about the nature of God and specific Christian doctrines. A welcome contribution."

> – **Paul Matthew Harrison**, author of *Deconversions: My
> Journey Through Evangelical Christianity*

"Mark Karris has written a wise and powerful book. Without exempting himself from a single page, he writes as a fellow traveler on the deconstruction/reconstruction journey. The reader never feels scolded or lectured to, but guided by someone whose mind is as sharp as his spirit is therapeutic. For all of us who grew up in the church and struggled to save it (and ourselves) from self-inflicted death by a thousand doctrinal cuts, this book washes over the reader like a balm in Gilead. Take, read, study—and then talk about it in community. Something new is coming. Mark Karris has seen it, and he wants us to see it to. As a charter member of heretics united, whose name is legion, I say, "Well done, good and faithful servant, well done.""

– Rev. Robin R. Meyers, PhD, retired senior minister of Mayflower UCC in Oklahoma City, Distinguished Professor of Social Justice Emeritus from Oklahoma City University, and author of *Saving God from Religion: A Minister's Search for Faith in a Skeptical Age*

"As a pastor in a community filled with 'religious refugees,' I deeply appreciate and see the immense value in the wisdom that Mark Karris has been able to provide in this new book. Karris journeys alongside of the reader as a compassionate guide, seeking to offer the insights and realizations that were birthed from his own experiences of deconstruction and reconstruction. Mark helps you make sense of the grief, confusion, and anger involved in deconstruction and then masterfully integrates theology, psychology, and personal experience to aid others in charting a new path ahead. If you're burnt-out and tired of religion, this book will provide some much-needed replenishment for your soul."

– Danny Prada, pastor of Heartway Church

"Mark has given us a very vulnerable, authentic and raw description of his deconstruction journey. He also shares his personal reconstruction process as a potential model for others willing to do the hard work of healing their wounding "splinters." In citing diverse research about those leaving church and their stories of trauma, he provides a valuable compendium of information that documents the dimensions of this phenomena. Mark's story will be a light in the 'dark nights' for others on their faith journey. The dechurched need to know they are not alone; they are not failures; they are not without the love of God guiding them on the journey and Mark gifts them with that assurance."

– Paul D. Fitzgerald, DMin, Founder of HeartConnexion Seminars and Spiritual Director

"In my work as a spiritual director and friend to people experiencing a painful faith deconstruction, I am always grateful for material that helps give language and hope for the messy and beautiful road to greater freedom in our faith. Mark Karris is right—the numbers are legion—and so many are seeking tools and guides to not just survive but thrive. *Religious Refugees* will help readers not only find themselves in the story but also offers what so many are seeking—tangible and accessible ways forward."

– Kathy Escobar, co-pastor of The Refuge, and author of *Practicing: Changing Yourself to Change the World* and *Faith Shift: Finding Your Way Forward When Everything You Believe is Coming Apart*

"There is an incredible scarcity of resources for people who are leaving the church, seriously questioning their beliefs, and trying to figure out how to live in the real world. It's for this reason I welcome such helpful books, such as Mark Karris' *Religious Refugees*, into the slowly growing collection of supplies available to this rapidly increasing demographic."

> – **David Hayward**, the NakedPastor, cartoonist, author, and coach

"Anyone who has been through spiritual Deconstruction already knows how painful it can be. Thankfully, Mark Karris has written a book that not only explains WHY it hurts, but helps to guide us out of the darkness and into the light of spiritual Reconstruction. We need more books like this one, and more compassionate guides like Mark, to show us the way forward."

> – **Keith Giles**, bestselling author of *Jesus Undefeated*

"The deconstruction/reconstruction is painful. It's lonely. And there are no pat answers to the questions that haunt us. But there is, thanks to Mark Karris, at least a life-affirming guide book to give us hope. The authentic spiritual journey that begins with resentment and bitterness, can end in extraordinary grace, fierce compassion, and transformational forgiveness."

> – **Dr. Roger Bretherton**, Associate Professor, University of Lincoln
> (UK), Chair of the British Association of Christians in Psychology

"Deconstruction can be such a jarring experience. It can feel as though the ground is giving way beneath your feet. Oftentimes, the only comfort is having people you can trust who can guide you and assure you that you're not alone. Mark is one of those people. This book promises to be an incredible comfort and resource for those traversing the daunting journey from deconstruction to reconstruction. Mark's competencies in theology and counseling, along with his personal journey, provide a powerful combination in this book. In reading, you will find profound insight, as well as incredible concrete steps to walk this deconstructive/reconstructive path. Well done, Mark!"

> – **Ben DeLong**, author of *There's a God in My Closet:*
> *Encountering the Love Who Embraces Our Skeletons*

"A beautiful manifesto of hope for this generation of deconstructed disciples. Thorough, encouraging, and cutting edge, *Religious Refugees* is precisely what the present generation of ex-vangelical, divinely-inspired dissidents needs. Karris not only offers a helping of solidarity in this incredible work, but also offers hope and a way forward. Get it, read it, and get it into the hands of every faithful questioner you know. I think it is a prophetic masterpiece!"

> – **Jeff Turner,** author of *The Atheistic Theist: Why There*
> *is No God and You Should Follow Him*

"This book is incredibly helpful for those who have been hurt or have become alienated from the church. For those who no longer find comfort practicing their faith in traditionally conservative types of churches and find it difficult associating with others in the church due to rejection, this book is extremely valuable. The strong point of the book is helping the dechurched experience the profound reconciliation, healing, and forgiveness of God as revealed through, in, and by Christ. This book is liberating for all Christians, including those who might find some types of deconstruction too radically dismantling of orthodoxy."

– **Fr. Thomas Acklin**, O.S.B., Senior Fellow of the St. Paul Center for Biblical Theology, spiritual director, and author of *Spiritual Direction: A Guide for Sharing the Father's Love*

"If you've recently become aware that the God who loves you moves in a *more* redemptive and mysterious way than your church once told you and you are scared out of your mind for what that means for your journey ahead, then with the utmost care, wisdom, and competence, Mark wrote this book for you. I am excited at how many lives this crucial book will touch!"

– **Meggie Lee Calvin**, bestselling author of *I Am My Own Sanctuary: How A Recovering Holy-Roller Found Healing and Power*

"Mark Karris' *Divine Echoes* was great. *Religious Refugees* is just as good. Scratch that; it may be better! I can't exactly put my finger on why, but I think it's simply because of just how needed a book like this is. With so many people struggling with their faith, deconstructing things to the point where they can't find a semblance of what they once knew because of all the theological rubble, in comes Karris with perhaps the timeliest book I've read in the last five years."

– **Matthew J. Distefano**, author, blogger, podcaster, and musician

"This is the book is the best book on the topic of deconstructing and reconstructing one's faith I have ever read! Millions of Christians are changing their beliefs and leaving church. But they're not abandoning Jesus. Instead, they are following Jesus on a journey of rediscovery. Mark is a faithful guide who tells fellow travelers where they may be going, what they may expect, and how to navigate the twists and turns on the road ahead. If you have doubts and questions about your church, your faith, your theology, or your place in this world, read *Religious Refugees*. This excellent book will shed light on your path."

– **J. D. Myers**, RedeemingGod.com, author of *Nothing but the Blood of Jesus*

"In *Religious Refugees*, Mark Karris, relying on his experience as an ordained minister and licensed therapist, leads us on a journey to understand why people are leaving the church, what deconstruction looks like, and the internal wars that accompany such a journey. Then, with tender care, he helps us establish a 'way forward.' My only regret about this book is that I didn't have it sooner. Get yours today!"

– **Karl Forehand**, podcaster, speaker, and author of *Apparent Faith: What Fatherhood Taught Me About the Father's Heart*

All rights reserved. No part of this book may be used or reproduced, stored in a retrieval system, or transmitted in any form or by any means, electronic, mechanical, photocopying, recording, scanning, or otherwise, without written permission from the publisher except in the case of brief quotations embodied in critical articles and reviews. Permission for wider usage of this material can be obtained through Quoir by emailing permission@quoir.com.

Copyright © 2020 by Mark Gregory Karris.

First Edition

Cover design and layout by Rafael Polendo (polendo.net). Cover image by storyblocks.com.

Snippets from Part II and III adapted from *Season of Heartbreak©* by Mark Gregory Karris. Published by Kregel Publications, 2017. Used by permission. All rights reserved.

Excerpts used from *Death and Life by a Thousand Cuts©* by Mark Gregory Karris. Published by *Counseling and Family Therapy Scholarship Review,* 2019. Used by permission. All rights reserved.

All Scripture quotations, unless otherwise indicated, are from the Holy Bible, New International Version®, NIV®. Copyright © 1973, 1978, 1984, 2011 by Biblica, Inc.™ Used by permission of Zondervan. All rights reserved worldwide. www.zondervan.com.

Scripture quotations marked KJV are from the King James Version of the Bible. Scripture quotations marked NLT are from the New Living Translation Version of the Bible, Holy Bible: New Living Translation. Wheaton, IL: Tyndale House Publishers, 2004. Print. Scripture quotations marked NRSV are from the New Revised Standard Version of the Bible, copyright © 1989 by the National Council of the Churches of Christ in the U.S.A. Used by permission. All rights reserved.

To protect the privacy of individuals, names and identifying details have been changed. As a licensed therapist, the author takes confidentiality seriously and has completely changed details of any story when necessary.

ISBN 978-1-938480-55-3

This volume is printed on acid free paper and meets ANSI Z39.48 standards.

Printed in the United States of America

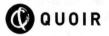

Published by Quoir
Orange, California

www.quoir.com

RELIGIOUS REFUGEES

(DE)CONSTRUCTING TOWARD
SPIRITUAL AND EMOTIONAL HEALING

MARK GREGORY KARRIS

ACKNOWLEDGMENTS

I am grateful for my wife and son who inspires and energizes me to write for more of a shalom-filled future. I am profoundly thankful for Nathan Ray Jones and his editing prowess. Special thanks to Andrew McFadyen-Ketchum for helpful editing, feedback, and encouragement. I want to give a big shout-out to Quoir Publishing for believing in me. Most importantly, I want to express tremendous gratitude to all the religious refugees whose precious voices are strewn throughout these pages.

TABLE OF CONTENTS

INTRODUCTION

For inquisitive, status-quo-offending folks like me, being in the church has been like staying in a long-term abusive relationship. The problem is I love the girl so much. At least, I think it's love. Maybe it's infatuation. Perhaps it's Stockholm syndrome. I'm not sure. Anyway, I stayed because I had this stubborn hope she would change. I dreamt of being the valiant hero who came along, swept her off her feet, and dramatically transformed her into the stunning princess she was meant to be. Unfortunately, nothing I did seemed to work. Over the years, things just seemed to get worse.

Time after time she abused me. She verbally assaulted me. She tried to control me. She manipulated me. She gaslighted me. She stabbed me in the heart with a rusty and serrated knife. But like a lovesick idiot, I kept coming back. I thought, "Maybe tomorrow it will be different. Maybe tomorrow she'll love me for who I am, in all my theological quirkiness." But she didn't. And after some reflection, I finally came to the realization we needed a break.

After many years of incessant doubts, deep reflections, and inner angst, I finally had enough gusto to depart from my passionate lover: the church. The decision to take a momentary break was made in an instant, but the deconstruction process had been going on for a while. For a long time, I felt like I'd been trudging through a murky pond with alien-looking fish taking nips at my legs while I was stepping around jagged, rusty nails on the pond floor. It is never easy to leave behind what you consider to be a part of your identity and it certainly wasn't for me.

To be honest, whether we realize it or not, we are all in the process of deconstruction. I think most spiritual seekers are. Death and deconstruction make up the water in which we all swim. We suffer the cuts of a thousand deconstructive deaths in our lifetime. And it's from those cuts that reconstruction, transformation, and new life can emerge. Some of us can masterfully deny death's deconstructive sting by engaging our superb defense mechanisms. And we can keep the cognitive dissonance at bay through denial, rationalization, and busyness. But whether we like it or not, nothing is static. Nothing remains the same. All of life, including our theology, is fluid. We are on the roller coaster of life and death, moving swiftly on tracks that are revealed to us only a few feet at a time.

Like many other God-lovers who are outside-the-box thinkers, I have been told I am going to spend eternity in Hell. People have fiercely shouted at me, calling me a heretic and a false teacher. They've told me I have no right to teach others about the Bible. Some have even told me I am deceived and probably have demons that need to be cast out. Others have scolded me and confidently declared God was angry at me. They warned that punishment would be knocking at my door in the months to come if I didn't change my ways.

One of the most important paths I have taken in my own reflective journey involved writing a book on petitionary prayer. Writing allowed me to clearly articulate the need for deconstructing what I had always been taught on the subject. I knew in my bones there had to be a way to pray for others that was more effective, did not increase suffering in the world by making people complacent, and didn't make a good God look really, really bad. When it was published, I excitedly handed it to the pastors at the new church I was attending, hoping it would invite dialogue. As an ordained pastor, I was hoping that, in time, I would be invited to the table to serve faithfully alongside them. Instead, they passive-aggressively kicked me out of the church. "Mark, you can stay as long as you want, but know that you could never serve in any capacity—and that includes teaching or preaching."

They could not handle my messing around with the sacred cow of prayer. They were squeamish at my questioning of whether every passage of Scripture should be taken literally. That moment was the final unraveling of my last frayed, fragile piece of straw, and it helped me make the difficult decision to take a long-overdue hiatus from religious life as I knew it.

It seemed I wasn't alone. Over time, I met a tsunami of "dones" who were on the run just like me (You know it's a movement when society coins a technical term for us). Dones are swiftly moving far away from their once-beloved Christian faith—at least from the Christian faith as they knew it. They have had enough of religion, particularly of noxious, exclusionary religion. They are distancing themselves from a religious framework that depicts a God who created a fiery place called Hell where people are tormented for eternity for not believing the right things about Jesus. They also can't hold their dissonance at bay when asked to proclaim, "Yes, God as depicted in the Old Testament—a God who killed babies, destroyed millions of animal and human lives in a flood, burned people alive for not following orders, and commanded people to be stoned to death for disobeying him—is the same God fully manifested in Jesus."

They are sickened by the fact that their tribe subtly or overtly excludes people based on race, gender, sexual orientation, class, and differing theological viewpoints. They can't understand how their pastor, or religious family members, can actively support leaders who act in ways, and share viewpoints, that are in complete contradiction to Jesus' way of life. They have simply had enough.

Some have other reasons for struggling with their relationship with God. They find their faith frazzled because the simple, pat Christian clichés and responses to life's difficulties and complexities seem more appropriate for third graders in Sunday school than for mature, adult believers. Being told that "God is sovereign and in control of all things" simply doesn't make sense amidst the rampant evil and suffering they see all around them. They think a God who is in control of all things and still wills and *allows* a woman to be raped, a dear friend to be murdered, a pandemic to ravage people, or an innocent child to die from cancer, is simply untenable as part of some master plan.

This season of questioning one's faith and religious beliefs can be excruciatingly painful. I know it was for me. It feels like walking on a wobbly waterbed rather than on solid ground. It feels unsafe and dangerous. It feels lonely and isolating. The fear of rejection from God and from others feels suffocating as emotions such as shame, guilt, fear, anger, and sadness take center stage. The consequences of such a prismatic array of emotions are sleepless nights, hiding, pretending, unhealthy addictions, isolating, ruminating, and engaging in a whole variety of other coping behaviors.

Many Christians refer to this unsettling time in their lives as the Deconstruction/Reconstruction (D/R) journey. The D/R journey is shorthand for those who are going through a seismic shift in their religious and spiritual orientation. Of course, most people, throughout the course of their lives, change a religious belief here and there. They may also experience some growing pains along the way. The D/R season, however, is so palpable that many experience a profound sense of disorientation. I call the signs and symptoms of this disorientation *Religious Disorientation Growth Syndrome* (RDGS). Symptoms include:

1. Doubting or denying one's religious beliefs that were once held as true.

2. Subtle or intense anxiety about a person's relationship with God.

3. Increase of painful emotions, such as anger, loneliness, shame, guilt, sadness, and despair.

4. Isolation and criticism (feared or realized) from members within their own family and/or religious community.

5. Existential angst concerning a person's identity and future self.

RDGS causes people to suffer emotionally, spiritually, and even physically for more days than they care to experience. And, paradoxically, this disorientation can be a powerful catalyst that leads to tremendous emotional, mental, and spiritual *growth*. I have witnessed countless people experience profound transformation after wisely traveling through their D/R journey.

Throughout the twentieth century and even today, this process is common at Christian colleges, but is typically confined to people in their 20's. It is so common that, as recently as August of 2019, Christianity Today ran an article entitled "Doubt Your Faith at a Christian College? That's Part of the Process," which noted that this phenomenon traces all the way back to the 1920's. The difference now is that people going through this struggle at Christian colleges are surrounded by a community of other students with a shared experience. At first, the experience feels isolating, but after one or two late-night discussions with their buddies, those students quickly realize they're not alone. Even the professors, who often play the role of mentor, have usually been around long enough to anticipate this phase.

But for those of us who attended a secular university, didn't attend college, or who simply visited or revisited this experience later in life, it is riddled with isolation and disorientation in a very profound way.

There is a fear associated with walking away from the church—an even greater fear in walking away from the God we once knew. Like childbirth or the loss of a loved one, it is a painful process. There is no getting around that.

This book will explore the D/R journey through the lens of psychological research, theology, philosophy, and, most importantly, practical real-world experiences of those who are going through—and have gone through—this often painful and confusing process.

As a licensed therapist and ordained pastor who has gone through the D/R journey, I'm offering a compassionate guide for those who desire to successfully navigate the complexities of their faith and learn how to increase their emotional and spiritual vitality. The main thrust of this book is intended to help Christians on the journey to spiritual formation and emotional healing. While this book can be beneficial to read individually, it's transformational potential is best experienced in community, especially with discussion questions at the end of each chapter. It is also ideal for compassionate counselors, spiritual directors, or pastors working with those who are struggling with spiritual concerns.

The late and brilliant Rachel Held Evans wrote:

> There are recovery programs for people grieving the loss of a parent, sibling, or spouse. You can buy books on how to cope with the death of a beloved pet or work through the anguish of a miscarriage. We speak openly with one another about the bereavement that can accompany a layoff, a move, a diagnosis, or a dream deferred. But no one really teaches you how to grieve the loss of your faith. You're on your own for that.[1]

I am writing this book because of my passionate desire that no one feels alone during their difficult D/R journey. The feeling of aloneness is one of the most brutal aspects of the deconstruction, healing, and reconstruction process. If I can reduce the overall confusion of those on the D/R journey, if I can decrease their bewilderment of why they are experiencing such strong emotions, and if I can offer them a map of possible ways to grieve and move forward toward healing and reconstruction, then I will have accomplished my goal.

I realize I am a very situated human being. I am a white, middle-class, cisgender, heterosexual, finite male who can only speak from my limited and particular experiences. So, I take great caution to *guide*, and not *dictate*, what folks should believe or behaviors in which they should engage. I make claims about God along the way, but please know that I make them *not* as someone who knows definitively. Like everyone else, I understand and see God through a cracked, darkened, and kaleidoscopic glass. Nonetheless, with a limited understanding of God, I forage in partial blindness for God-truths and forge ahead.

I have divided this book into three parts. In Part I, "The Big Picture," I focus on the larger dynamics involved in why people, like us, are struggling with our Christian heritage and what the process from unshakeable faith – to deconstruction – to reconstruction looks like. The opening chapter is where I trace out an overview of the research into the stark reality of those who are leaving the church (or certain forms of the church). This includes some of the more anecdotal evidence regarding why the *dechurched,* or *religious refugees,* are leaving (or being forced to leave). I use Chapter Two to outline the different stations of the D/R journey (otherwise known as stages, phases, or seasons). Confusion is one of the key elements that accompanies leaving our former understanding of faith and/or our former faith community. With that in mind, the purpose of this chapter is to provide a map of where we may have been before the deconstruction process, where we find ourselves amidst deconstruction, and the hope that reconstruction provides.

I have titled Part II, "The Inside Scoop." It explores the inner experiences and processes that are common for those of us on the D/R journey. The goal is to make sense of the emotional and spiritual mayhem so that, as we go through the process, we can grieve well, heal, and eventually engage in the reconstruction phase of our spiritual journey.

Chapter Three tackles the beginning stage of our radical religious upheaval, particularly by looking at how newly emerging beliefs battle against our old beliefs, creating a type of violent internal war—a cognitive dissonance we must resolve if we are to stay sane. Two case studies from my own life will serve as a means of fleshing out this conflicting process: one dealing with the topic of divine sufficiency; and the other, divine violence. In Chapter Four, I give an overview of painfully familiar experiences of hurt, grief, and trauma that the dechurched go through in their faith shift. I spend Chapters Five and Six diving deeper into our psyches and exploring the topics of emotions and defenses. Spiritual health and emotional health are two sides of the same coin. Learning to make sense of our emotional experiences, and the various defensive mechanisms this journey triggers, is hopefully a welcomed gift that helps us wisely navigate the spiritual frenzy we find ourselves in.

Part III, "The Way Forward," is where I delve into the types of pathways formed by connections, practices, and principles that will hopefully prove instrumental for your own deconstruction and reconstruction journey and, ultimately, for the rest of your life.

I begin this third part by discussing the blessing of an Unholy Huddle in Chapter Seven. It is instrumental to gather fellow travelers who journey with us into the unholy abyss of the deconstruction process, while at the same time embracing the so-called *unclean* aspects of who we are—those difficult, shameful, and painful parts of our stories that we try to hide. Chapter Eight invites us all to love and be kind to ourselves in the midst of our spiritual struggle—a topic often neglected in Christian churches. Self-compassion is the key here, so the primary focus of this chapter is on the research and everyday application behind this life-changing attitude and practice.

In Chapter Nine, I turn to barriers that hinder intimacy with God. Two important obstacles typically keep people from a loving relationship with God during the shifting sands of the D/R journey. One has to do with our fight or flight system and the other has to do with our "soul wear," or internal image of God. I have found a practice, from the field of neuroscience and informed by memory reconsolidation, to be particularly helpful for deconstructing and reconstructing healthier images of God.

With Chapter Ten, I venture into specific theological territory that was key to my own D/R journey. Here I touch on the unconventional love of God—God's perfect, moment-to-moment, uncontrolling, and co-operative love—and how that concept proves useful in working through the theological minefield of such topics as: our image of God, evil, petitionary prayer and social justice concerns, miracles, and trusting God. In Chapter Eleven, I come back to more practical suggestions in which I share a few uncommon prayer practices that myself and others have found helpful in connecting with God— namely centering prayer; weeping and crying out; and imaginative, meditative prayer.

Chapter Twelve brings us to the topic of forgiveness. Forgiveness is a powerful gift that releases us from the poison and bitterness that unforgiveness cultivates within us. I outline a research-based model of forgiveness that can enable us to reconstruct and re-story—or rewrite the story of—our spiritual journey with more energy and clarity. I close out our discussion by venturing into the power of love, service, and living according to our unique values in Chapter Thirteen. Wherever we land theologically, once the dust settles from our deconstruction and reconstruction journey, we want to make sure that our lives are immersed in the beauty of love and service to others.

I encourage you to take in the good, savor what you can, and vigorously spit out the bad. There are enough replicas and automatons in the world. Ultimately, my desire is for you to be true to who you are and where God—who is Love—is leading you.

For most of my life I was lost. I was always searching and looking for home. Perhaps, so I thought, I would find it in a house ... or in a community ... or in a spouse... or in a mentor ... or in a successful career. It took me a long time to realize that home is not a building, it is not a location, it is not an achievement, and it is not found in another person. I am home, and home is within me. I carry home wherever I go. If you're a religious refugee and migrating away from toxic religion, my hope is that, as you read this book, you may find the same home within yourself. May you live out of that home where Love resides, not just for your sake, but also for the sake of others.

PART I

THE BIG PICTURE

This section will examine the research of sociologists and the lived experiences of those who left the church hurt, traumatized, and disoriented. It is not a reactive attempt to blame the church for the problems experienced by a subgroup of Christians. Exceptional churches, incredible pastors and leaders, and other Christ-like Christians have changed countless lives for the better. I am merely attempting to better describe, be curious about, and empathically understand those whom researchers call the "dechurched." Additionally, in this section, I will venture into the various possible stations of experience the dechurched go through—from faith, to doubt, to wavering, to slightly evolving, to disorientation, to angst, to saying goodbye, and finally to becoming a new kind of Christian. Sometimes having a map makes traveling a little bit easier.

CHAPTER ONE

WE ARE LEGION!

....

*"Trauma is personal. It does not disappear if it is not validated.
When it is ignored or invalidated the silent screams continue
internally, heard only by the one held captive. When someone
enters the pain and hears the screams, healing can begin."*

— DANIELLE BERNOCK

....

No one wakes up and excitedly tells themselves, "Today is the day I
want to start unraveling my faith, throwing myself into the throes
of social rejection, despair, and one of the most painful seasons of
my life." Rather, it's like realizing, halfway through the day, that you
have a massive, splitting headache—it just happens. Sure, we could
continually deny, suppress, and repress our doubts, troublesome questions, and piercing splinters of toxic beliefs, but the energy it would
require simply becomes too costly. The D/R journey comes at us like
a snowball, slowly moving down the hill in a harrowing winter, building and building and finally crashing through our psyche, leaving us
completely disoriented.

It's not your fault that your faith is shaken and your core beliefs
about God, the church, the Bible, and yourself are shifting. Life
happens. Shift happens. Life changes with or without our gracious

consent. In every generation people think, "We are the only ones going through this." However, throughout history there have always been deconversions, reconversions, renovations, reformations, and people who have experienced the agonizing dark night of the soul. Yet, at our present time in religious history, some unique dynamics are brewing that are worthy of reflection. Like a check engine light in a car, they may be warning us of deeper issues bubbling beneath the pristine and polished Christian-surface that point to the origin of the D/R journey so prevalent for folks today.

Around six to ten thousand churches die each year.[1] Those are staggering numbers, aren't they? Sadly, a lot of heartbroken pastors, leaders, and congregants are behind those statistics. One of the fastest growing religious trends in America, when it comes to religious polls, is the rise of the "nones." These "no-religion folk" have catapulted from 12 percent in 2003 to 21 percent of all adults in 2017.[2] They were typically raised without a religious upbringing and can identify themselves as atheists, agnostics, or as those who feel pretty neutral about religion. Nearly two-thirds of all young adults, who once were attending church regularly, have dropped out at one time or another.[3] Twenty-seven percent of Americans consider themselves "spiritual but not religious," a category which has increased eight percentage points in the past five years. On top of all of that, a large percentage of Americans, thirty-four percent to be exact, are "dechurched."[4] The dechurched are the "been there, done that, got the t-shirt" folks (we will talk more about them in a minute).

These present-day religious shifts validate what the late Phyllis Tickle emphasized in her book, *The Great Emergence*. According to Tickle, "The Great Emergence" is a radical and much-needed shift, occurring every five hundred years or so, when the church has an epic theological, doctrinal, ecclesial, and spiritual rummage sale.[5] These shifts and statistics are all a part of what Brian McLaren calls *The*

Great Spiritual Migration. In a positive and hopeful tone, McLaren opines that spiritual migration is "not *out of* our religions, but out of our cages and ruts, not as jaded ex-members, but as *hopeful pilgrims moving forward in the journey of faith.*"[6] Diana Butler Bass, a connoisseur of religious culture and trends, writes, "People believe, but they believe differently than they once did. The theological ground is moving; a spiritual revolution is afoot. And there is a gap between that revolution and the institutions of religious faith."[7]

IDENTIFYING THE DECHURCHED

I wrote this book in light of the growing number of "dechurched," so let's explore their experiences in more detail. Sociologists Josh Packard and Ashleigh Hope, authors of the book *Church Refugees: Sociologists Reveal Why People Are Done with the Church but Not Their Faith,* performed one hundred in-depth interviews with people who were disengaging with the church. You probably hate labels as much as I do, but see if you can identify with Packard and Hope's brief definition of the "dechurched": "They're done with church. They're tired and fed up with the church. They're dissatisfied with the structure, social message, and politics of the institutional church, and they've decided they and their spiritual lives are better off lived outside of organized religion."[8] From their interviews, Packard and Hope were able to narrow down common themes as part of people's reasoning for distancing themselves from, or leaving, the church:

- They wanted community … and got judgment.

- They wanted to affect the life of the church … and got bureaucracy.

- They wanted conversation … and got doctrine.

- They wanted meaningful engagement with the world ... and got moral prescription.[9]

Kathy Escobar's *Faith Shift: Finding Your Way Forward When Everything You Believe is Coming Apart* adds a few helpful subcategories for those disillusioned by church.[10] She describes *spiritual refugees* as "men and women of all ages and backgrounds whose beliefs have shifted, whose certainty is lost, and whose faith expression is now displaced." She describes *church burnouts* as "people who may have given their lives to congregations, ministries, or theological perspectives, but their passion has waned." And her third subcategory, *freedom seekers*, are people who are "tired of feeling stuck and caged by the systems they have lived in. They long for more."

David Kinnaman is the president of the Barna Group, a respected research group that explores the intersection between faith and culture. In his book, *You Lost Me: Why Young Christians Are Leaving Church ... and Rethinking Faith*, Kinnaman and his colleagues gathered data from hundreds of thousands of interviews from over a period of twenty-seven years. The purpose of their study was to explore people's faith, church experiences, what pushed them away from the church, and what connections to the church they have chosen to keep.

Kinnaman explains his own subcategories he uses to describe the group he calls "the dones."[11] *Nomads* are frustrated and disillusioned with Christianity, but they are not angry and hostile. They have left the church and are ambivalent about faith, yet remain genuinely spiritual. *Prodigals* are angry. They are done with the toxic religious aspects of the Christian faith. Now that they have left, they are free to be their true selves. And then the *Exiles* are still in it to win it, or at least in it to make a difference in the church they love. They are also passionate about the world they live in. However, exiles are profoundly disappointed and confused with the lack of loving and creative cultural engagement by many Christians. Here are the broad reasons

Kinnaman lists for why Christians distance themselves from church (or ditch it altogether):

> They find the church to be *overprotective*, stifling creativity and cultural engagement. *Shallow* with their formulaic slogans, easy platitudes, and proof texting. *Anti-science. Repressive*—religious rules. *Exclusive*—they want to find common ground, even if that means glossing over real differences. *Doubtless*—the church is not a place to express doubts.[12]

Do any of these labels and descriptions resonate with you? Whether you consider yourself a Done, Spiritual or Religious Refugee, Church Burnout, Freedom Seeker, Dechurched, Nomad, Prodigal, Exile—or whatever label or non-label you feel best describes you—the reality is the same: You are going through (or have gone through) a profound shift that has catapulted you into a season of doubt, distressing emotions, anxiety-provoking and painful social realities, and existential and identity concerns.

You are not alone! We are legion! We are many. And, for good reason.

Christians, including church leaders, unfortunately engage in a whole lot of victim blaming. They harshly blame confused, doubting, and hurting Christians, calling them "lost," "heretics," or simply "wayward sinners." Instead of optimistically considering that the large number of people on the deconstructive journey are part of Spirit-inspired events such as *The Great Emergence* or *The Great Spiritual Migration*, they call the mass exodus of dechurched Christians *The Great Apostasy* or *The Great Spiritual Damnation*. Some church leaders blame Satan, false doctrine, a corrupt culture, and the dechurched themselves while neglecting to take a broader and systemic look at themselves, their decisions (and the choices of those who came before them), or other possible causes of the D/R phenomenon.

Here's the deal: You are *not* a bitter, prodigal son or daughter who chose to take all the beautiful things you learned, along with your rich inheritance of the Christian faith, only to squander it in some big debauched and satanic soirée. Instead, the well of your heart has been poisoned by various elements of current Christian principles, practices, policies, and attitudes at the hands of well-meaning churches.

REASONS FOR DITCHING THE CHURCH

I've compiled my own list of the main reasons people are becoming disenchanted with the church. Based on the qualitative and quantitative data (stories, interviews, assessments, and statistics) compiled by sociologists and psychologists, this list also includes the stories of many people I have personally engaged with as a therapist, friend, or on social media as I listened with compassion.

POLITICS AND BUREAUCRACY

In the face of church politics and bureaucracy, some people feel they are unable to make a difference in the church. For example, some have powerful gifts to share, but because they're divorced, gay, too young, too old, not attractive enough, not articulate enough, not white enough, not abled enough, not educated enough, or simply female, they are not allowed to uniquely contribute to the life of the church. When bureaucracy or politics play too much of a role in the church, people can often feel left-out and sidelined. They feel as if there is an in-crowd and an out-crowd. They may have tried to start a ministry, or to engage in a particular area of the church, but for reasons they never understood (unless the reasons have been made explicit), it felt like they were perpetually trying to chisel through a thick brick wall. Ultimately, this has led to their disillusionment and feeling as if they don't belong.

Jason was educated, a gifted communicator, and passionate about God and the health of the church. Although he considered the Bible his sacred text, he was not able to teach, preach, or lead any kind of workshops because he held slightly different views on the inspiration of the Scriptures. He stated, "I feel stuck. I feel heartbroken. I feel like there is something wrong with me. The leadership knows my character. They know I love Jesus. They know I have been trained in homiletics and have performed workshops in the community. But why is it that, if I believe slightly different ideas about the formation of the Bible, I am automatically out of the running for using my gifts in the church? It is just sad."

Cora, a 66-year old woman who participated in Packard and Hope's study, had been a Christian for decades. She shared her story about how the church's politics and bureaucracy got in the way of her following the passion God placed in her heart:

> It was fine as long as I was doing what I was told. As long as I was plugged into what someone else had put forth, it was no problem. But when I wanted to do something on my own, it was a whole other story. The last thing I tried to do was start a little group to help the elderly people in our congregation, where we would just go and mow lawns and wash windows and do things for people who needed it. But that never came about. There were so many rules and regulations just to mow lawns that I just backed off of it. It's weird, because we were such a big church you would think this little thing would be easy. But I talked to the missions minister and he told me to come up with a name for my group, propose a budget, write out a mission statement, come to the board hearing and figure out a way to report back every month. I told him, "Really? I just want to mow lawns. Why do we have to do all that?" He told me the board didn't like things going on in the church unless they could oversee it. And here's the kicker, they weren't offering me anything in return. No budget, no help recruiting or organizing. It was just about control. So by that time, I was like "Okay, never mind. I'll just do this on my own."[13]

Since church politics and bureaucracy are overseen mostly by men, there can be strains of misogyny and patriarchy, interlaced with theology, that are oppressive to women and marginalized people. During a recent "Truth Matters Conference," John MacArthur, the poster-child of conservative evangelical Christianity, was asked to give a word association about Beth Moore, a well-known female Bible teacher. MacArthur's response was, "Go home." He then proceeded to say, "There is no case that can be made biblically for a woman preacher. Period. Paragraph. End of discussion." On the recording, you can hear some members of the crowd laugh in delight and excitedly clap.[14] Unfortunately, this view is all too common in the American church (and churches abroad). Many Christians, however, who value dialogue and equal opportunities based on call and gifting, don't find MacArthur's sentiments to be a laughing matter.

CLONE WAR SYNDROME

There are other Christians who left the institutional church because they couldn't overcome the obstacle I call *Clone War Syndrome.* Some churches think they are in a perpetual war with the surrounding culture and with other expressions of the church. Diversity is feared and stifled for the comfort of homogeneity. These types of churches are in the business of creating clones. There is no room for messy dialogue, discussion, and dialogical encounters with people of differing theologies or ways of being in the world. It would be too anxiety-provoking and messy, especially for churches that crave safety and neat theological and moral boxes. Churches suffering from Clone War Syndrome are religious machines that seeks to bake cookie-cutter Christians.

Regrettably, the cost of fear-based cloning is the stifling of creativity and curious souls. Writing about the dechurched who left the church, Packard and Hope observed, "They felt the ability to ask questions and explore various aspects of their faith wasn't supported in the church, and it was a major factor in their decisions to leave."[15] With the power of the internet, people now have the ability to travel to exotic, cognitive-dis-sonance-producing, theological places with the click of a button. Stale, simple, myopic, and repetitive Christian teachings on Sunday mornings are no longer going to reach the hearts and minds of many church goers. So, discouraging complex and innovative theological thought is like pouring coarse sand in the fuel tanks of the souls of thoughtful and creative people. It's true, however, that some people like things simple. But inquisitive others seek to traverse the wonders of the mind and soul, as well as all creation, for glimmers of the Divine.

In the *Bielefeld-Based Cross-Cultural Study*, another large study, researchers examined folks who deconverted from Christianity and came to similar conclusions about the unique personality and spiritual traits that prevent people from becoming passive sheep who accept church as usual. The researchers engaged in one-hundred interviews with those who left the faith either in Germany or the United States. They summarized the results:

> The ideal deconvert would be characterized by the predominance of gains: a person who open-mindedly explores new religious orientations is ready for inter-religious encounter, rejects fundamentalism, authoritarianism and absoluteness claims, has advanced and transformed in faith development, and, especially when living in the United States, owns a strong sense of personal growth and autonomy.[16]

As you can see, any type of cloning, constriction, authoritarianism, and close-mindedness is anathema to some Christ-loving folks. It is not about being overtaken by sin. It is about a spiritual ache and an evolution of consciousness. It is about people who will not settle for God-in-a-box and who desires to embrace the wondrous God of the cosmos and beyond. Here, from the Barna study, are some additional criticisms Christians gave as they unknowingly diagnosed their church with Clone War Syndrome:

- Christians demonize everything outside of the church.

- Christians are afraid of pop culture, especially its movies and music.

- Christians maintain a false separation of sacred and secular.

- Christians do not want to deal with the complexity or reality of the world.[17]

Some pastors and leaders may chalk it up to "rebellion" and "hardheartedness to the timeless truths of God's word," but they are clearly missing the opportunity to patiently and lovingly engage with these expansive, creative, and spiritual souls. These are the same souls Packard and Hope refer to as previously being "the most dedicated people in any congregation."[18] Some church leaders don't realize that, by their refusal to change, adapt, and recontextualize the gospel message and other sacred doctrines, they are forcing people out of their congregations and creating religious refugees—those who are leaving their home of religion and migrating toward healthier emotional and spiritual destinations. They are inadvertently creating a new mission field. My hope is that church leaders will patiently take time to earnestly learn about the dechurched by being in close relationship with them. And I encourage church leaders to learn their language and operating system and humbly pray about how best to love them and incorporate them into the life of the church.

MORAL PRESCRIPTIONS

Some of the dechurched faced obstacles of moral prescriptions. These Christians were aching to be the Spirit-led answer to the ills and injustices they saw in the world. They desired to be empowered, encouraged, and equipped to do good works in the community. Instead, all they heard on Sunday mornings was how to engage in a four-step sin-management plan to avoid the frightening fires of Hell. Or, if it wasn't sin-management, they were repeatedly told that the earth was going to burn down in the end times "so why be a tree hugger when people's souls were at stake?" For dechurched people, sermons were geared more toward personal holiness and eternal-torment-prevention rather than inspiring the congregation to fiercely, potently, and tangibly love others in their communities.

Packard and Hope, writing about the angst of the dechurched caused by this moral prescription dynamic, explained, "Preaching a message about the evils of drinking seemed like so much small change compared to big-ticket items such as poverty, racism, and gender inequality."[19] In other words, people's God-sized passion for issues of social justice (or simply, *God's justice*) was so great that they felt forced to leave because of the myopic, exclusivist, and narrow vision of the church. Harper, a 43-year-old Christian female, shared, "Instead of existing for the world, they exist for themselves. And that to me didn't match the biblical narrative; it didn't match what I could see was needed and possible out in the world."[20]

Diane, a retired pastor whose ministry focused on issues of social justice, wrote:

> Why am I "done?" As an older woman, I don't find "community" in the church, especially because my friends have moved on to other, more relevant communities, or have themselves become "dones." I don't have my faith nurtured by the words, don't like being preached at, and frankly, just don't believe in the institution any more as a force for good in the world. Even before I went to seminary, I questioned much of the church but felt I could do more good by working within the system than by throwing rotten tomatoes at it. And I did work within the system for decades to try to help bring about social justice

on an institutional level. But I was just one person and eventually got tired of butting my head up against the wall. I found I did much more good and lived out my faith working with and for the disenfranchised of my local society outside the walls of the church.[21]

SHALLOW-ITIS

Another obstacle is what I call shallow-itis. For many dechurched people, church became a place where you faked it to make it and *not* a place to be real and to authentically feel. The canned sermons, repetitive prayers, and the let's-sing-the-same-upbeat-chorus-fifty-times worship songs, encouraged people to ignore their angst, pain, hurt, lament, questioning, and doubts. The problem is when church is all about positivity, singing solely upbeat music, and hearing shallow responses to complex individual and societal problems, some Christians just can't stomach it.

Rahim, a Christian who chose to leave the institutional church due to his encounters with "fake Christians," said, "I would rather hang out with unbelievers than Christians because they keep it real. I don't have to hide or pretend in front of them. And they don't have to do that with me." Peter, a Christian who has been having a harder and harder time remaining in church, said to me, "I feel like church is a show. Why in the world are there fog machines and colored lights with everything meticulously crafted and orchestrated like a Broadway show? The pastor is always smiling. Christians are always smiling. Doesn't anyone have any problems? Am I the only one who feels like an outcast with mental health issues?"

People are looking for a holistic, real, and raw religious community-experience. They want to worship with every last bit of their wounded heart, fractured mind, divided soul, and lack of strength. In their church, they never felt they had permission to do so because of the implicit rules that encouraged people to talk only about the good and to avoid the not-so-good. There are already enough shallow and oxymoronic fake-reality television shows on prime time. They are not looking for the same kind of experience in the church.

With *shallow-itis* also come shallow responses to complex issues. Let's take the topic of disability in the church. Many churches are shallow in their practical aesthetic responses toward those with disabilities. And many Christians do not possess the confidence to adequately pray for those who have disabilities. When they do pray, they can recite hurtful Christian clichés that cause some to feel bad. Sometimes, Christians' verbal responses to a person's disability can be downright shallow and cruel. The late theologian Nancy L. Eiseland, born with a congenital bone defect and a strong advocate of those with disability concerns, wrote:

> As a person with a life-long disability, growing up in the church exposed me to a wide range of religious responses to disability. These folk theodicies are summed up in the familiar remarks: "You are special in God's eyes. That's why you were given this disability"; "Don't worry about your pain and suffering now, in heaven you will be made whole"; and "Thank God, it isn't worse." I was told that God gave me a disability to develop my character. But at age six or seven, I was convinced that I had enough character to last a lifetime. My family frequented faith healers with me in tow. I was never healed. People asked about my hidden sins, but they must have been so well hidden that they were misplaced even by me. The religious interpretations of disability that I heard were inadequate to my experience.[22]

Obviously, there are many reasons for Christians to be disturbed or to distance themselves from the faith they once knew. One of the most compelling reasons, shared by participants in various studies and by other well-known Christians, was the judgment they experienced from people in the church.

CHURCH SHOULD NOT FEEL LIKE A WAR ZONE

Judgment is antithetical to building an authentic and diverse community because it is harmful to the human spirit and sabotages relational connection. Let's use technology as an example. Every time we turn on a screen, we are judged by creative, innovative advertisers who spend millions of dollars to succinctly and persuasively tell us who we are not and what we are missing. We then judge ourselves for not being attractive enough, successful enough, white enough, black enough, smart enough, hip enough, rich enough, and simply not being enough.

In the same way that we feel inadequate when we see advertisements, we may feel judgment from God for never measuring up to some unattainable religious standard. When we go to church, we expect to be challenged. Community is hard. Following Jesus can be hard. But we don't expect to be harshly judged by fellow journeyers. It seems that Christians ignore Jesus' wise encouragement to "judge not" unless we have engaged in prayerful introspection of one's own log-sized inadequacies (Matt. 7:1) or Paul's provocative, pastoral, and self-reflective question, "Who are you to judge someone else's servant?" (Rom. 14:4). Unfortunately, this is to the detriment of individual and communal flourishing.

Let me share the experiences of a few people who were judged by fellow-Christians as they traveled though their D/R season of life.

Rachel Held Evans, in her book *Searching for Sunday: Loving, Leaving, and Finding the Church,* experienced seismic shifts in her Christian faith over the years. She wrote about the judgmental responses she received from her Christian community at large:

> My friends and professors diagnosed the crisis of faith as a deliberate act of rebellion. After graduation, rumors of my purported apostasy circulated around town, and I found myself on the prayer request lists of churches I didn't even attend. My best friend wrote me a letter

comparing my doubts to a drug habit and explained that she needed to distance herself from me for a while.[23]

Famous Christian artist Lisa Gungor, author of *The Most Beautiful Thing I've Seen: Opening Your Eyes to Wonder*, wrote about her internalized fears of judgment because of her intense questioning of things she once held dear. Internalized fears of judgment usually have their origin from outside sources, are taken in, and are accepted as if they are a person's own ideas. Lisa wrote, "Me, the good girl once on the 'straight and narrow,' with Grammy-nominated songs and singing about God all over the world, now blinded by evil, or her evil husband, and forever to burn in the eternal pit of despair because I was doubting."[24]

Philip Salim Francis is a researcher who studied seventy-eight men and women, either graduates of Bob Jones University and Oregon Extension alumni, who grew up and embraced American evangelicalism. Francis wrote about his work in the book, *When Art Disrupts Religion: Aesthetic Experience and the Evangelical Mind*. He discovered that the arts played an instrumental role in each of the participants leaving their faith. Whether it was film, music, theatre, poetry, writing, or other creative aesthetics, the "transcendence," "real presence," "power and depth," and "wonder, awe, mystery" experienced with the arts caused them to deconstruct their conservative Christian faith.[25] The aesthetic-ruptures became born-again moments that forever changed the trajectory of their lives. In regard to the rejection the participants received because of their doubt, Philip writes, "These Bob Jones and Oregon Extension alumni almost universally claim that in the communities in which they were raised, doubting in matters of faith was frowned upon and doubters were regularly regarded with scorn … Doubt was an indication of immorality."[26]

Glenn, a wild, creative pastor and a successful podcaster, who loves Jesus and the church, told of his experiences of judgment from Christians:

> I've been unfriended and blocked by people on Facebook. I have been called a heretic, a wolf, a lost soul, a snowflake, and SJW (social justice warrior) Christian. I've been told that my thoughts are like tepid water that can't be stomached; an ear-tickler who tells people what they want to hear. A wannabe pastor. I've been ghosted by friends and other friends comment on my stuff only when they adamantly disagree with something I say.

Marty Sampson is a well-known worship leader and avid songwriter. If you were in an evangelical church for a bit, chances are you sang a few of his songs as he wrote for Hillsong and other well-known worship bands. In August of 2019, he shocked the Christian community by stating, "I'm genuinely losing my faith"[27] and went on to describe some of his questions and doubts. His announcement was published a few days after Joshua Harris, the author of the famous and controversial book, *I Kissed Dating Goodbye*, told the world he was no longer a Christian. There was much love, grace, and overwhelming positive support for Marty, but the brutal judgment, so indicative of what many of us receive for just doubting and questioning, was downright awful. I jotted down just a few Facebook posts:

- He brought it on himself for not being rooted and grounded in love and God's word.

- He should have taken that to his pastor and started a praying session to get himself back in order.

- APOSTASY is an end times sign ... That's what's happening to Christianity. It's just that simple.

- He was never saved to begin with. Just another hell-bound hipster.

- He is just an artist and a singer ... but never a true worshipper!

- Whatever demon has taken over his mind won't let him listen obviously.

- Go away, sort your head/heart out, come off your self-made pedestal and maybe you'll find God again. Don't lead other snowflakes into the abyss.

- Wonder why Marty Sampson is so upset. He shows he wants to be used by the devil.

Christians can be judged because of their doubts and questions, their looks, their music, their friends, their drinks, the shows and movies they watch, their social class, the politicians they choose, the amount of social justice activities they engage in, their age, their race, the amount of Bible knowledge they have, their sexual orientation, the time they spend in prayer, and the list goes on and on. As the experiences of Marty Sampson and others demonstrate, one of the most common judgments Christians face is due to their emerging beliefs.

Sociologists Packard and Hope discuss the implicit or explicit rules churches have for requiring people to align with particular beliefs before they're allowed to engage fully in the life of the church. They write, "This is not only a dubious way to practice Christianity according to our respondents, but also a profoundly ineffective way to build community."[28] A sense of community will suffer when churches focus more on propositions and theological points than on people. People are much more than brains. They are wholistic beings with varied thoughts, an assortment of backgrounds and experiences, and varied needs to uniquely express themselves. They desire to feel a sense of belonging amidst diversity rather than feeling like they can only find acceptance if they believe exactly the same as everyone else.

Christians' passive-aggressive judgments are the most common and are just as painful as those that are explicitly stated. Packard and Hope write, "By far the most pervasive type of judgment our respondents described was felt or perceived rather than overtly expressed. This typically occurred between congregants and included dirty looks, ostracism, jealousy, whispering, and rumors."[29] While a lot of positive and validating encouragement come from some Christians, it is the negativity that stays with us and lingers. That is because we have what neuroscientists call a negativity bias. Rick Hanson, renowned psychologist and author of *Hardwiring Happiness,* writes, "The brain evolved a negativity bias that makes it like Velcro for bad experiences and Teflon for good ones."[30]

Our nervous system continues to remind us about the painful Velcro-prone experiences of judgment, rejection, and lack of safety. It does that to help us avoid experiencing the same distressing events over and over again. The truth is that we cannot feel a sense of belonging and safety when church life is like an emotional warzone where the bullets of critical judgment (toward the self and others) lurk around every corner. We know from a neuroscience perspective that if we do not feel safe, the part of our brain that takes in information goes offline. In other words, we can't learn if we don't feel safe around one another. It is no wonder that some of us may want to run. Christians can do better. They will need to if they want to avoid incurring more traumatized victims.

People want to experience church as a safe place to connect with God. They want an environment that can help them grow relationally and spiritually so they can make an indelible impact in the world. Judgment and rejection by those considered to be the family of God can make church and church folk feel unsafe. It could also become an obstacle to the inner transformation that is necessary for our external, Spirit-led revolutions.

YOUR D/R JOURNEY IS NOT YOUR FAULT

You may be familiar with the story in the Gospels of the Gerasene demoniac or the healing of the demon-possessed man. Parallels can be drawn between this ancient story and what has happened with contemporary religious refugees. Let's explore Mark's version in chapter five since, in all likelihood, Matthew and Luke copied and expanded his account.

Jesus traveled by boat with his anxious disciples across dangerous and chaotic waters to the region of the Gerasenes. Immediately, a man with an evil spirit, who was profoundly suffering and obviously not in his right mind, approached Jesus. He then fell on his knees in front of Jesus. While most people would turn away in fear or move into attack mode, Jesus didn't dismiss him, judge him, or criticize him. With profound courage and compassion, Jesus sought to address and alleviate the reasons for his suffering. Within moments, Jesus got to the bottom of his misery and the demon-possessed man was eventually healed. The man, who was once considered a monster, was miraculously "dressed and in his right mind" (v. 15) and restored to his community.

There are many perspectives one can take when reading about this man's healing. I can't help but read this story as an allegory for those who are currently suffering in the midst of their D/R journey.

I see the demon-possessed man as a person who was severely traumatized. He suffered trauma in part due to the tyranny of Roman occupation. Jesus asked him, "What is your name?" Then the demon replied, "My name is Legion, for we are many." Then Jesus sent the demons into a bunch of dirty pigs that "rushed down the steep bank into the lake and were drowned." Any hearer of this account in Jesus' time would have immediately thought of the oppressive Roman occupation. "Legion" literally meant a large number of Roman soldiers, usually around four to six thousand of them. New Testament scholar Stephen D. Moore writes about the colonial implications of Mark's narrative, "Not to put too delicate a point on it, the Romans are here shown up for the filthy swine that they are, and triumphantly driven back into the sea from whence they came—the dream of every Jewish peasant resister, as one of our own sages has observed."[31] So, as you can see, this story is not just about Jesus healing a demon-possessed man. It is a story exposing oppressive forces and subversively demonstrating the power of Jesus to heal systemic, individual, and communal trauma.

It is easy to look at individuals and blame them for their own problems and suffering. However, this story from Mark's Gospel reminds listeners after the death of Jesus, and eventually readers like us, that there are systemic and structural issues at play that wreak havoc in people's lives. The demoniac—which is a sad term because it dehumanizes the suffering person, leaves him nameless, and reduces him to a label—was living in isolation. He was staying in the "tombs" (v. 2). He "had often been chained hand and foot" (v. 4). He was in such relentless emotional pain that "he would cry out and cut himself with stones" (v. 5). Why? Was he suffering because of his genetics or the terrible sinful choices he made? Neither!

He symbolically represented all of the God-lovers in Jesus' day who were suffering due to the brutal and oppressive Roman occupation. He represented the inner anguish that occurred due to not being able to peacefully worship and live congruently in the world they inhabited. It's possible the man was suffering with what psychologists might call Dissociative Identity Disorder (DID), previously known as

Multiple Personality Disorder. People (usually in childhood) experience DID when the weight of trauma becomes so severe that they are no longer able to bear it. Their psyche then fragments and splits. Actually, this is a clever defense mechanism to save the person from complete emotional annihilation. If one part/identity/personality can split and take the weight of the trauma, then the other personalities do not necessarily have to. Perhaps the violent proclivities of Roman practices and barbarous persecution, where loved ones were unfairly imprisoned and lost their lives, took its toll on the demoniac.

It is also possible that the man was traumatized by members of his own community. The text tells us, "No one could bind him anymore, not even with a chain" (v. 3). Who initially put him in the dingy and desolate tomb? Who bound him with rusty and heavy chains? Was it initially done against the man's will? Could members of his own community have violently and coercively put him in the tombs just like people do to some who are mentally ill today—forcibly putting them in restraints and throwing them in a dark cell to rot in solitary confinement? Who wanted him out of sight and mind so that no one needed to bother with him?

Some people today become exceptionally worse after being in solitary confinement. Is that what happened to the man in the tombs? Could members of his own community have bruised and battered him? Could kids have come along and thrown rocks at him? After seeing Jesus come too close, was it one of his traumatized and terrorized identities who said, "Swear to God you won't torture me" (v. 8). Is this why the text says, "When they came to Jesus, they saw the man who had been possessed by the legion of demons, sitting there, dressed and in his right mind; and they were afraid." Afraid? Afraid of what? Certainly they were fearful of Jesus. After all, he just sent their precious money-making pigs (that were not exactly kosher) into the murky water to drown. But were they also afraid of what the

47

once-possessed man might say? Were they concerned about the guilt they might have to face because of how they unlovingly treated the precious man; a man created in the image of God?

Some churches are functioning like powerful, foreign occupiers attempting to squash identities, individual desires, and anything that doesn't fit in with their pathological ideologies that masquerade as divine intentions and holy prescriptions. Consequently, an untold number of Christians are hurting today because of the sneaky leaven of burdensome and pernicious religious practices, policies, attitudes, and propositions. They are unknowingly treated like the demoniac and occupied peasants. They suffer while Christians use broad-brush and demeaning labels to "other" them. They receive various messages telling them it's their fault for distancing themselves from God (at least perceived distancing from the viewpoint of the critics) and the church:

- If you just prayed more.

- If you just fasted more.

- If you just read the Bible more.

- If you would stop sinning.

- If you would go to church more.

- If you gave more money.

- If you stopped listening to those podcasts.

- If you stopped reading those books.

- If you got rid of that unforgiveness.

- If you stopped questioning and just trusted more.

The list goes on and on. It is blame, blame, and more blame. Then, after these Christian demoniacs are traumatized and gaslit, they are passive-aggressively pushed or pressured out of the church into the darkened tombs of the world. For many, the feeling of aloneness is utterly unbearable. Some church folks hope that by distancing themselves from us heretics, they do not have to be reminded of their own lack of empathy, judgment, intolerance for diversity, cognitive dissonance, bigotry, infatuation with savior-like political leaders, hypocrisy, oppressive policies, power trips, aversion to new ideas, and overall un-Christlike ways. Sometimes, those who are traumatized simply say, "Enough!" and walk or run away.

Ironically, who may have actually been have kicked out of the church so church leaders (the occupiers) could dish out their overbearing rules, regulations, and restrictions? Could it have been … God? The result, both of religious foreign occupation and of kicking out Divine love, is spiritual trauma.

SPIRITUAL TRAUMA

Elizabeth Baker, a Christian writer and editor from Texas, shared how she has been negatively affected by Christian teachings and practices that do not seem to line up with the life and teachings of Jesus:

> I don't sleep through the night anymore. I suffer from near daily panic attacks and almost constant anxiety. The source of my joy, my security, and my identity has vanished, leaving me with an angry grief that almost no one in my immediate circle understands. I have relationships that were once life-giving but have turned toxic. I feel manipulated, deceived, and abused. And why? The church that raised me is gaslighting me.[32]

Like Elizabeth, when people finally awaken and realize how their once-beloved faith has sadly failed them (or worse, mentally or emotionally abused them), the result can be spiritual trauma. Paul Matthew Harrison, author of *Deconversions,* writes, "When our worldview shifts or we become disillusioned with what once brought us stability, peace, comfort, and hope, it can be terribly traumatic."[33] Reba Riley, who has written about her deconstruction journey, calls the experience "Post-Traumatic Church Syndrome".[34]

Dr. Marlene Winell, psychologist and author of *Leaving the Fold: A Guide to Former Fundamentalists and Others Leaving Their Religion,* specializes in working with those who suffer due to their former religious experiences.[35] Winell calls the aftereffects of toxic religion *Religious Trauma Syndrome.* In discussing the seriousness of this tragic phenomenon—both the traumatic realization of how sick their religion made them and the process of exiting—Winell writes, "Leaving a religion, after total immersion, can cause a complete upheaval of a person's construction of reality, including the self, other people, life, and the future. People unfamiliar with this situation, including therapists, have trouble appreciating the sheer terror it can create."[36] Linda Kay Klein, author of *Pure: Inside the Evangelical Movement That Shamed a Generation of Young Women and How I Broke Free,* writes:

> Evangelical Christianity's sexual purity movement is traumatizing many girls and maturing women haunted by sexual and gender-based anxiety, fear, and physical experiences that sometimes mimic the symptoms of post-traumatic stress disorder (PTSD). Based on our nightmares, panic attacks, and paranoia, one might think that my childhood friends and I had been to war.[37]

YOU ARE NOT ALONE

Beloved friend, you are not crazy. There are really good reasons for why you may be experiencing the level of spiritual struggle that you are. You are a religious refugee. You have been forced out (or are being forced out slowly) by the church because you are different, because you are open, creative, inclusive, sensitive, and passionate, and because you have a more expansive vision for church than what a narrow-minded, judgmental, fear-based, boring, inauthentic church can provide. You have been given a scarlet letter "H" for Heretic. You have been verbally assaulted, placed in chains like you're some, wicked demoniac, and kicked to the curb like an orphaned child.

You are not alone. We are a part of a growing community of folks who have been hurt, disillusioned, and traumatized by some of our experiences within the Christian religion.

I believe Jesus, the universal Christ, the one ubiquitous Spirit who sustains and fills us all, has experienced your inner ache, witnessed your crying out, and grieved as you cut yourself with stones of criticism, shame, and fear. Perhaps what we need to do to start the healing journey is continually do what the demoniac did: "He ran and fell on his knees." It was an act of surrender as he fell into the presence of love, mercy, and compassion. He understood that it was only Love and Truth that could set him free.

I don't believe in a quick fix, snake-oil spirituality: "Hey, just give it all to Jesus in this moment, all of your pain will be gone, and you will receive all of the desires of your heart for eternity." Sometimes there are moments of miraculous transformation. For many of us, though, it is a long, continual process of exposing the demons of fear, shame, and pain that were forced into us and then excising them with compassionate others by our sides. As we do that, we let those vexing life-zappers run into the turbulent watery abyss where they belong. Then, as we vulnerably allow the Divine to clothe us, signifying and solidifying that we are the beloved, we can begin, moment by moment, to be put in our right minds once again. Once we can see and think clearly, we can speak truth to power, not only with our words, but more importantly, with and through our lives.

QUESTIONS

1. What are your thoughts on whether or not the Deconstructive/ Reconstructive process is a choice?

2. What shifts are occurring in Christianity in the West? Why do you think they are happening right now?

3. There are different labels researchers are giving to those who are shifting in their faith: Done, Spiritual and Religious Refugee, Church Burnout, Freedom Seeker, Dechurched, Nomad, Prodigal, Exile, etc. With which label do you identify with and why?

4. When you think about your church experiences, how have you been affected by: *Politics and Bureaucracy, Clone War Syndrome, Moral Prescriptions*, and *Shallow-itis?*

5. What instances of judgment have you experienced from other Christians?

6. Why do you think critical judgment is antithetical to building an authentic and diverse community? What would healthy judgment look like?

7. In what ways did Jesus bring healing to the demon-possessed man in Mark 5? How are those ways similar to the healing Jesus wants to bring to those considered *dechurched?*

8. How can the church effectively reach out to the *dechurched* and those who are deeply hurting from past church experiences?

CHAPTER TWO

STATIONS OF THE D/R JOURNEY

"Few of us follow a straight line in our spiritual story: we squiggle and wiggle, stop and start, progress and regress, rest and recoup, charge ahead recklessly and take sharp turns or stumble into ditches that turn out to be portals."

— SARAH BESSEY, *OUT OF SORTS*

Let's zoom out and explore a broader overview of several stations through which a person could travel on the D/R journey. My hope is that this reorients you for a moment, providing a map of where you have been, where you are, and where you might be going.

First of all, I prefer the word *stations* over *stages*. I know it's a semantic quibble, but it seems to me that the word *stage* conveys an air of judgment. Stages assume that people move on to higher and higher planes of experience—and, of course, the higher the stage, the better off a person is thought to be. I also prefer *different* over *higher*, because people should be accepted as they are. They shouldn't be judged for where they are on their life's path. Though a stage-approach doesn't necessarily imply judgment and a better-than attitude, using the word *station* simply avoids those associations altogether.

Stations also make me think of places where fellow travelers gather. A few people remain in a seemingly unchangeable, fixed pathway throughout their lives, but most of us are changing, evolving, and traveling somewhere. Because nothing is perfectly neat and orderly, we can return to familiar stations as needed. And unlike stages—fixed parameters that try to cover everyone's experiences—stations imply that there is more out there that may not yet be described.

STATION ONE: FEELING AT HOME

Station One of the spiritual journey is a time when a person feels at home, in a place of comfort, ease, and security. When you walk into the house, you know exactly where things are. It's reassuring to know that when you come home you will see the same dusty pictures on the wall of family with out-of-fashion clothing and outmoded haircuts. Home is where you can ease your tired feet and be your imperfect, messy self. It's a place where you feel a sense of belonging, especially when you spend time with a family who loves you.

This station of the Christian experience can be thoroughly fulfilling. Knowing that you are home—in *your* community, with *your* God, with *your* beliefs, and with *your* religious rituals—gives you a profound sense of comfort and safety. This feeling of home produces a buffer against the stressors of life and protects you from the blitzing existential and harsh realities that surround us all. There is no deep doubting in this station; questioning here is for the sole purpose of learning and building on what a person already knows about God, life, family, and the church.

There is a difference between *coming home* and *feeling at home.* I had a "coming home" experience when I went from being a person who was religionless, depressed, suicidal, and hopeless, to coming home to the sense of God's love and a church that accepted me as one of their own (which doesn't necessarily mean they accepted me for who I was). Other people have a different story of faith. They don't have the flashy Damascus Road kind of experience that instantaneously changes them into a holy rollin' Jesus freak. They grow up in the church and always feel at home there. Church is family and family is church. Even if it's dysfunctional, for those in Station One, it's still family.

I remember meeting Jesus and coming home to my new church. There was something refreshing in knowing I would see the same familiar faces when I went through those doors. It was so special to hear Brother Ritchie or Sister Lisa say with a warm smile, "Hey, Brotha Mark! Praise the Lord!" I experienced so much joy in receiving the holy hugs and warm embraces. Of course, it was side hugs for the sisters. I wasn't sure about the rationale or biblical precedent for such a greeting, but I knew that to brush up too close to them would cause some sort of unholy catastrophe. Ultimately, no matter what difficulties came my way during the week, it gave me great solace to know that, at some point, I would see my beloved family.

Not only did my church feel like home, it also provided emotional security by way of engaging in patterned religious rituals. I knew I would see my church family a couple of days every week. But I also knew, and could predict, what would happen every Sunday morning. There would be shouting to God in corporate prayer, announcements, an offering, four worship songs, a sermon, an altar call, three more songs, prayer and the pastor's last words, dismissal, and a potluck downstairs. The routine was something I craved, especially given my background. I'll tell you more about my story as we go along, but all you need to know right now is that most of my childhood and adolescence had been immersed in an utterly chaotic whirlwind of abuse, neglect, drugs, and violence. Given my past experiences, my new church and feeling-at-home experience—with all of its consistency, patterned rituals, and sense of family—was heavenly to me.

Another component of my faith in Station One was reading the Bible, something that made me feel very special. I will never forget the feeling I had when I opened the Scriptures and saw Jesus' words in red. It was mesmerizing. Every word captivated me. To know that these were the exact words Jesus spoke, without one edit in over two thousand years (at least that was what I was told)—that was too much for my little brain to comprehend. I felt so special knowing that God had written and preserved those words for me. The Bible was my *Basic Instructions Before Leaving Earth*.

My at-home feeling in the church was rooted in the routine, a sense of belonging, and a love for God's words. It was also the result of the comfortable blanket of packaged black-and-white beliefs offered to me by my fellow church members. They gave me manuals and tracts, telling me everything I needed to know about Apostolic Pentecostal doctrine. Between those manuals, tracts, and the Bible, no guesswork was required for any of us. We had the truth. We had the answers. We were part of the *in crowd* and everyone else was on the outside. And, the best part? Because of our denomination's perfect, unblemished doctrines, I knew I was one of a chosen few who were truly saved. My speaking in tongues sealed the deal. All of those packaged answers were like decadent ice cream to my parched, chaotic soul. Let's just say there were a lot of benefits to feeling at home in Station One.

STATION TWO: SPLINTERHOOD

I will discuss *splinters* in greater detail in the next chapter, but for now, let me introduce the topic to you. Station Two occurs when conscious or unconscious thoughts (splinters), and the resulting cognitive

dissonance, cause an immense amount of tension. Cognitive dissonance takes place when a person holds to two ideas that appear to be
contradictory. It will be experienced by a person who, for example,
believes that "gay people will spend eternity in Hell," but is simultaneously also starting to believe that "God loves gay people just the way
they are." The tension usually starts off subtly and is something from
which people can easily distract themselves. Over time, however, the
cognitive dissonance becomes impossible to ignore.

Kathy Escobar calls this station "the stage of shifting." She describes
it as "the strange transitional phase between the clear boundaries of
where we've been and where we might go spiritually."[1] People enter
this station because the splinters, or contradictory beliefs, cause so
much discomfort and irritation to one's psyche that it becomes harder
and harder to ignore. Marlene Winell calls this station "separation."
She writes:

> Questions and doubts arise, perhaps gradually. Bits of new informa-
> tion become harder to integrate and new life experiences do not fit
> with standard dogma. It can feel unsettling when it seems that prom-
> ises are not being fulfilled or that unexpected problems are occurring.
> That is, there are fewer pluses and more minuses. Your faith feels like
> a tapestry coming apart.[2]

As I write this, Marty Sampson seems to be making a pit stop
at Station Two. He can no longer ignore his splinters or incessant
thoughts that have caused tremendous cognitive dissonance. And as
he continues to expose these splinters, Sampson finds himself in a
liminal space, not knowing where his doubt and questions will lead.
He dared to be courageous by sharing some of his splinters on social
media. Here are a few of his concerns:

- How many preachers fall?

- How many miracles happen? Not many.

- Why is the Bible full of contradictions?

- How can God be love, yet send four billion people to a hot place, all 'coz they don't believe?

- Christians can be the most judgmental people on the planet.[3]

At some point on his journey, all of Marty's doubts and questions clustered together and he could no longer ignore them. As a result, he began to feel overwhelmed. The splinters in his mind, and his subsequent emotional turmoil, then caused him to question important aspects of his faith.

Like many people, Marty didn't ask to be in the Station of Splinterhood. It just happened. After hearing countless stories of people experiencing the D/R journey, I see clearly that this early station is not a choice. Though life-events can trigger the birth of the splinters, those who dwell in Station Two didn't ask to become disoriented and out of spiritual alignment. This experience—this gap between the world as they knew it and the foreign world of ideas that crashed in on them—just happened.

George was a participant in a research study written about in an article entitled "Breaking Up with Jesus." In his interview, he talked about the D/R process as not only being out of his control but also initially happening outside of his awareness. He wrote, "This is going on in the unconscious; the brain working this through, ruminating over this, one isn't fully aware one is doing it."[4] Katie, another participant in the same study, tried to fight and resist the D/R journey. She beautifully articulated an experience common to many people in Station Two: "You are kind of fighting it at least half the time, because you desperately want to hold on to what you believe, what's giving you purpose and meaning up to this point and it's just slipping through your fingers and you can't hold on to it no matter how hard you try."[5]

Everyone's experiences are so diverse that no one moves through the stations in a linear progression. Sometimes people feel at home in Station One but never really unpack all of their boxes. It's almost like they are home, but part of them has always had one foot in one station and another foot in the other.

People struggle to embrace the feelings of being at home for many different reasons. One reason could be that they always felt like an outcast or had a difficult time trusting people. They listened to the pastor's sermons but felt like the words were intended for more spiritual listeners. Or perhaps they always listened with a hermeneutic of suspicion, never entirely trusting what the pastor said was true. Some part of them felt like they belonged and had found a place they could call home, but another part of them was always on high alert. That fearful side was scared of the vulnerability that intimacy demands—which, in their case, and particularly in their growing-up years, may have led only to rejection and pain. Sometimes we bring our emotional baggage to church before anyone at church ever hurts us.

STATION THREE: "TO BE OR NOT TO BE"

In Station Three, splinters are being exposed. Confusion and cognitive dissonance are like a woodpecker, incessantly and annoyingly pecking away at our psyches, eventually forcing us to do something about it. The main question we ask ourselves in this station is: "To be or not to be?"

Does the good and faithful Christian choose to go back to the comfort and security of their home in Station One? Or do they choose to overcome their anxiety and become an active adventurer, traveling boldly to a new destination at an undisclosed location?

It's always hard for people to let go of the good that they know in hopes of receiving a greater good in a future that they don't know.

Some ask themselves whether or not they should just stick with the familiar good. They may be people who are able to compartmentalize and push the splinters down deep into the unconscious as needed. Or they think that if they could find a few satisfying answers to their questions and doubts, then they would rush back home to tell their family the good news: "I'm not a heretic! I'm a good Christian. I'm keeping the faith." In Station Three, they make the choice either to remain homebodies or to daringly walk a road less traveled.

Before Marty's cognitive dissonance, he may not have thought much about the reality of preachers falling into sin. But let's imagine that wasn't the case and, every time he heard of a preacher falling, he began to doubt God's work in their lives. In those moments, if Marty wasn't careful, his mind could have led him to question the reality and existence of God. In other words, if God's spokesperson and right-hand man wasn't genuine and real, then maybe God wasn't either. That was too much for him to fathom, so, on an unconscious level, he pushed down those doubts, far outside of his awareness. That is called *repression*, a defense mechanism that occurs without conscious awareness.

Let's also imagine that Marty engaged in *suppression*, a defense mechanism which happens on a more conscious level. Once he was aware of his splinters, he intentionally chose to distract himself from his cognitive dissonance and ignore his anxiety. He kept himself busy, reading his Bible and spending more time in prayer or ministering to others—anything to keep his awareness away from the unpleasant trouble brewing within his thoughts. This very complex process may have taken place with his contradictory thoughts about miracles, biblical contradictions, Hell, and his tension with judgmental Christians.

Marty probably used both conscious and unconscious defense mechanisms to cope with the chaos in his own head. That's true of all of us. But, there comes a time in Station Three when all of us, Marty included, have to choose either to go home to what is familiar or to journey ahead toward foreign, potentially perilous, territory. It's never easy to question beliefs we once held sacred. We never know where the path will lead once we step onto it.

STATION FOUR: RETURNING HOME DIFFERENT

A person in Station Four has felt the wonder of a church family while also experiencing the nuisance of contradictory beliefs about theology and identity. They now make their choice in how to proceed. Instead of traveling to uncharted terrain, they choose the safety of returning home. Despite some slight shifts in their beliefs, they essentially return to the smooth, hot, tasty cocoa of beliefs they once held dear. They return to the tried and true, familiar people, practices, propositions, and principles with which they've always felt comfortable. They have arrived back in the same place they started—just a little different.

There's nothing wrong with the choice to travel back home. It's not the end of the book. Instead, it's just one small chapter in a story that is continually unfolding. Perhaps the slight anxiety about newly emerging beliefs has dissipated for people in Station Four. They've read books, listened to podcasts, met with like-minded people, and integrated new ideas that reconfirmed and fortified what they originally believed. In this case, cognitive dissonance can disappear.

Some return home out of fear. The fear of God's judgment can be an incredible motivator to stay on the well-worn path. Fear of losing friends, family, and a loss of identity can scare the heretical hell out of people. Ultimately, the security of being home feels better than the insecurity of traveling abroad. But, remember, none of this is linear. We don't know where anyone's journey will take them. At some point they could reenter Station Two or Three again, and then they could either go back home once more or venture into the unfamiliar wilderness.

Many pastors travel through Stations Two and Three and then decide to remain at home. They do so for many reasons, most of which are rooted in fear. Some fear that if they reveal their struggles, doubts, and questions, they'll be perceived as unfit for their position. They may fear that church members would consider them heretics who have given themselves over to the dark side. Can you imagine the struggle they must endure in making a decision to move to another station of spiritual experience that may cost them their job? The fear is even greater if they can't utilize other, work-related skills to support their family.

I have heard firsthand from pastors who were in the midst of this kind of internal conundrum. Many have shared with me their terror just thinking about publicly acknowledging their doubts about important doctrines that their church holds dear. Knowing that they would be kicked out of the church, and perhaps be unable to provide for their families, forced them to hide. This is no easy predicament. It's sad their professional roles don't allow them to be exactly who they are: imperfect followers of Jesus on a messy spiritual journey just like everyone else.

A pastor with a spouse and kids may also feel the pressure to stay home for fear of harming his/her family. It's one thing to have a personal faith shift but another to allow that shift to profoundly affect others. Whether that would actually happen, doesn't matter. The fear of causing spiritual harm to their family is genuine. One pastor I spoke with said, "I am afraid of letting my wife know about my spiritual struggles, because I don't want to bring her down. I don't want to destroy her faith, or my kids' faith for that matter."

Wives who have husbands as a pastor can find themselves in the same uncomfortable predicament. When discussing Station Four, Sandra, whose husband is a pastor, responded:

> When it's the pastor's wife, it's just as excruciating. I feel stuck in Station Four because I *am* different, but to leave the church when my husband is an elder would destroy my marriage, our local church, and have a ripple effect into the denomination. I can't talk to him about it because he doesn't understand. I can't talk to people in my church because I'm the elder's wife. I can't talk to most elders' wives (in other of our churches) because they're still in Station One and probably always will be. Sometimes it's a lonely existence.

People already have complicated lives and prefer to not make them messier and more difficult than they need to be. So, they may not want to drastically change what they believe. At the very least, they don't want to accept the fact (nor do they want others to know) that they have drastically changed their beliefs. Others may choose a different apologetic scaffolding to support what they have always believed. In either case, they choose to remain home. And though they are home, they are different. They are changed. As the ancient philosopher Heraclitus said, "No man ever steps in the same river twice, for it's not the same river and he's not the same man." Experiences always change us to some degree. People either have renewed vigor to champion what they initially believed, or they come home with perpetual doubt, continually hiding their true selves and living an incongruent life.

STATION FIVE: DISORIENTATION

In a later chapter, I'll explore the disorienting grief process people go through on the D/R journey, but I want to discuss it briefly here. Some enter the Station of Disorientation willingly. Others are overtaken by it. Some travel through it gracefully with only minor distress. Many travel through it woefully and painfully, while some suffer to the point of experiencing trauma and PTSD symptoms.

People travel to Station Five when they are no longer able to ignore their splinters of contradictory beliefs or when they experience life-altering events that forever change them. Even in life-altering events, it's what a person comes to believe afterward that can be potent enough to change the course of their life. All of the troubling thoughts and emotions a person has been avoiding can react like a beach ball, forced beneath the surface, wildly popping back up out of the water. In this station, everything has forced itself out into the open, bringing confusion, loneliness, and, for some, despair.

The blinders are off in Station Five. Having been fully awakened, people are in anguish at the reality they face. They see themselves, God and the church, the past and the future, in a different light than before. For some it can be like living a horror story. The monsters of anxiety, fear, shame, anger, panic attacks, sleepless nights, nightmares, rejection, and confusion crawl around seeking to take their lives away. Author Reba Riley shares typical signs of "post-traumatic church syndrome" experienced by people in Station Five:

> Prayer is out of the question; the Bible is something you use to mop up spilled coffee; you can't darken the door of a place of worship without sweaty palms, vertigo, chest pains, nausea, and vomiting … I didn't mention the more destructive side effects of spiritual injury: anger, grief, despair, depression, failure to believe in anything, moral confusion, loss of gravity, and emptiness.[6]

Station Five is a place of loss, grief, and disorientation. It is a season of visceral emotional experiences, confusing cognitive struggles, and ruptured relationships. But listen. This station, if we allow it, can also be a springboard into profound growth and transformation! What feels like a disorienting crisis of faith can become a bright light, enabling transformative insight, leading to a new life of congruence with increased love and connections.

STATION SIX: ANGSTVILLE

Our next stop is Angstville. This station is where people predominantly experience anger, doubt, cynicism, and negative emotions and attitudes that become the filter through which they see everything.

Anger is a naturally occurring emotion experienced by many in the previous station, Station Five. It is a paramount emotion in the grieving process. I think people *should* be angry at systems of ideological and theological oppression that sank deep into their being and negatively affected their relationships with God, themselves, and others. Unfortunately, in Station Six, anger is their predominant emotion, the one they experience on a daily basis. It's almost like they're stuck in a time warp with the trauma of their Christian past looping continuously through their mind.

In this station, a person can't bring themselves to forgive or to stop harshly judging Christians. They hate God, or at least they are apathetic toward God. They are prone to engage in angry social media jabs at Christians, the Bible, God, or whatever else gets in the way of their efforts to convince others of the terror and toxicity of Christianity. People in this station are unable and unwilling to move on. They miss out on the opportunity to use their anger in adaptive ways that contribute to healthier living for themselves and others.

Some people in Station Six remain Christians, but are embittered toward Christianity. Others leave their faith altogether. And ironically, those who claim to have left Christianity exert such energy toward deconstructing and destroying it that it's very clear they still have a relationship with God and the church—though not a very amicable one.

Matthew, a friend of mine who was a Christian for twenty-two years, has taken an indefinite sabbatical from Christianity. He's an example of someone who views the world through a lens of anger. He told me, "Christians suck. The Christian God is a tyrannical asshole. Anyone who remains a Christian is just a dumb fool who can't think for themselves. All the time I wasted on that fairy tale ... I could have been doing other things with my life." You can find Matt in various social media groups—the groups that haven't yet kicked him out—using his "fierce intellect" to destroy Christian arguments.

Doubt, like anger, is also common among people in the previous station, Station Five. Doubt is normal and natural for them, especially after previously believing they were holding to the absolute truth about God, the Bible, the future, and humanity. By its nature, trauma primes us for doubt, especially when we believed so passionately. Once you burn your fingers on a red-hot stove, you tend to be very careful about touching it again. That means believing wholeheartedly in anything during the D/R journey can be problematic.

At Station Six, however, doubt is a reactive experience that refuses to let anything good in. Doubt becomes cool, hip, habitual—a part of our identity. Doubt becomes, in fact, our new faith. Keith Giles writes, "Uncertainty is the only thing you feel certain about. Doubt is the only thing you believe in. Questions are the only answer ... The freedom that comes from not giving a crap anymore is intoxicating. We find ourselves on the outside looking in and—even if it's a little bit painful—it starts to feel like home."[7] Too much doubt limits the amount of beauty and love that people can take in. How can anyone heal if they can't let in the good?

Cynicism—believing the worst about everyone and everything—is another common attitude in this station. A cynic assumes that people will act out of their worst intentions instead of their best. Once you realize that a cynic parked at this station has been traumatized, and badly hurt, it starts to make sense. But, even though it might make sense, there are consequences to looking at the world through this cracked, shadowy lens. Neuroscientist, Andrew Newberg, and Loyola Marymount University professor, Mark Waldman, authors of *Born to Believe*, write about the toxic effects of cynicism: "This [cynicism], as every psychiatrist and cardiologist knows, can lead to anger, bitterness, contempt, hostility, and depression. In the long run, the hormonal and neurological changes caused by these emotional states can seriously compromise physical health."[8]

At some point, we have to say *No* to stale anger, depressing doubts, and calloused cynicism. Carrying around the hurt that perpetuates such feelings and attitudes has a cost. The unfortunate reality is that people who are hurting tend to hurt other people. Wounded people tend to wound. At some point, we have to choose the difficult path of healing and reconstruction.

In some ways, it's unfair to portray people as having a choice to move on from this station. Really, who has the right to determine the expiration date of a person's natural grief processes? Who's to say that someone has been angry or cynical for long enough and now it's time to move on? I don't think anyone does. Nevertheless, after personally watching some folks spend years rehashing traumatic events and grimly judging others, including God, it's clear that some other dynamic is going on. There comes a point at which they may be choosing a primary identity as "one who is victimized." Contrast this with those who identify as victims but then have the bravery to heal and overcome that past for their own sake and for the sake of others.

The therapist side of me is torn. I'm aware that a unique dialectic—two opposing assertions that are both true—is at play with people in the Station of Angstville. When two contradictory truths can be held together, they can paradoxically bring insights into a higher level of consciousness. For example: what happened to us as religious refugees is not our fault. We should be accepted for who we are, and where we are on our path toward healing from spiritual trauma. That needs to be made perfectly clear. We were drawn into a vast array of systemic issues that robbed all of us of our divine humanity. The result is a group of people who are traumatized and terrorized. *And*—not *but*—we are now responsible to do something about what happened to us. It's our choice: remain bitter or fight and claw our way to something better. We are paradoxically accepted *and* invited to change at the same time.

People can hang out and chill in Angstville as long as they want. Some may want to do so until the day they die and that's their choice. But, honestly, I don't think most people want to stay here; they just don't know how to get out. They don't have the skills to grieve well and reconstruct their faith. They may not have loved ones who walk alongside them and help them heal. Perhaps there were times when people tried but were pushed away, including the very people God may have been inviting to compassionately walk with them. People in this station can be prone to self-sabotage. But if they can dig deep and fight for healing and integration, then what started as post-traumatic church syndrome can become post-traumatic growth.

STATION SEVEN: FAREWELL AND GOODBYE

Religious refugees are looking for a home. Some find one—just not in the Christian tradition. Some Christians move through Stations 1–6 and then say farewell and goodbye to God and the Christian faith forever. They grieve about their past and find a freedom they never thought could exist for them. And it's not a fake sort of freedom. They aren't deluding themselves, thinking they're free when they're actually entrapped in sinful lifestyles forever seeking to numb their traumatic past. No, these are people who choose not to have anything more to do with Christianity and, as a result, they experience a sense of freedom.

Where people in Angstville may shout, "F- - - you, Christians! I'm free!" those in Station Seven say, "Yes, there were toxic aspects to the Christian faith I was a part of; still, I don't have any hate in my heart toward Christians or their faith. I wish them well. It's just not for me. I've moved on. I'm happier and experiencing more freedom then I ever did as a Christian."

Paul Matthew Harrison, in his book *Deconversions*, eloquently discusses his journey from having a vibrant Christian faith to "belief in something more."[9] Harrison, a Christian with a sharp intellect, sought out to make sense of his Christian faith and the various doctrinal packages that came with it. He also had a profound ache to know God intimately. Unfortunately, his search brought him neither adequate answers to his theological questions nor an intimate relationship with God. In the wake of God's perpetual silence to his cries for closeness, he decided to stop being a Christian.

"Tired of the evasion and runaround," Harrison writes, "exhausted from seeking but getting no answers, and finding the skeptical arguments against Christianity convincing and the defenses wanting, I concluded that I could no longer be a Christian."[10] As you might expect, he experienced what many of us religious refugees have experienced in the wake of drastic spiritual change—judgment. "A woman at church had discerned that I was being oppressed by demons, then laid hands on me and proceeded to take authority over and cast out a 'spirit of intellectualism.'"[11]

Harrison put an enormous amount of energy toward processing and working through his grief over his Christian experience in a healthful way. He was determined to learn from his experience and flourish as a human being. Later in his journey, he was able to say, "These disillusionments forced me down a path of having to take a look in the mirror, accept difficult truths, learn from my mistakes, and make changes in my beliefs and actions. I took responsibility for my life and began correcting my course. I began growing up."[12] After a long time, Harrison was able to heal to such an extent that he did something unexpected—he went to church. In his memoir, Harrison talks about seeing the church experience with fresh, empathic eyes. Instead of arrogant, coarse judgment, he was able to see the positives in the flawed, yet profound, communal nature of the service. Although he didn't believe in the metaphysical aspects of what the pastor was saying or what the worship leader was singing, he found an appreciation for the event. He wrote:

> In this church, people gather to celebrate their peace, hope, and joy. They share wisdom and learn from one another. There is self-reflection, character-building, and the will to change and grow. They listen to, pray for, and support each other. They focus on something bigger than themselves and allow for awe and wonder. They want to make the world a better place and take action to do so.[13]

I have found that Harrison, and others in this station, are not so clouded by anger that they can't see the beauty and goodness in imperfect human imagination and concepts and rituals about the Divine. They might still be angry at how particular Christian doctrines hurt and oppress others, but they are able to respond with genuine compassion rather than reactive rage and anger. They seek to live in a way that uses any anger as fuel for their passion for social and spiritual justice. They may not be religious, but they can be genuinely spiritual and live according to their own values, not values imposed on them by religious authorities. Harrison sums up the creed of those in Station Seven:

> All worldviews contain some element of mystery, paradox, contradiction, irony, or absurdity. Life is full of things about which we have conflicting feelings and tentative understanding, so the attempt to

create or find rational coherence and understand everything in your life and in the world around you is a doomed project from the start. I've decided to end the project of seeking answers to ultimate questions and get on living in the world without them.[14]

Some folks can choose reconstruction even if that means building a life without a relationship with God or the church.

STATION EIGHT: EXTREME MAKEOVER—HOME EDITION

Welcome to Christianity 2.0! Station Eight is where Christians have engaged in an extreme makeover, completely renovating their spirituality. They have moved through the feelings of safety and security at home, become aware of emerging contradictory beliefs, experienced profound grief and disorientation, and have now finally moved to a place of acceptance in which they choose growth and spiritual metamorphosis. Writing about this part of the recovery process, Marlene Winell says:

> Fortunately healing can occur. You can work through your pain and allow your inner strengths to emerge. In the rebuilding phase, people re-discover their self-worth. They rejoin life on a different basis. Perceptions and beliefs are reconstructed. You too can find new principles to live by and new meaning for your life. Some of your values may remain the same, but you sort through what you have been taught and keep what is valuable.[15]

Though people in this stage have done a complete overhaul of their theological beliefs, they remain connected to Jesus. Many still love, honor, and seek to base their lives on Jesus' teachings. The idea that God is manifest in Jesus is taken very seriously. They might say, "You want to see what God looks like, look at Jesus." To them, all of Scripture, and all of the portrayals of God in Scripture, must bow down to the beauty and majesty of Jesus. Christians in this station believe in the Jesus who is depicted in the New Testament and the universal Christ who is above, below, and beyond the Scriptures.

Followers of Christ in this station tend to avoid bibliolatry of any kind. They are not bound by a need to view the Bible as an inerrant, golden text with one overarching, cohesive metanarrative that was gently hoisted down from Heaven by almighty God. Despite an acknowledgment that the Bible holds both human and divine fingerprints, they immensely value its diverse perspectives as a means to learning and growing, that "they may be equipped for every good work" (2 Tim. 3:17). They see the Scriptures as a sacred communal text that informs their faith and take careful consideration not to use it in ways that oppress or marginalize others.

People in Station Eight view church differently. They definitely do not see church as an ornate building. Instead, they see it as a community of people. And because people can travel anywhere at any time, church can be informal and organic. Wherever two or three are gathered to talk about life, faith, and God, it is a precious spiritual experience. Packard and Hope discuss this shift of perspective in their book, *Church Refugees*. They write:

> Most often this took the form of a weekly dinner or meal, but there were many other manifestations, including book clubs, movie-watching groups, online chat rooms, forums, and musical gatherings. While none of the experiences might seem inherently spiritual, our participants characterized them as expressions of their faith.[16]

Those hanging out in this station like to be understood as a human *becoming* rather than a human *being*. *Becoming* entails process, whereas *being* has to do with a sense of arrival. They are learning, growing, and morphing into only God knows what. So, as you might imagine, they don't appreciate being pinned down by labels. No single, unchangeable label captures the complexity of who anyone is. Labeling others is an attempt to dehumanize and erase the diverse complexities of individuals and groups in order to gain power over them. Frank Schaefer writes, "You will always be more than one person. You will always embody contradiction. You—like some sort of quantum mechanical physics experiment—will always be in two places at once."[17] We will always be complex beings with different subpersonalities, all of whom have unique feelings and thoughts.

Those of us who have arrived at this station can be considered both a theist and an a/theist.[18] Why? We believe God is more than we can think and imagine, and we distrust what our feeble minds can conceive of God. We have fundamentalist parts and progressive parts. Some have Christian parts and Buddhist parts. We have secure parts of ourselves and insecure parts. We have adventurous parts and parts that enjoy familiar comforts. Some parts are healed and others are wounded. We have parts that want to be close to and connected with people and we have parts that just want to be alone. Most people have multiple sub-personalities and don't want to be labeled or dissected; they just want to be known and loved. Those in Station Eight are very conscious of ensuring that people are understood and loved in their complexity, so they seek to avoid labels whenever possible.

Although people in Station Eight have received a makeover, that doesn't mean they've reached a state of nirvana and are free from all suffering. They still have doubts, struggles, relational issues, and existential concerns just like everyone else. They still deal with "phantom theologies." Though they no longer believe, for example, that God is violent and cruel, or that God hates gay people, or that God has designed a torture chamber called Hell for sinners like them, there are times when those theologies sneak up and cause them momentary distress. The difference between this station and others is that theological and faith concerns are not earth-shattering.

Here, people believe that change is inevitable. Beth Allen Slevcove, author of the book *Broken Hallelujahs*, astutely writes, "We think we know who God is and who we are in relation to God, our understandings are shattered through some experience, God comes along and eventually gives us a new and greater understanding of God, and just when we think we've got it figured out, the cycle repeats."[19] For those in this station, there is less of an anxious desire to cling to the security of a static faith and more openness to the constancy of change and a faith that is ever-evolving.

Those in Station Eight embrace the fact that they are always changing, but also in a space of restful adventuring. They feel more freedom to become who they are and how God made them to be. They have confidence that love will guide them the rest of the way. They may cycle through other stations again (including Splinterhood and Disorientation), but for now, life, God, and faith make sense. I like to put it this way: It makes sense to them that their faith doesn't always have to make sense. Renowned spiritual writer Alexander Shaia, in his book *Radical Transformation: The Four-Gospel Journey of Heart and Mind*, writes, "The genuine path that opens before us does not lead in the direction of greater control, but rather toward a new kind of intimacy. It releases us into learning to live within great unknowing, instead of being frightened of incomprehension and attempting to exert power over it."[20] People at Station Eight embrace mystery, awe, and wonder. They are home and want everyone else to feel at home, too.

QUESTIONS

1. Can you describe a time in your life when you were hanging out in Station One: Feeling at Home?

2. Why do we long for acceptance, comfort, belonging, and safety?

3. Can you describe two contradictory beliefs that have caused cognitive dissonance for you in the early stages of the D/R journey?

4. What are the unique dynamics involved in a pastor's D/R journey? What advice would you have for a pastor who is struggling with doubts, questions, and disorientation?

5. Author Reba Riley discusses the destructive side effects of spiritual injury: anger, grief, despair, depression, failure to believe in anything, moral confusion, loss of gravity, and emptiness. What symptoms have you experienced during your faith shift?

6. What are your experiences hanging out in Station Six: Angstville? How have you experienced anger, doubt, and cynicism as you have been deconstructing and reconstructing your faith?

7. What are your thoughts about the dialectic between acceptance and change?

8. How do you fit in, or not fit in, to Station Eight: Extreme Makeover—Home Edition?

PART II

THE INSIDE SCOOP

I designed this section to help you understand the nature of grief and the emotional process you are going through during your confusing and grueling D/R journey. If you're anything like me, the initial disorientation, and tumultuous aftermath of a faith crisis, may leave you feeling confused and alone. You feel as though you are not only moving into uncharted territory, but, even worse, like you are the only one inhabiting this strange, new land.

Let me encourage you. With a greater understanding of the origin of your disorientation—particularly with the emergence of newfound beliefs— and the nature of hurt, grief, trauma, and your overall emotional processes, you will be able to reduce your suffering and diminish your feeling of aloneness. You'll also develop a greater ability to grieve well, heal, and move toward healthy reconstruction.

CHAPTER THREE

THE SPLINTERS

....

"What you know you can't explain, but you feel it. . .that there's something wrong. . .You don't know what it is, but it's there, like a splinter in your mind, driving you mad."

— MORPHEUS, FROM *THE MATRIX*

....

Have you ever had a sharp ache pop up out of nowhere and, instead of being curious about it (you know ... self-diagnosing yourself with a terminal illness on WebMD), you just went on with business as usual? I mean, who has the time to slow down, be still, and ask: "What's with this annoying pain I have never felt before?" No way! Work has to be done. People have to be seen. Emails have to be read and written. The dazzling show of life must go on! Then, over time, the pain you denied becomes more and more palpable. Eventually, you can't ignore it. It must be examined and must be tended to. You finally come to realize: something has to change.

Isn't that essentially the same way we discovered our religious splinters? You know what I'm talking about, right? They are those sharp, pesky pieces of neural dissonance pushing down deep into the recesses of our puzzled and entangled psyches. Those annoying *things*, whatever they were at first. Those irritations of the mind we couldn't quite name. Those splinters that kept us from nonchalantly skipping down the Christian road without a care.

Splinters start off as ideas and then become entrenched beliefs. They come from teachings and doctrines that we were exposed to, or picked up from situations or events we experienced, and eventually become foreign matter to our soul. There are two types of splinters we will now explore.

CYTOTOXIC AND THEOTOXIC SPLINTERS

Let's discuss the first set of splinters: Cytotoxic splinters. The word "Cytotoxic," from a purely biological perspective, simply means *toxic to cells*. This toxicity can promote cell damage or even death. From a spiritual perspective, Cytotoxic splinters come in the form of religious beliefs that, although they initially felt normal and right, can over time become troublesome and toxic. Those pesky ingrained beliefs are lodged in our psyches and can eventually cause suffering to ourselves and those around us.

The sort of Cytotoxic splinters I have in mind have their origin in man-made religion. They have a veneer of godliness but are inevitably exposed for what they are: that which is contrary to love. Rather than encouraging people to open up and invite inclusivity, they tend to foster exclusivity. They are marinated in pride and fear. They are rule-based instead of relationship-based. Although, at one point in time, they may not have felt like splinters, they may start to as your journey progresses. They have long-term negative consequences that not only affect the host, but indirectly affect those the host encounters. Richard Rohr, an internationally known Franciscan friar, writes: "If you do not transform your pain, you will surely transmit it to those around you and even to the next generation."[1] In other words, our splinters—what we believe about ourselves, God, other people, and the world around us—matter.

This newly found status of splinterhood, particularly for Cytotoxic splinters, may be due to the introduction of a new and contradictory belief, a sudden rise in consciousness, a developing rival value, or a disconfirming reality. Typically, an increase in the strength of a contrasting belief, value, or shifting reality creates a greater potential for disorientation. The result is similar to what your body does when it encounters germs and foreign entities. What once felt like part of the psyche becomes foreign to it, and, like all foreign entities, the psyche becomes irritated by its presence.

On the other hand, there are *Theotoxic* splinters (*Theos* is the word for God in Greek) that also invade the psyche as foreign entities. Unlike the splinters previously discussed, Theotoxic splinters are core beliefs that come from teachings, doctrines, situations, or events that, while painful, are designed to increase our capacity for love, inclusion, mercy, and forgiveness. Theotoxic splinters can be very painful and initially cause just as much inflammation as Cytotoxic ones. Why? God-infused splinters like these inflame our ingrained pride, selfishness, critical spirit, and other anti-Christ attitudes and sensibilities that objectify and dehumanize others. The aspects of our soul that are not conformed to the image of Christ consider them toxic and want nothing to do with them.

A great example of a Theotoxic principle is found in Proverbs 25:21-22. The author says, "If your enemy is hungry, give him food to eat; if he is thirsty, give him water to drink. In doing this, you will heap burning coals on his head." In other words, acts of love (such as lovingly encouraging someone who may dislike you) can be painful, irritating, and bothersome for the recipient. However, like we read in Proverbs, it is potentially a good pain that can reorient a person and lead to a radical change in perspective. This is what Theotoxic splinters are like: burning coals of Spirit-infused neurons that heal. These holy splinters can initially be painful, but they can also burn away maladaptive and outdated beliefs. The result is repentance—a word that signifies a powerful paradigm shift that reorients a person toward the heart of God.

In our case, Cytotoxic splinters are natural —or traditional— beliefs that grow to become foreign, whereas Theotoxic splinters are foreign—or nonconforming, less common—beliefs that grow to become natural, fully integrated Divinely-infused beliefs. Each can create a similar sensation of pain, but, depending on the type of splinter and the circumstances behind it, can signify different things. Both Cytotoxic and Theotoxic splinters infect the surrounding areas of our mind and heart like a retrograde virus, seeking to insert a DNA copy of its genome into the cells of our souls. The key is to open ourselves to Theotoxic splinters, allowing them to penetrate the soil of our hearts and minds and replicate.

The more love-filled and inclusive one's heart becomes, the less at home traditional beliefs, that lack such love and inclusivity, will feel. It is in that milieu that Cytotoxic splinters are fully solidified—as the Theotoxic ones become natural and force what was previously natural to become foreign. Once the light of the Theotoxic splinter exposes the Cytotoxic splinter for the Trojan Horse it originally was, the difficult task of extraction begins. An ancient Christian writer refers to it as the need to "demolish arguments and every pretension that sets itself up against the knowledge of God" and to "take captive every thought [splinter] to make it obedient to Christ" (brackets mine).[2]

The Theotoxic splinter usually starts with a brief entrance into our awareness and then encounters an immediate response from our psychological immune system. Because the splinter is deemed as a foreign invader, it gets blasted with a dose of denial, possibly in the form of suppression. For example, we could be going along our merry Christian way, praising God, reading our Bibles, going to after-church events, and strolling through life. Then, suddenly, we momentarily experience a sharp sting we should probably remedy. However, because acknowledging the splinter would be too costly to our identity, and carries the potential byproduct of social exclusion, we deny it exists and keep trudging along.

For many, the longer the splinters stay lodged within their psyche, the greater chance they have to cause infections. Infections left unaddressed can produce toxins that eventually drive people mad. For others, a type of psychological granuloma—a cellular structure of immune cells that create a barrier around what the body experiences as foreign substances— may form around the splinter. It is a harm-prevention mechanism. And in the case of splinters that people are trying to avoid, the person's defense system creates a type of granuloma that walls the splinter off from their consciousness. As a result, instead of pushing the splinter out and healing the irritation, some people take their splinters to the grave.

For many, defense mechanisms fail. At some point, the sting and irritation of the reality they have been covering up are far too strong to ignore. The incongruence between what a person is starting to truly believe due to Theotoxic splinters, and the content the old Cytotoxic splinters are dictating, is insurmountable. The gap becomes too wide. Their core self finally takes a stand and says, "Enough! It is time to face these competing splinters head on!" Unfortunately, at that point, the effect of their immune responses on their soul, due to the internal war of competing beliefs, could have already taken its toll—especially if the Cytotoxic belief is connected to a network of other splinters (since we rarely have just one). Due to the severity of the infection, the pus of anxiety, shame, depression, anger, and burnout could be in full effect (more about that in our next chapter).

I need to address a necessary caveat here. I cannot say definitively that Theotoxic splinters and Cytotoxic splinters are universal. Yes, I may think that some are true and defend them vigorously, but I can't, from a God-like position, state emphatically and judgmentally to others that "This set of beliefs are from God" while "This other set is from man-made religion, culture, or the Devil." That means I do not define Theotoxic splinters and Cytotoxic splinters from the absolutist position of, "Thus saith the Lord." Rather, I define them from the position of one being led by his experience of God. Perhaps it is an oversensitivity of mine to not play God in others' lives. But that very tendency in others, I believe, is partially why we are in this disorienting deconstructive mess to begin with.

I may see that a Theotoxic belief can be clearly found in the life and teachings of Christ. And my religious community may see it that way as well. We can passionately and prophetically declare that some ideas should not be appreciated and/or tolerated. More importantly, we can *live out* our subversive truths with confidence and passion. At the same time, there are over 30,000 different Christian sects and denominations. I have to leave room, even if only a millimeter of space, to the possibility that I could be wrong on some doctrines. Sometimes, it is not about being right or wrong; it is about appreciating (or respectfully tolerating) the vast diversity of Christian beliefs and experiences that exist all over the world.

Let's look at two practical examples of Cytotoxic splinters and Theotoxic splinters in action within issues of spirituality. In the first example, I will deal with the topic of divine sufficiency, one of my earliest deconstructive/reconstructive experiences. In the second one, I will explore, in more depth, the topic of divine violence.

GOD IS (NOT) ALL I NEED

Before college, I was a part of a small Oneness Pentecostal church. It was the first church I belonged to after getting *saved* at the age of twenty-one. And, boy, did I get *saved!* I was a depressed and hopeless cutter with suicidal tendencies who was also dealing with the tragic effects of childhood neglect and abuse in an environment characterized by violence and drug-use. A week after being so hopeless that I tried to get AIDS, with the hopes of dying a slow death (a long, X-rated story), I lifted up my hands in a field not far from my house and invited Jesus into my heart. It was a powerful experience! I wept like a baby. Then, a week after meeting Jesus for the first time, off to church and to organized religion I went. High ho! Unfortunately, I ran from one dysfunctional family to another.

If you know anything about Apostolic Oneness churches, you know they have some extremely conservative teachings. I don't know if they are any different today, but back then, if a person never spoke in tongues, they were clearly not saved. Women were not allowed to cut their hair, and some were even told they would go to Hell for doing so. Likewise, men couldn't have long hair, and if they did, the same fate befell them.

I remember being at a men's conference with hundreds of people in attendance. The famous Pentecostal giant, T. F. Tenney, was the guest speaker. As he railed about the need for holiness codes for the church, he shouted a line I will never forget. Talking about Christians smoking cigarettes, screaming at the top of his lungs, he proclaimed, "If they are smokin' now, they will be smokin' later!" The whole crowd was cheering and yelling, "Amen! Praise God! Praise the Lord!!" I was thoroughly confused. I just started weeping. I thought to myself, *How could these people celebrate that Christians who smoke cigarettes will be going to Hell?* The dissonance in that moment was something I never forgot.

On another occasion, a bunch of United Pentecostal Churches came together for a picnic. Surprisingly, picnics were not on the "demonic activities to stay away from" list. At the event, I talked to a guy I had never met before and asked him what church he went to. He told me he used to be a member of one of the local churches, but got kicked out. When I asked him why, he said, "Because I couldn't stop masturbating." As a fairly new Christian, I was shocked. It was not like he was an exhibitionist; he didn't randomly do his thang in public. He was a young, single guy, who, on occasion, masturbated for release and pleasure. Without going into detail, I must admit that upon hearing this, I was frightened for my ecclesial future (😉)!

To go along with a subtle fear of anything pleasurable, I was explicitly warned not to hang out with people who believed in the Trinity. To them, the Trinity was a demonic, pagan, and polytheistic doctrine contrived in the 3rd century. Obviously, amidst all of the rules, fear, and exclusivity, the church I was part of was a very cultish situation.

Every Sunday at church, there was an altar call. At that most holy place, you would find me pleading with God to have mercy on me: a pathetic, evil worm of a human being who continually needed to be saved. I was so tightly bound up in rules and legalism that I thought I would defile the temple of the Holy Spirit if I drank soda. I believed that impure products could not enter God's sacred vessel, the container of the Holy Spirit. Over time, all of the rules, regulations, and hypocrisy took its toll. I finally had enough and, to the dismay of my "spiritual covering," I ran away to a non-fundamentalist Christian college. While it was a difficult transition, college was a life-changing experience as there were many liberating lessons to learn.

Some professors, students, and guest speakers at my college taught me an idea (both implicitly and explicitly) that went like this: *God is all you need; needing anything else is idolatry.* Theologians refer to this idea as Divine Sufficiency. My Pentecostal church communicated a rule-based message of Jesus-as-my-king. But in college, Christianity was Jesus-as-my-all-sufficient-lover and intimacy-based—a much more clear, direct message.

I didn't realize it at the time, given where I was coming from, that even the belief that *God is all you need; needing anything else is idolatry* was a Cytotoxic splinter. That was the case even if, at that time, it appeared Theotoxic. It was a toxic belief I held to that would eventually cause me immense pain. Why was it toxic? It encouraged me to isolate myself from others. I thought that if God was the only one who could bring me true healing and happiness, then why would I go to an imperfect and sinful person for help with those things. It also fostered an earn-it and work-for-it mentality which was exhausting. Don't get me wrong. There is nothing wrong with spiritual disciplines, but they are counterproductive when you are encouraged to use them to obtain an illusory and impossible goal.

At first, I didn't think anything of it. Needing God and God alone seemed like a lofty and holy ambition. Other people I met seemed to get to that heavenly state, so I assumed it was a spiritual feat that could be attained if a person was disciplined enough. Perhaps it was the illusion they portrayed or an experience I simply projected onto them. Nonetheless, I was going for it. I was going to cease being an insecure and needy little boy trapped in a man's body. I was determined to become a spiritual giant who needed nothing, and no one, but God.

Over time, the belief that *God is all you need; needing anything else is idolatry* would feel like an aching splinter. There were countless times I chose to ignore it. On one occasion, a nagging voice rose within me that screamed, "That's bullshit. God is *not* all I need," but, I quickly dismissed it. It seemed like, underneath the surface, an unconscious battle was going on. I must have picked up a Theotoxic splinter along the way that contradicted the original Cytotoxic belief in divine sufficiency. Perhaps the message that came from the Theotoxic splinter was simply, "God is not all you need. You also need other people."

I continually suppressed the message coming from the Theotoxic splinter. If I gave up on the idea that God is all I needed, I feared rejection from the spiritual elite. I thought that I would be a failure and unspiritual if I didn't experience utter enlightenment like the rest of the folks with their glistening halos. So, I continued to work toward God being my everything. I engaged in all the spiritual disciplines I could think of. I hoped to achieve the mysterious, yet attainable, Oneness with God—a static and mystical state in which I needed no one but God.

After repeated attempts at pushing the stubborn Theotoxic splinter down, it eventually rose to the surface. It was almost like the Cytotoxic and Theotoxic splinters were in an epic battle (in actuality, they were). They were contradictory neurons, in the form of beliefs, fighting for space inside my brain. Eventually, there came a point when I either had to remove the Theotoxic splinter or push it back down to an area in my psyche that would no longer be accessible.

I spent a couple of years seeking a mystical union with God. Then, during a season of grieving a past relationship, and after a few weeks of full-on grieving mode, I found myself at a service singing a Vineyard worship song all about needing God and God alone. I felt the need to stop singing mid-chorus. Surprised at what was happening, I began to tear up as I realized that I could no longer sing the lyrics with authenticity. I began to feel overwhelmed with shame. So, I bowed my head and uttered something to myself I never expected to say: "God is not all I need."

Even though I was praying, fasting, reading the Bible, and submitting myself to God, I hungered for something more: a real-life, flesh-and-blood human being (or two) who could compassionately sit with me in the middle of my incessant loneliness and pain. I needed wit(h)nesses—people who made time to be compassionately present and wholeheartedly *with* me; people unafraid to enter my dark experiences and *witness* my sorrow.

In the middle of the church service, I put my gloves on, got out the antiseptic, and chose to begin the arduous process of extraction. I lifted my head and proudly declared to myself, "God is not all I need. I need other people." I finally allowed the Theotoxic splinter to have its way. While there were a few miniscule pieces of the Cytotoxic splinter still lodged within me, over the years they fell out on their own. I felt liberated. I was finally able to own the message God was trying to communicate to me.

Over time, this new belief of mine became more solidified without any toxicity. It transformed from a Theotoxic splinter to a fully integrated, Divinely-infused belief. I came to realize that we all have God-designed aches and hungers that God alone cannot fill. One of these is human connection, something that monks, priests, and nuns figured out a long time ago. They live together and aren't off in a cave somewhere like a bunch of self-sufficient hermits. I started to find many biblical passages to confirm our interdependence such as 1 Cor. 12:21: "The eye cannot say to the hand, 'I don't need you!' And the head cannot say to the feet, 'I don't need you!'" In other words, we need each other. I need you, and you need me.

The Cytotoxic splinter that *God is all you need; needing anything else is idolatry* was out. I felt free to name my truth. Regardless of the super-spiritual grins on the glowing faces of the spiritual elite at my college, I felt liberated to state to myself and others: "I am needy! I need the warm presence of non-judgmental friends. I need the wildness and beauty of the outdoors. I need food. I need air and water. I need music. I need a place to lay my head. I *definitely* need underarm deodorant and a toothbrush. And, of course, I need God." Other things besides God fill me, bring me joy, keep me healthy, and sustain me. And that's okay!

Some of you reading this are thinking, "Duh, I could have told you God is not all we need." I know, I know. Looking back on that experience, it should have been a no-brainer, but we all are in different spaces and places on the spiritual journey. One person's Theotoxic splinter is another person's long-held spiritual splint—a treasured belief that has long upheld them, kept them strong, and enabled them to live and love as God intended. I now know that God who is in all, manifests all, and sustains all can be found in everything I need. So, in a way, I still believe God *is* all I need, particularly if all that exists is pulsating with Divine DNA.

I could write a whole book on the Cytotoxic splinters I have taken out and the processes that led to their demise. Keep in mind, though, that this book is not meant to be a theology textbook. I am not out to prove my case against Cytotoxic splinters in a deeply theological, thorough, and systematic manner. I am more interested in sharing with you what was going on in my head and heart while coming to a decision to remove a Cytotoxic splinter that negatively affected my relationships with God, self, and others.

THE JOURNEY FROM DIVINE VIOLENCE TO THE VIOLENCE OF DIVINE VIOLENCE

Years ago, amazingly, I wouldn't even cringe at the idea of God commanding genocide (Joshua 1:12); flooding the planet and giving sharks a smorgasbord of human entrees (Genesis 6-9); killing precious Egyptian babies (Exodus 11:5); burning people to a crisp (Numbers 11:1); striking down seventy people for being curious and peeking into the ark of the covenant (1 Sam. 16:19); ordering someone to be stoned to death by an entire community for working on the sabbath (Numbers 15:32); being prejudiced against people with disabilities and those who looked different (Leviticus 21:17-24); or committing a host of other Hitleresque monstrosities. I suppose I was just going with the Christian flow.

There were times when the Cytotoxic splinter that *Every passage of Scripture must be taken literally, and, therefore, a holy and just God does use violence to punish disobedience*, would feel uncomfortable, but I had to push those feelings down. Why? Because the text clearly and unequivocally quoted God commanding violence. It was staring at me from the page. The biblical text clearly depicted God, angry and wrathful because of sin, violently punishing and killing people. It would have been heretical to many people in my Christian circle, to question the veracity of passages in the Bible that described divine violence. I was told that to suggest God did *not* call the religious community to enact divine violence because of sinful disobedience—when passages of Scripture clearly showed God doing so—would be the same as questioning the inerrant "Word of God." That was a problem. After all, you know who else questioned God's truth? You got it! Satan.

If I had a cubic foot of helium for every time a Christian brought up the Genesis story to me—the one with the wily serpent who tried to get naïve Eve to question God's word saying, "Did God really say?"— I would be flying in space right now, passing members of the elite Space Force on their mission to save the world. In essence, I was told that questioning whether or not God really did violently kill babies (or had God's angelic hit-creatures do it) was tantamount to being inspired by Satan. I heard responses to my doubts, such as:

"How dare you question God!"

"Mark, I am praying for you! I know God will lead you to His truth"

"Pride comes before a fall!"

"Don't let Satan deceive you."

"God is not just loving, but God is just and holy! Sin demands punishment!

"Mark, just trust in God's word."

I was in a bind. I knew God hated Satan. And in my naïve mind, it was not a stretch to assume that God would abhor me for listening to that sly, slithering snake. To entertain the idea that biblical writers were culturally conditioned to describe sub-Christlike portrayals of God would have been irreligious.[3] It was not a giant leap to think that these sincere Christians, some of whom were pastors and leaders, would deem me a heretic for doing so. Not to mention I would be out of a job for questioning the word of God, seeing that I was working full-time in a conservative-minded church. You better believe I shoved that splinter down as far and as fast as I could!

Church folks also brought up the slippery slope argument, one that sounded very scary to me at the time. It was hinted to me that if I started questioning God's word (which is really people's interpretations of people's interpretations of God's word), then I would be led straight down a demonic slope, swiftly into a life of miserable debauchery. In no time, I would be performing séances and humbly worshipping Grand Master Lucifer.

"Don't go down the Devil's path, Mark!" they warned.

"Without God, you can do no good. Leave the truth of God's word and curses will follow," said one confident preacher.

After all of these subtle, and not so subtle messages, it was apparent that I didn't need people to scare me. My inner critic, on its own, would have a field day providing me with apocalyptic, doom-and-gloom messages of what would happen if I didn't trust God and His word. I believed that a consequence of my doubts would be suffering the fate of a horrible and unrecoverable depression. Perhaps I would find myself homeless, roaming the streets with a debilitating addiction, unable to break free. Why? God's blessing and favor on my life would instantly dissipate because I was rebelliously doubting Him and His word. It would be a life without God and a life without goodness, so I falsely imagined. So, I continually engaged in the fine art of suppression, pushing the doubts I harbored about the biblical text down, further and further.

My naysayers also made the point that if we couldn't trust the Bible to accurately portray God in the Old Testament, how could we trust what the gospel said about Jesus? Couldn't the gospel writers have made stuff up too? While, back then, their slippery slope argument caused me to push my doubts deeper down into my awareness, I now think they actually have a good point. I don't think it is fair to state that writers of Hebrew scripture may have been at times creative storytellers accommodated by God in their sub-Christlike portrayals of God while, in the same breath, claiming every New Testament authors' jot and tittle is a one-hundred percent literal, objective, non-exaggerative, absolutely-truthful account of what Jesus said and did.

In other words, I don't buy into the proposal that God needed to accommodate biblical writers' imperfect perceptions of God only in the Hebrew Bible. Despite the impressive 5,800, either complete or partial, Greek manuscripts of the New Testament, the notion that we have a perfect translation of God's word is intellectually dishonest. I concede that both Hebrew Bible and New Testament authors may have filtered God's inspiration through their own biases and worldview.[4] That is a can of worms I am willing to pry open. I believe most biblical writers throughout the generations were in relationship with God; were wrestling with God; were inspired by God; were trying to make sense of their communal story with God in the midst of trauma and travail. And while inspired, they did not always perfectly tune into the frequency of inspiration. Thankfully, there is enough inspiration found within the biblical text to wrestle with and be inspired by for our communities of faith. We can also be confident that there is enough inspiration that points to Jesus, the express image of the invisible God.

Other Christians shared with me a different side of the slippery slope argument: "Isn't your hermeneutic just a slippery slope towards relativism and cafeteria-style Christianity? Isn't that like saying, 'Oh, delicious! I will take that verse. Yuck! I prefer not to take this verse. Ooh, give me some of that,' and so on? If we can't trust the Bible to accurately describe God and Jesus, what is our faith built upon?"

I'll be honest with you. For a long time, I thought they were right. Their slippery slope argument inspired me to cling ever so tightly to my "perfect God-breathed text," which included clear pictures of divine violence. I didn't want to "pick and choose" and be one of those "deceived liberal fools." I wanted to follow the whole counsel of God's word.

But today, I think differently. There are roughly 174,000 words and 32,000 verses in the Bible. I think we are all cherry-pickers who pick and choose what verses primarily guide our lives. As far as a foundation goes, I think it is safe to say that Jesus, the Universal Christ; the Word of God; and the Way, the Truth, and the Life is the Foundation.[5] While the Bible *points* to Jesus, the Bible cannot and does not *contain* Jesus. As precious as the Bible is as a sacred text, burn every one of them in the world and the Word of God lives forever! Okay, now back to that darn splinter.

While there was the entrenched Cytotoxic splinter—*Every passage of scripture must be taken literally, and, therefore, a holy and just God does use violence to punish disobedience*—there were a couple of major Theotoxic splinters that were burrowing their way sharply into my mind and heart. The first was: *God cannot be less loving and less wise than we are.* The second was: *God is love and love does not perpetrate gratuitous violence. Therefore, not all Scriptures should be read literally.* The battle of the splinters was on!

MY COMPASSION, GOODNESS, AND WISE DISCIPLINE METER MUST BE OUT OF WHACK

When I brought my questions to people, questions about some biblical writer's violent portrayal of God, assuming these writers were culturally conditioned and simply viewed God as any other tribal deity from that time period, they would say: "Well, God is just. God is holy. God hates sin. And there are consequences to disobedience. God is just in his discipline." If those people were right, then I needed to take my compassion, goodness, and wise discipline meter immediately to the repair shop. Randall Rouser, a systematic and analytic theologian, writes that "If human beings really are wrong about a moral intuition this basic and intuitive, it is difficult to see why we should trust any of our moral intuitions at all."[6] It boggles my mind that my notion of what constitutes as love, goodness, compassion, and healthy discipline could be considered so marred by sin that, in actuality, my views are deviant and ungodly. To some, what appears to be loving and just from my standpoint (a belief that a lovingly just God would use wise, health-promoting, non-violent discipline) is just a satanic mirage. But could that *really* be? Has sin so poisoned my heart and twisted my mind so greatly that I call that which is good and just (God's violent and retributive punishment of sin) evil?

For example, I think that commanding violence—including stoning, burning, maiming, and killing, which God is said to have done plenty of in the Bible—is inhumane, ungodlike, and missing an invaluable and moral sense of restorative justice. Restorative justice seeks to transform relationships and communities. As John Howard Yoder, professor of ethics and theology, puts it: restorative justice should "contribute to the creation of structures more worthy of human society."[7] Restorative justice is completely contrary to seeking the brutal and violent cessation of life. It is creative and forward-thinking. It leads with fierce compassion and seeks to restore wounded and wayward human beings to a right relationship with God, self, and others. Doesn't that type of justice make sense? After all, if you're a mangled corpse due to the mob of angry folks with stones in their hands who think they are following God's orders, the only transformation that's going to happen is metamorphosing from a human being to nutritious bird, bug, and bacteria food. Dead people don't learn valuable lessons that help them become ethical members of society.

I supposed then, based on what people were telling me, that if I had the good, wise, and compassionate mind of God, I would value the killing of disobedient people. Why? I would value what God values. Now, I am not saying I would take pleasure in it. Surely, God does "take no pleasure in the death of the wicked" (Ezek. 33:11). But I would still grasp the horrific nature of sin that preachers kept talking about. I would have a proper picture of a glorious, righteous, and holy God who always does what is good and just. Right? Then, instead of cringing when I read about God killing babies, I should boldly say—in humility, perhaps with a faint tear coming down my cheek—"Praise God, the mighty Egyptian baby killer, for His just acts!" Instead of questioning whether God really commanded genocide— or commanded people who sinned to be maimed and stoned to death (much unlike Jesus' response to sin)—I should proclaim, "All of God's violent commands are praiseworthy, just, and good!"

No. I could not. I simply could not muster up enough faith to believe God did the violent things written about in the Bible. I couldn't put my conscience away.

The final tug on the Cytotoxic splinter of divine violence happened when I became a father. I simply could not imagine violently punishing my child (or giving someone else permission to do so) because of his disobedience. I could never kill my child for not listening to me. I could never use violent and gratuitous physical force to discipline him. Karl Forehand, author of *Apparent Faith,* puts it succinctly: "The Scriptures were written by people who often portrayed God as a parent using the term Father. If God is Father and if He is love, then His love for His children must at least be better than the love I have for my children."[8]

Am I supposed to believe that a God, who is vastly more loving and just than I am, would be less loving and just than me? No matter where you are on the liberal/conservative divide, I am sure we can agree that maiming, burning alive, stoning, and drowning our children, when they selfishly go against our wishes (even if they were our adult children), is not the most compassionate, just, wise, and loving thing to do. Right?

"God is not just a God of love; God is holy and just!" some people shout.

Okay. Let's say that God's righteousness necessitates God's desire for justice, a desire to make things right. Certainly, justice seems to be a need for us. When something unjust happens to us, when someone hurts or offends us, we usually demand that wrong to be made right. We usually demand payment of some kind. We demand justice! When that pained part of us wants and demands justice, what is it that God requires of us? And does that requirement provide a glimpse into what God's true impulse is in the face of injustice?

Here is my concern with the "God demands justice for sin" motif. It seems to me that God asks us to forgive, without the need for violent physical punishment, when people act unjustly toward us. So, how is it that God demands justice in the form of violent physical punishment if people sin against Him, but God calls us to extend love, mercy, and forgiveness when people sin against us? Something is amiss here. Why is our primitive impulse toward justice—"an eye for an eye,"—to be superseded by love, mercy, and forgiveness, while God's impulse to violently punish due to an offense, and giving in to that impulse is to be applauded as holy and righteous? Wouldn't that make us more lovingly just than God?

God's knowledge of discipline should be vastly superior to the researchers, parenting experts, healthy development strategists, and transformation gurus of today. We know that violent punishment is cruel, harmful, and negatively impacts the brains of developing children. We know that the healthy carrot is better for us all—including adults—than the Negan-like stick. And we've been taught a plethora of non-violent techniques to discipline children and adults that promote compassion, equity, and overall moral citizens. Could God, who by definition is a wiser and more intelligent disciplinarian than we are, possibly use primitive violence and killing as the primary methods of loving discipline and justice? I think not.

I am tired of playing the "Well, God accommodated their primitive ways" card. If Jesus, as God, could say to the misinformed beliefs of the people of his day, "You have heard it said. . . but I tell you," I am sure God could have used the same approach back with the Israelites. They wouldn't have needed to hear something new if God had gotten it right in the first place.

After pushing down the Cytotoxic splinter of divine violence countless times, my Spirit-guided conscience and rational faculties finally had enough. I juxtaposed the beliefs dozens and dozens of times before there was a shift in perspective from "Every passage of Scripture must be taken literally, and, therefore, a holy and just God does use violence to punish disobedience" to "God cannot be less loving and less wise than we are. God is love and love does not perpetrate gratuitous violence; therefore, not all Scriptures should be read literally". It took many separate occasions over many years, along with many conversations with likeminded peers, to finally come to a place where I could not believe God, *the* role model for compassion, wisdom, love, holiness, and justice, would use horrific violence to punish

God's people. There came a point when I could not believe, with a clear conscience, that God looked like every other tribal god of the Ancient Near East. I could not believe the worst, that a Divine sense of discipline and justice most resembled a twisted composite of Hitler, Stalin, and Mao Zedong.

So, I made a confession to my Christian friends: "I know all of God's actions are good, just, and praiseworthy, but I cannot praise God for killing children. I cannot praise God for commanding genocide. I cannot praise God for commanding people to be stoned, maimed, and burned alive for missing the mark of God's ideal. If that is good, then it seems that my justice, goodness, and compassionate discipline meter is broken and can never be fixed. And, in truth, perhaps I don't want it fixed if it means that I would have to confidently believe the very thing I detest."

I came to a place where I could be honest with myself and ask, "Is my meter really broken?" And over time, I realized that perhaps it was working just fine. Maybe my growing understanding of compassion and loving justice was perfectly on point. Even though it is a finite view that is shared by many, perhaps God's loving justice does not encompass brutal and violent displays of punitive power. It could be that God, who epitomizes wise and loving discipline, is far more loving than we could ever think or imagine. It may be that God cannot be less loving and less wise than we are. It may be that God *is* love, and love does not perpetrate violence. Every passage of Scripture can teach us valuable lessons, but perhaps not every passage of Scripture should be interpreted as one-hundred percent accurate, objective history.

STACKING THE DECK WITH LOVE

I needed to go through one more process to fully root out the splinter that *Every passage of Scripture must be taken literally, and, therefore, a holy and just God does use violence to punish disobedience.* When we get rid of an old, rickety framework, we have to replace it with a new, healthy one. I had to begin looking at Biblical passages through a lens that helped me determine which were accurately portraying God and which ones were not.

The Bible was written by more than forty authors across three continents. If there were oral traditions for both the Scriptures in the Hebrew Bible and New Testament (as many scholars believe), then there were many more than forty authors. These various authors clearly did not see eye-to-eye on topics of theodicy and the nature of God, violence, love, Heaven, Hell, sin, etc. Their texts are multivocal and kaleidoscopic in nature.

After many years of reading, wrestling, and reflecting on the biblical text, I cannot with a clear conscience hold to a flat reading of Scripture where all texts fully disclose and reveal the true nature of reality and of God. There is no way I can say, "Yes, God killed those Egyptian children," or "Yes, God righteously killed those millions of sinful and rebellious men, women, children, and animals in a catastrophic flood." I also can't say, "Yes, God savagely burned people alive for not being obedient." The list goes on and on. I have come to a non-anxious resolution that the biblical authors were, at times, culturally conditioned.

Pete Enns, a biblical scholar, theologian, and master of deconstruction and reconstruction, writes in his book, *How the Bible Actually Works,* "The problem of divine violence becomes far less of a problem when we remember why some biblical writers portray God violently. They are making sense of God with the ancient vocabulary available to them in their world. And like most things in the Bible, God is presented in diverse ways along with the changing experiences of the ancient Israelites and then the first followers of Jesus."[9] Sometimes, God is a projection of ourselves. If that is the case, we should expect

God, or our portrayals of God, to grow, morph, and change throughout the centuries.

I finally removed the last piece of the Cytotoxic splinter that *Every passage of Scripture must be taken literally, and, therefore, a holy and just God does use violence to punish disobedience* when I decided to stack the hermeneutical deck in favor of love. Since the biblical writers did not always get it right about God, love is going to be where I start. Love is going to be my filter. Love is going to be where I end.

The Pentalateral Hermeneutic of Love (PHL) is a lens with which I currently look through the Scriptures. It helps me determine what passages may be culturally conditioned and sub-Christlike portrayals of God. The PHL also helps me consider what passages have a higher likelihood of reflecting and refracting the incredible, beautiful, and loving character of God.

The five-part lens consists of:

1. The fruit of the Spirit (Galatians 5:22)

2. The biblical definition of love (1 Corinthians 13:4–7)

3. The only explicit parabolic picture Jesus gave of God the Father found in the story of the Prodigal Son (Luke 15:11–31)

4. Perfect love described in Matthew 5

5. The radical self-giving, others-empowering life of Jesus Christ, who is the full revelation of God.

Maybe, just maybe, it is not an accurate portrayal of God if, in a passage of Scripture:

1. God is exhibiting the works of the flesh (e.g. hatred, jealousy, rage, etc.) rather than the fruit of the Spirit.

2. God acts in a way that is not patient, kind, and protective but rather is easily angered and keeps records of wrongs.

3. God does not forgive or compassionately invite sinners back into God's presence.

4. God is not kind to the ungrateful and wicked and extending mercy to the just and the unjust.

5. God does not look like Jesus who forgave his enemies, extended mercy, forgave without payment of some kind, and cried because his people would not return to him.

A Hermeneutical Grid to Help Decipher Which Scriptures Accurately Depict the Character of God

PERFECT LOVE

Does the character of God displayed by the text line up with a God who perfectly loves His enemies (Matt. 5)?

FRUIT

Does the character of God displayed by the text line up with the Fruit of the Spirit found in Galatians 5?

JESUS

Does the character of God displayed by the text line up with Jesus, who is the express image of the invisible God?

FATHER

Does the character of God displayed by the text line up with the only explicit parabolic description of the loving, compassionate Father offered by Jesus in Luke 15?

DEFINITION OF LOVE

Does the character of God displayed by the text line up with the definition of love found in 1 Corinthians 13?

PENTALATERAL HERMENEUTIC OF LOVE

The PHL obviously doesn't solve every biblical issue, but it provides me with a fairly coherent framework that helps me to understand that passages portraying God as vindictive, vicious, and violent are not necessarily objective history. I can imagine something else must be going on with the text. Or, I could be reading my violent-God biases in the text itself. Sometimes there are violent events that occur, but does the text *explicitly* state that God committed the violence? I can value the texts before me, not as I want them to be, but in the raw, unfiltered, and R-rated versions that they really are. I can avoid sugarcoating them and believe that the biblical authors could have witnessed real, horrific events while simultaneously understanding that they interpreted what they witnessed through their cultural framework and the tribal view of God they held at the time. There are also a myriad number of ways that biblical scholars can help us examine the text. In the end, I can appreciate how my spiritual family saw things centuries ago. I can honor their experiences and humbly learn from them without taking every word they say as the exact word or act of God.

One thing is for sure: I can trust that God is love. And love doesn't violently punish and kill others (or have others do it). Love exposes the violence of divine violence. I can also trust that God must be a wiser and more lovingly just disciplinarian than myself and esteemed others. Advocating for restorative practices—and not punitive ones—for the healthy development of children and adults, so they can contribute to healthy communal ideals, seems to be divine rather than demonic. I can now say with confidence that *God cannot be less loving and less wise than we are.* And, *God is love. Love does not perpetrate gratuitous violence.* And, as a result, *not all Scriptures should be read as literal events that occurred in history.*

The splinter of *Every passage of Scripture must be taken literally, and, therefore, a holy and just God does use violence to punish disobedience* is one toxic splinter. Here are some additional overt and covert Cytotoxic splinters I have tweezed out from my Christian experience over the years. Remember, these are mine. I suspect you have your own list. We can lovingly agree to disagree if what I consider tragically toxic is something you tenaciously treasure:

- Human beings are primarily and intrinsically sinful and evil.

- Because humans sin against God, they are deserving of eternal suffering and torment.

- God uses Hitleresque violence to discipline those who are disobedient.

- God's truth can only be found in the biblical text.

- The body and its desires are wicked.

- The Bible is completely free from contradictory positions on God and the godly life.

- Masturbation is always unholy and sinful.

- Other religions are demonic and have nothing to offer Christians.

- God plans, wills, and controls *all* things.

- If you give the church money, God will bless you. If you don't, God will not.

- Pastors and those in leadership are somehow holier and deserving of more intrinsic worth than those who are not.

- Mental illness is caused by demons. They need to be cast out for people to be healed.

- Propositions and having the right knowledge of God is more important than loving people.

- God has only one will, and, if you stray from that will, your choices moving forward are doomed.

- Praying (or talking to God) increases God's love unilaterally in people's lives; and the more people pray, the greater the chance of God increasing God's love [prayer chains anyone?].

- God should only be considered to have masculine characteristics and should solely be thought of as "Him."

- Human beings are more important than all other creatures, and all creatures are for humans' consumption and purposes.

- You can be healed of sickness if you just have enough faith.

- Self-love is contrary to Christian values.

- God loves some and hates others.

- God is in the heavens and occasionally intervenes in human affairs.

- Questioning deeply beloved Christian doctrines is unspiritual, divisive, and demonic.

- Men are superior to women and should be the only ones who lead a church.

- In the end times, creation is going to burn, so we shouldn't care about taking care of it now.

- Those who identify as LGBTQ+ are automatically bound for Hell.

- Emotions are not to be honored and listened to; only God's truth should be valued.

Our splinters, especially when they are in the form of core beliefs, are powerful. Religious beliefs intertwined with grand stories take on a life of their own. They mold us, shape us, and direct us in ways beyond our comprehension and apprehension. They create our reality and determine our destiny. While we can easily change what our favorite jeans are, or what restaurants we like to go to, changing our religious beliefs and religious narratives is immensely challenging. Yet, that is what reconstruction is all about. Reconstruction is re-storying. It is about determining what stories we want to shape our identity, our faith, and our future.

This radical reorientation, of what and how we believe, comes knocking at our door uninvited. We can either welcome the guest or choose to go about our business as usual. We can choose the red pill and go down an adventurous path of the unknown or we can choose the blue pill and live a life of illusory security. If you are reading this, you have most likely taken the red pill. Your mind clamored for congruence; your spirit sought to lay hold of liberation. It was either that or let the splinters drive you mad.

The battle for spiritual peace comes with a price. Sometimes we have so many unremitting splinters in need of extraction, and so many new ones that sound like the Sirens' singing their alluring songs of love, that we are left completely disoriented. This phase of disorientation, and the grief process that accompanies it, is where we now turn.

QUESTIONS

1. How would you describe the difference between Cytotoxic and Theotoxic splinters?

2. What are three Cytotoxic beliefs that you once believed to be true, but now find toxic?

3. Can you describe a few Theotoxic beliefs that initially brought discomfort but now feel comfortable to believe?

4. Why do you think it is so hard to change religious beliefs?

5. What are your thoughts around the belief that *God is all you need and needing anything else is idolatry?*

6. What are your thoughts around the belief that *Every passage of Scripture must be taken literally, therefore, a holy and just God does use violence to punish disobedience?*

7. What is helpful or not helpful about the *Pentelateral Hermeneutic of Love* in identifying subChristlike portrayals of God in the Bible?

8. In the list of overt and covert Cytotoxic splinters, which ones do you agree or disagree with? What ones are not found on the list that you would include in yours?

CHAPTER FOUR

MAKING SENSE OF THE MAYHEM

"Some people's lives seem to flow in a narrative; mine had many stops and starts. That's what trauma does. It interrupts the plot. You can't process it because it doesn't fit with what came before or what comes afterwards."

— JESSICA STERN

Montu was the world's tallest and fastest rollercoaster when it opened in 1996 at Busch Gardens in Florida. It was revolutionary at the time it was built as visitors would be completely inverted and experience 3.8 times the force of gravity. Beneath parts of Montu's track was a Nile crocodile exhibit, making the ride both visually stunning and terrifying as daredevils plummeted toward the pit of hungry reptiles. It was truly a sight to behold and, for the thrill-seeker, it was a treacherously amazing experience. Oh, I almost forgot the best part! This rollercoaster full of zigs, zags, and adrenaline-filled free-falls was named after Montu, the ancient Egyptian *god of war*.

It's the perfect name when you think about it. People who are struggling in their faith, and who feel like they are at war with God (and God's representatives), experience the same feelings as visitors riding on an unpredictable, out-of-control, zigzagging roller coaster. Once they start exposing the splinters that are causing their enormous cognitive dissonance, their whole life feels like it is starting to unravel. It is utter disorientation, complete inversion, 3.8 times the force of gravity.

Walter Bruggeman describes this disorientation of faith, writing, "It constitutes a dismantling of the old, known world and a relinquishment of safe, reliable confidence in God's good creation. The movement of dismantling includes a rush of negativities, including rage, resentment, guilt, shame, isolation, despair, hatred, and hostility."[1] Along the way, people can feel a profound heaviness, as though pinned down by rollercoaster-like g-forces. They can feel overwhelming dread and disorientation as they look down at the hungry crocodiles wanting to eat away at a hopeful and stable future. At other points on the rollercoaster, just like they're rolling down a straight, smooth section of track, people can feel steady, secure, and optimistic about the spiritual adventures ahead.

Even secular researchers are studying this phenomenon called spiritual disorientation, seeking to find a correlation between a person's mental health, beliefs, and inner wrestling with God—what they call *divine struggle*. "Divine struggle," researchers argue, "is related to lower levels of positive indicators of mental health, such as self-esteem, problem solving skills, life satisfaction, meaning, and positive affect, as well as to higher levels of negative indicators of mental health, such as anxiety, anger, depression, and general emotional distress".[2] They are exactly right. Disorientation, a divine struggle, incessant spiritual zig-zagging, and feeling like there is a war going on inside our soul, is what many are acquainted with on the D/R journey.

The divine struggle means entering into the wilderness of piercing grief where the ferocious wolves of deconstruction are slowly nipping at our scarred heels. It means walking into the chasm of the unknown. The inevitable state of disorientation, which is a sign that change barged through life's door, can visit us often during this war within ourselves. And, from my experience, this is especially true at the start of our D/R journey, when we begin questioning our reality, faith, identity, and anything else that isn't bolted to the ground.

People typically avoid this journey because of the cognitive, physical, and emotional mayhem that comes along with it. The aftermath of disorientation and the overall experience of grief can oftentimes leave us feeling confused and anxious because we are entering into uncharted territory. Even worse, we can feel alone, as though we are the only ones inhabiting this strange new land. But I'm here to tell you that the rollercoaster doesn't have to be such a traumatic experience. In fact, I believe you can prepare yourself and minimize suffering and feelings of isolation with a greater awareness of the emotional and physical effects that show up on the D/R journey. You can know the best way to approach the ride by learning healthy ways to grieve, heal, and how to engage in the reconstruction process.

I FEEL HURT!

People who feel negative toward Christianity commonly say, "I have been *hurt* by the church." But what do they mean by "hurt?" Most of them are describing the cocktail of feelings such as anger, sadness, and fear they can literally feel pulsating through their entire body. It is both physical and emotional because they feel both types of pain in the same region of their brain. For those of us who can't fully relate to "de-churched" people like this, and since few of us are actually trained neurologists, here is an example that might help to make sense of their experience: The emotional pain they feel when they experience judgment and rejection by other Christians is the equivalent to the physical pain that comes from getting hit in the back of the head with a huge brick.

This intense feeling makes complete sense in light of recent work by cognitive researchers who found evidence that physical and emotional pain are located in the same part of the brain. They hypothesized that if it were true, people could feel both physical pain and emotional pain in the same regions of the brain, then acetaminophen (Tylenol) could possibly help reduce emotional pain. During their study, they administered acetaminophen to some participants and a placebo (a fake pill) to the others for three weeks straight. In the middle of those three weeks, the researchers intentionally made the participants feel rejection by excluding them from an activity. Afterward, they hooked them up to a functional magnetic resonance imaging (fMRI) machine to examine their brains. The conclusion was that those who received the acetaminophen reported "hurt feelings" less frequently than did the placebo group, demonstrating significant overlap between emotional and physical pain as registered by the brain.[3]

The emotional pain and visceral hurt we experience long after our negative experiences with people inside the institutional church, is very real. Unlike a badly bruised arm that people can see with their own eyes, it is nearly impossible to see the bruises on our hearts and understand how much they hurt. Rejection from our faith community, or having to reject it due to growing apart or spiritual abuse, cuts to the deepest core of our emotional, physical, and spiritual being. It hurts our brains. It hurts our hearts. It hurts our bodies. It simply hurts.

TRIBAL BRAINS

Rejection and ridicule from those of our religious communities hurts for a very good reason. It makes sense why choosing to leave our fold, to leave our religious tribe, is difficult and filled with inner anguish and turmoil. The latest neuroscience tells us that humans have an innate need to belong, feel safe, and be loved. In fact, we need it so badly that our nervous system encodes loneliness, isolation, and rejection as primal threats.[4] Loneliness and isolation can cause anxiety and stress hormones to ripple through our brains and bodies with devastating consequences to our immune system and overall well-being. It hurts so much because we are wired to connect and belong.

One of the reasons leaving faith, and more specifically our community of faith, is so painful, is because we have tribally-wired brains. Back in the day, men and women belonged to tight-knit groups and tribes. We sang the songs, followed the rules, and engaged in the rites and rituals that helped bond us together and maintain social order. No one dared to deviate because (1) it could leave the tribe vulnerable to attack and (2) non-conformity against the tribe, especially against the tribal leader, meant banishment—basically a death sentence. Our bodies evolved to accommodate the fact that people couldn't survive alone. So, for thousands of years, most human beings keep the status quo and that tricky tribal brain never entirely went away.

Because of our tribal brains, it's almost impossible to stop singing the songs, to break the rules, to disobey the religious leaders in our lives, and to become anything different than the docile sheep that we are used to being. Straying away from our group already causes enormous apprehension due to our tribally-wired brains. But throw the tribal God into the mix (usually a punishing, angry, and dissonantly loving deity) and you have double the anxiety and terror. No wonder leaving our tribal beliefs and community is one of the most confusing and herculean adventures in which we could ever engage in!

When we leave elements of our faith behind, we may not realize in the moment just how primitive and deep the fear can become. We are left with confusion and we may feel like we don't know what the heck is going on inside of our own heads. Chaos is the perfect word to describe this sense we have that we are not okay and we don't really know why. Our logical left- brain is not in sync with our emotion-laden, subconscious, right-brain. And, as a result, we end up listening to the voice of our fearful, amped up, tribal-wired unconscious nervous system that tells us all kinds of lies while we deconstruct our faith. Lies like these:

- I am going to be all alone.

- I am going to die in the wilderness of the world.

- I will be a lost soul and won't know who I am anymore.

- God will hate me forever.

- I won't be successful without other Christians liking me.

- I will cause other members of my family to fall away.

- I will be vulnerable to demonic attack.

- I will never recover from this.

- I will be miserable for the rest of my life.

- If God doesn't exist, then what is the point of living?

Don't worry. If you start hearing phrases like these, you are not possessed by crafty demons. You do not have "vile spirits of confusion, anger, and pain" that need to be cast out. Instead, you have underneath-the-hood processes that produce many fear-based messages which, at least initially, are largely beyond our control. If you went hiking, tripped over a rock, and broke your leg, it would be normal to shout a few choice words while you experience immense physical pain. It is just as normal to experience emotional pain and disorientation (and shout the same choice words) when a community you genuinely love is gone, or while you stray from your tribe's beliefs and rituals. And it is completely normal to experience levels of complex grief at the apparent loss of God. The D/R journey, at least in the beginning of its awakening, can be scary and painful.

TRAUMA

Desperate to experience the full goodness of God, Moses cried out to his Creator, "Now show me your glory!" (Exod. 33:18–20). Ironically, if God had done as Moses asked, one can only assume the fiery glory of God's holiness would have burned a hole right through Moses's eyes, fried his brain, and disintegrated him right where he stood. Moses's request was naively dangerous and was similar to including "stand ten feet away from the sun and take a selfie" on your bucket list. Not a good idea. In great love and mercy, instead of striking Moses dead right where he stood, God said to him, "You cannot see my face, for no one may see me and live." So, rather than see God's face, only God's back was revealed to Moses. God loved Moses and because of that love, God didn't give him what he wanted. Instead, God gave him what he could handle.

Just as humans would crumble, die, and disintegrate in the presence of such goodness (at least, that's how the sacred tale goes), we can suffer similar negative consequences through excessive badness, otherwise known as trauma. The brutal violence, loss, evil, and other kinds of trauma we experience throughout our lives can take their toll on us. Humans are resilient and can weather the most brutal of circumstances, but the truth is that trauma can crush us.

The word "trauma" comes from a Greek word meaning "wound" or "injury." Traumatic events can cause various degrees of injury to our souls that, in turn, affect our physiology, spirituality, and relationality.

For most people, trauma disrupts their emotional GPS causing over-powering emotions, ruminating thoughts, and even painful sensations in the body. Though every person goes through significant bad events throughout their life, not everyone perceives them as traumatic. Each individual has a unique level of tolerance to traumatic events that is determined by their upbringing, their feeling of support and safety at home, their level of safe supportive friends they currently have, temperament, and current life-stressors.

If your traumatic experience was due to interactions with your Christian tribe, then perhaps a description from trauma expert, Judith Herman, might resonate with you:

> Traumatized people feel utterly abandoned, utterly alone, cast out of the human and divine systems of care and protection that sustain life. Thereafter, a sense of alienation, of disconnection, pervades every relationship, from the most intimate familial bonds to the most abstract affiliations of community and religion. When trust is lost, traumatized people feel that they belong more to the dead than to the living.[5]

For some, the D/R journey is a "little-T" trauma that makes very little impact on their well-being. Others, on the other hand, experience the journey as "big-T" trauma that involves symptoms of PTSD (Post Traumatic Stress Disorder). The most common symptoms of PTSD include insomnia, nightmares, an amped up nervous system, flashbacks, shame, hopelessness, irritability, anger, difficulties concentrating, social withdrawal, and a host of other negative experiences. You know a person's psyche has been hit by a massive, life-altering avalanche when they have nightmares about going to Hell, experience panic attacks thinking about going to church, and deal with paralyzing anxiety due to the belief that God is mad at them. They feel an acute sense of confusion, depression, loneliness, and fear of constant ridicule, rejection, or punishment for questioning their own beliefs.

But what exactly causes religious trauma? Certainly, any kind of physical or sexual abuse that occurred at church is traumatic. The psychological damage done to those who are taken advantage of sexually at the hands of influential religious leaders is severe. Children who are continually beaten, and who are told it is God's will to rid them of sin and make them pure and holy, is reprehensible. Trauma like this can leave a lasting, lifelong impact.

Along with physical and sexual abuse, mental and emotional traumas within religious communities can contribute to the same untold suffering. This kind of abuse is typically induced by religious teachings under the guise of the supposed inspiration of God. These kinds of trauma are insidious because they are not apparent at first and might lay dormant in our minds for a long time. In other words, we might not experience or recognize the effects of these traumas until decades later. Marlene Winell, who coined the term *Religious Trauma Syndrome*, suggests that mental and emotional traumas, perpetrated by churches, can consist of:

1. Toxic teachings like eternal damnation or original sin

2. Religious practices or mindsets, such as punishment, black and white thinking, or sexual guilt, and

3. Neglect that prevents a person from having the information or opportunities to develop normally.[6]

One of the criteria for PTSD is that "a person has been exposed to a catastrophic event involving actual or threatened death or injury," or "a threat to the physical integrity of him/herself or others."[7] To be threatened with eternal damnation and torture at the hands of the most powerful being of the universe surely falls under the category of "threatened death or injury." For some, that threat is an assault on their soul, yet the repercussions of the traumatic experience may not be felt until years later.

Philip Salim Francis describes one participant's traumatic mental and emotional symptoms after she realized God had finally slipped away from her. He writes:

> In the months that followed the realization that she had lost God, Jeanie suffered greatly. She slipped into a depression ("for a month I couldn't get out of bed") and felt a constant feedback loop of self-criticism: "You are a sinner," "You are an evil, impure person," "You have killed God, like they killed Jesus," "You'll never amount to anything," "You are going to hell."[8]

Did you notice the negative thoughts that were contributing to her depression? After all of her time in a Christian community, is that all she has to show for it? Are cruel, self-deprecating self-talk and fear of future, eternal torture the best evidence we have that we're in a relationship with a loving, compassionate God and part of a community supposedly known by its love? I can't imagine so!

The result of such toxic negativity only comes from being in close, repeated contact with toxic religion. I believe that if she had not been in a church that taught fear-based doctrines, she likely would not have been in such a state. Even the most Bible-believing, conservative evangelical would agree that the fruit of the Spirit is not self-hate and debilitating fear of everlasting torment (at least I hope that is not the case). Don't you think that teachings focused on perfect love, extravagant grace, and the beauty and sufficiency of Christ would help cast out such harmful notions?

Some Christians may find relief knowing they are going to heaven one day. But they may also experience inner turmoil as they think about the "threat to the physical integrity" of their loved ones. Jose, a Christian friend of mine, said, "There is no way I can be joyful in heaven knowing my unbelieving mom and dad are going to be tortured for eternity. Sometimes I can't even sleep at night thinking about them going to Hell. It sickens my stomach. I know God is love but for the life of me I can't understand how a person's sins in this short life could land them in a position to be tortured without end." Jose is not the only Christian who deals with that much anguish and dissonance.

GOOD GRIEF

We have all experienced profound losses. As a result of those losses, depending on which station you find yourself, you may be experiencing overwhelming grief, which carries with it a rainbow of feelings. Some of us have also experienced big-T trauma. And one of the most mind-blowing truths about trauma experienced at the hands of religion is this: the deeper you have embraced and given your heart to the church, God, sacred rituals, and religious beliefs, the greater the trauma and more profound the grief.

The grieving process you are now going through isn't easy, but it's normal. It is your psyche's natural means of fully experiencing the feelings that accompany those losses. Grieving the right way can help you heal, teach you valuable life lessons, and spur you forward as you write and reconstruct the next chapter of your ever-unfolding life adventure.

Even though the grieving process is normal and necessary for your spiritual journey, the path is not linear. There is no God-ordained *Seven Steps to Freedom: An Approach to Grief After Deconstructing Your Faith* manual you can buy online or from a Bentley-driving televangelist with a glued-on smile (if you have one, burn it). People are far too complex, their stories and experiences too drastically different to benefit from a pre-packaged, neatly-designed, one-size-fits-all approach. In reality, grieving, and the D/R journey in general, is more like a zigzag; a lightning bolt; an up-and-down slanted, messy trail, as unique as the individual going through it.

Keep in mind that this is *your* messy D/R zigzag that will look slightly different from what everybody else has experienced. Don't let other people force their zigzag on you. Don't listen to people who avoid the spiritual wilderness and who have an aversion to all things messy and emotional. Don't let people guilt you into moving on too quickly or moving backward to what once was. Pay no attention to those who say, "Thus saith the Lord, "You have been in the wilderness long enough, so move on already." Listening to feedback from your closest friends and family is important, but ultimately this is your journey. You will have your own unique timetable for grieving the loss of a Christian faith you once knew and arriving at a place where you feel more whole. You have a uniquely designed, tailor-made path to healing. Only you can determine when you have walked far enough through the twists and turns of the valley of the shadow of deconstructive death toward reconstruction.

It bears repeating that you didn't ask for this D/R journey, it just found you. You didn't ask for the loss, confusion, guilt, shame, trauma, and pain. It knocked on the door and barged in before you got up off the couch. Author of *Broken Hallelujahs,* Beth Slevcove, says it well:

> One of the most essential lessons I've learned about grief is that we do not get to choose what to grieve. It chooses us. Grief turns life gray, and sometimes it takes a while for our eyes to adjust to what's there and to believe there is a deeper reality present underneath. Our job is to listen to our heart and body and acknowledge what is hurting us. Our job is not to decide what wounds are worth grieving or to judge as insufficient whatever is hurting us. We do not choose what to grieve, but we can choose to grieve what we find.[9]

Since *grief* is about loss, and *grieving* is about acknowledging, processing, accepting, and integrating those losses, I want to touch on a couple of common losses that are experienced on the D/R journey.

LOSING A COMMUNITY

One of the most profound losses for people on the D/R journey is the loss of connection with their faith community. For some, their church was their family. The relationships they had were imperfect, just like any family, but mostly encouraging and energizing. The loss of relationships, and the loneliness that can occur because of that loss, is palpable.

Sometimes the loss of relationships can occur because people equate non-conformity to a particular set of doctrines as tantamount to befriending the devil. Christians are taught to not have anything to do with the de-churched, or to use their language, "backslidden Christians and unbelievers." Christian brothers and sisters (remember, they're supposed to be like family) throw 2 Corinthians 6:14 in the heretic's face: "Do not be yoked together with unbelievers. For what do righteousness and wickedness have in common? Or what fellowship can light have with darkness?" And taking these verses out of context, they use them as permission to shun the non-conformist in their midst.

A. J. was a Baptist minister and is now part of the de-churched community. At the end of his D/R journey, he remained passionate about God, but dared to be candid about some of his struggles with traditional Christian doctrines. He wrote about his loss of relationships because he openly wrestled through his beliefs. He writes:

> I've lost many friends who believe I finally fell into the grip of the devil. No more preaching/ teaching opportunities, needless to say. No assistance when having challenges, especially financial, even though

I was very liberal towards friends and young upcoming ministers. . . So-called friends no longer answer your phone calls. People post pictures of an event you attended without your face in the pics. There is no one to talk with, because you refuse to argue with them."

Sometimes you can experience isolation and loss due to the choice of distancing yourself from your faith community. You either feel like no one can relate to you or you're afraid of contaminating someone else's faith. I recently surveyed some men and women about the D/R journey. I want to share a few of their responses because I think they are more than relevant to this discussion.

Stephanie writes, "I have felt so lonely on this journey of deconstruction and reconstruction. I feel like if I share the depths of my doubts, I will cause others to doubt and distance themselves from God. That would be cruel of me. So, I just suffer alone." Ben writes, "I've found it hard not having friends in my church (that I'm aware of) who can relate to my struggles. They just don't seem to be as bothered by things like the problem of evil, divine violence in Scripture and they're blissfully unaware of many of the problems/difficulties in the faith."

Lacey, a Christian since the age of six, writes, "I've lost relationships with friends and family. I feel like I have lost my identity and elements of my faith. This has been an incredibly lonely journey, as I do not feel free or safe to even discuss the things that I have both learned and unlearned."

Another characteristic of people in the D/R/ journey is a hesitancy to spend time with Christian friends. When they do, they feel like a salvation-project, someone to be fixed and saved rather than a person to connect with. Sarah writes about her experience as a project, "I also feel very set apart when I do hang out with friends who actively participate in church. It's hard to talk about your situation without it feeling like they're trying to bring you back. That has been a very lonely process."

Sometimes, overcome by our own deconstructive zeal, we can neglect the journey that others may be on. And many times their journey is nothing like ours and is one devoid of deconstructing and deep questioning. We can end up pushing those people away. Rachel Held Evans wrote about this dynamic in her own life:

> I was so lonely in my questions and so desperate for companionship, I tried to force the people I loved to doubt along with me. I tried to make them understand. This proved massively annoying to those friends who preferred to enjoy their dinner and a movie without a side of existential crisis—so basically, everyone. I was reckless at times, and self-absorbed, and I'm still mending some relationships as a result."[10]

The loss of relationships and subsequent loneliness is unbearable for some. It is no wonder why, in the vacuum of losing one's tribe, folks turn to pseudo-lovers such as maladaptive addictions just to get by. The harmful choices they make to deal with their antsy tribal-mind and profound longing for connection gets the best of them! Whether we consciously dwell on our loner-state or not, our unconscious deems our aloneness as a threat. "We are apart from the tribe!," it shouts. "We are all alone in the world. Will we will ever fit in again?" The painful loss of friends, and even family, along the D/R journey is real.

LOSS OF SECURE CONNECTION WITH THE BIBLE

Some Christians, on the D/R journey, experience a sense of loss due to the tenuous relationship they now have with the Bible. What was once a comforting sacred text in which every passage of Scripture was

God-breathed, is now an ambiguous book that is better left on the table collecting dust.

People can feel like they've lost their divine compass after they lose their connection with the Bible. Justin, a Christian for 25 years said, "If we can't trust the Bible, then how do we know what God wants from us?" Francis, a Christian for 10 years stated, "If the Bible is not God's word, then how can we even know who Jesus is? How can we know how to get saved or go to Heaven?" If the Bible wasn't 100% written by God, through human vessels, some can feel like they are floating in the ocean without a rudder.

Many people, who have long been narrow-mindedly looking down at the Bible, unexpectedly and excitedly look up from its pages only to see a whole new world to explore. Others, though, feel a loss and existential dread. Some anxiously wonder how to definitively answer life's most important questions: Who is God? Who am I? What is our purpose? What is going to happen to us after we die? Some people's existential anxiety becomes so great that, without knowing the exact answers to these big questions, they lose the motivation to live. Their loss of a connection with the Bible is to be taken seriously and so is their need to grieve such a loss.

LOSING GOD

Finding out the God that you know is different than who God actually is can be a serious loss for many people. Even though some push through and remain in an ambiguous and complicated relationship with God, there is often a lingering feeling of betrayal. Since I am a therapist, let's be precise, though. Betrayal is not a feeling. It is the stimulus or the act of breaking a person's trust that causes a loss of trust and connection. The consequence of betrayal causes us to feel angry and/or sad. In this case, we experience a lot of emotional pain because of our perception that God has betrayed us.

The experience of betrayal is confusing. By whom do we feel betrayed? Who gave us our faulty picture of God? Did God betray us? Did we betray God? Did we betray ourselves? Was it our pastor or family's fault? This long list of questions is the result of the disappearance of trust, something that is normally built upon patterned moments of mutual love, understanding, and connection. When we realize God is not who we thought God was, we become guarded. Have you ever been in a relationship with someone you trusted, but after hearing new information about them, you completely changed how you related to that person? That's the dynamic we're talking about here. It is naturally hard to trust someone we thought we knew. When we don't know who God is, after "knowing" God for a long time, we become cautious. Here are some questions people typically have about God when they are experiencing the loss of the God they thought they knew:

- Is God a loving God? Or, is God a violent God? Or, is God an apathetic God?

- Does God like some people more than others?

- Is God found in all religions or primarily in Christianity?

- Is God in control of all things? If not, how can we trust that God will protect us?

- If there are errors in the Bible, and God can't even preserve the inerrancy of the biblical text, then how can we trust God at all?

- Does God send people to Hell, or will all be saved?

- Is God indifferent to what happens to us?

- If I was deceived this whole time, then why the hell did God not say anything to me?

- Does God even exist?

The loss of trust in the God we thought we knew can contribute to an anxious mind and troubled spirit and the questions about God's character, nature, and the precise manner by which God works in the world become endless. Before their D/R journey began, a person might have been reflective by nature, but what was once done from a place of relational security is now being done out of insecurity. Fear is driving the questions—not love and childlike curiosity. The incessant questions seem to be on repeat, forever looping on a daily basis. A fractured relationship like this can create a desire to distance one's self from God. I mean, let's be honest, who in their right mind wants to hang out with a shady character that appears to be some kind of Dr. Jekyll and Mr. Hyde?

Janet Hagberg and Robert Guelich, authors of *The Critical Journey: Stages in the Life of Faith,* write about this stage of disorientation and loss that is so common to those deconstructing their faith: "Some call it 'the dark night of the soul,' a time of feeling withered and alone, searching and not finding, or grieving and feeling a loss. Sometimes we feel so alone we think God has left us. Sitting alone in dark ambiguity is the result."[11] The feelings of aloneness, anxiety, confusion, and sheer discontent of being in relationship with a real but invisible, intimate but totally silent God, can be enormously depressing.

Instead of remaining in this complicated relationship with God, some lose a relationship with God entirely. Lisa Gungor, writing about the loss of her faith, acknowledged, "When you have lived your entire life certain there is some great God in the process of saving everything, and when your entire life is framed around the notion, the loss of it is a deep grief."[12] The death of relationship with God can be traumatic.

One day you feel a connection with a loving, all-powerful Creator of the Universe. And, the next day, you wake up and discover that God no longer exists. Talk about spiritual whiplash!

Grieving the loss of God is complicated. Those who decide to stop believing grieve the loss of a God who they now believe never existed. Philip Salim Francis mentions this complex process when he writes, "In the loss of God, they discover that they cannot mourn the passing into nonexistence of a once-existent being. They find themselves beset with all the feelings of the bereaved but often without clarity as to the nature of the loss or the procedure of mourning."[13] When a loved one passes away, we can grieve the loss of their presence, as they were once an integral part of our life. We cope by rummaging through old photo albums and reminding ourselves that they have passed from one plane of existence to another. But how do you adequately grieve the loss of a God you now believe never existed in the first place? Those people who no longer believe in God are actually grieving their idea of the non-existent God who was intricately involved in their lives. For those who give up God all together, this might be the most challenging part of the D/R journey, one that takes an enormous amount of time to process.

LOSS OF IDENTITY

When I left, or rather ran away, from the Christian cult I was in over a decade ago, I embarked on a fearful zigzag toward an unexplored destination. My friend was attending a less conservative Christian college and I packed my bags and sprinted there. Going to school was a monumental experience for me. You see, I had really wanted to be the first person, on both sides of my family, to go to college. My dream was that I would learn, grow, and avoid the ignorance, death, and dysfunction that infested my family for generations.

Before my exodus, the pastor of that cult discouraged me from going to school for fear of "contaminating God's word in my heart." More importantly, he didn't want to lose his *armorbearer*, a concept used in the Hebrew Bible that referred to the right-hand man of powerful leaders who were headed to battle. In our modern religious context, the concept is used to justify having a servant to take care of a pastor's practical needs while he prepares for the epic battle of prayer and sermon prep. So, I obliged. Who was I to go against the man whom I naively perceived at the time to be "the Lord's anointed"?

Yet, after some time, I knew I had to go to college. It wasn't like I was fully and consciously aware of all of my reasons. I just knew I needed to get the hell out of there. Actually, I needed to get myself out of religious hell. In a way, going to college was my first act of rebellion. And while it felt scary at the time, it also felt really, really good.

Leaving the familiar would end up being the best decision I ever made. But it also left me disorientated. During one brisk night during the first week of school, I was on the unusually cold, hard floor of my dorm room in the fetal position, feeling like I was going out of my mind. I was distraught, scared, and sobbing uncontrollably. I was frantically questioning everything. I didn't know what was real. I didn't know whom to trust. I didn't know what "truth" meant. God? Who the hell was that? Who the heck am I? Am I going insane? Will I be locked up in a mental institution like my brother? Will I have a future? In that moment, I experienced my first of many panic attacks. Though I experienced many losses, it was the grief caused by my loss of identity that surprised me the most.

Loss of identity during the D/R journey can be traumatic for some. When we are fused with God (or other people's views of God) and our tribe's beliefs, norms, and practices, we can lose contact with the uniqueness of how we were created. We lose sight of the fact that we were wonderfully created by God dancing with randomness, evolutionary processes, and the million choices made by previous ancestors that eventually led to our birth. We can lose ourselves in the religious soup of the group. And after a while, we start walking and talking like everyone else. The moment we start to think for ourselves and question the reality that has been presented to us, we are catapulted into a new land. Then, as we unplug from our religious Matrix and become born again—*again*—our first steps into a vast new world can shake us to our core.

It also doesn't help that we are taught, confusingly I might add, that we are loved AND that we are terrible sinners with desperately wicked hearts who deserve to burn in Hell forever. The message is: "The self is bad, and God is the only one who is good." Therefore, our uniqueness is suppressed for the sake of a pseudo-form of cookie-cutter godliness. Marlene Winell writes, "Selfishness and pride are considered terrible things in a traditional Christian context. Thus, when you leave the fold, it can be very difficult to know how to think for yourself. At one time, your individual identity was subsumed in a local expression of the body of Christ. Now you may need to get to know yourself and learn how to appreciate your uniqueness."[14]

Katie, a participant, in the *Breaking up with Jesus* study, shared her struggle in losing her worldview and ultimately her identity after deconstructing her faith. She writes, "… that it is your world view, it's how you understand your place in the world, how you understand the things that happen to you, how you understand what you are supposed to do with your life. And then that all falls apart and you have got to try and find a way of making sense of everything again from a completely different place."[15]

Author of *Post-Traumatic Church Syndrome,* Reba Riley, writes about leaving her faith and then struggling to find her identity:

> Placing your identity in Christ" is lingo for church-approved codependence: you allow your church's brand of Jesus to dictate what you

do or don't do or don't wear, eat, read, discuss, watch, and listen to. You let your church's Jesus pick out your lipstick and your friends, run your bank accounts, and prescribe your wardrobe. Having my identity in Christ was the problem, the entire reason I fell apart when I could no longer believe. When I left my faith, I didn't have anything of my own.[16]

Some on the D/R journey find that, when the foundation of their beliefs starts to crack, there is an undeniable shaking of their sense of self and they find themselves in quite an existential dilemma. For years, they plugged their brains into the Mothership of religion, reducing the need to think critically about their beliefs, to wonder about the nuances of life, or even ask difficult or divergent questions about God. Their brains have been wired together with a book, a priest or pastor, and other people in the faith-community. From their tribe slowly pumped the liquid of homogeneous beliefs.

There are countless people who adamantly believe Christian doctrines, and, when asked deeper questions about them, pull out the platinum mystery card from their back pocket. To me, this is evidence of our being tethered to the religious Matrix. Christians may say, "God's ways are above our ways. It is a profound mystery we must accept in faith." Then, if they are asked, "Can you show me where in the Bible that doctrine is found?" they look at you dumbfounded. Then, they defensively sidestep the conversation and talk about how much of a heretic you are for even asking the question. The truth is they believe their doctrines simply because they have been taught and told to believe them – never having to question anything and intently search out answers for themselves.

Coming untethered from the religious Matrix is quite unsettling and even traumatic for some. The loss of a community, the loss of a secure connection to the Bible, and the loss of God and their identity cause a perplexing affliction. Yet, the process of differentiating and adulting can also be liberating! The pure delight of learning how to trust in the Divine within you as well as learning about what *you* think, what *you* love and desire, what *your* purpose is, and what brings *you* joy—alongside wise and compassionate travel companions—can be worth the price of admission.

In the next chapter, we narrow our lens and focus on the common emotions that are stirred up in the midst of hurt, trauma, and grief.

QUESTIONS

1. For many, the D/R journey can feel like a roller coaster. What metaphor would you use to describe your journey?

2. Describe what aspect of this season of your life causes the most hurt and emotional pain? What are some of the most profound losses for you?

3. What about the idea of the "tribal-wired brain" resonates or doesn't resonate with you?

4. How has your relationship to the Bible changed from when you first became a Christian until now?

5. Can you describe a loss involving your relationship with God since you have been on the D/R journey?

6. As your faith has shifted, what thoughts and feelings arise as you think about a loss concerning your identity?

7. What does it mean to find your identity in Christ?

8. Though you may have experienced many losses during your D/R journey, what are some of the things you have gained?

CHAPTER FIVE

THE ELECTRICITY OF EMOTIONS

"The core of your being is formed by what and how you feel. When you avoid your feelings, you're squelching your identity and thwarting your true potential."

— RON FREDERICK

In the same way that electricity is fueling Montu at Busch Gardens, powerful emotions are fueling your unique and highly personal grief process and spiritual disequilibrium. In Latin, the word *emotion* means "to move." It's the perfect definition because the reality is that emotions are moving you in all sorts of directions as your disorientation starts to settle in and unsettle you to the core of your being.

Emotions are some of the most electric and compelling forces on the planet. Grief, for example, can be so strong that it affects your ability to concentrate at work or school. Anxiety can be so great that it causes insomnia, affecting your ability to fall asleep and stay asleep. Despair and shame can trigger negative thoughts, such as "I am worthless" and "God hates me." And think also of those roller-coaster bouts of deep sadness. One minute you are tearing up, the next minute you think you are okay, and then suddenly you feel heavier than a fifty-pound bag of bricks.

On this D/R journey, maybe you've never felt sad or even cried. Perhaps the only emotion you ever feel is anger. And you find yourself in a bad mood more days then you care to admit. You're angry at your boss. You're angry at your dog. You're angry at God and the church. You're angry at yourself and the world. Or maybe you're confused because you don't know what the heck is wrong with you, but you know you do not feel okay. All of that is to say that emotions are powerful and can affect you in all kinds of ways.

It's normal to experience strong jolts of emotion in the middle of your faith shift. After all, you loved deeply. You gave your heart to both God and the church. And you are now grieving a profound loss of connections, attachments, intimacy, conversations, rituals, and beliefs. You have every right to feel the way you do. Let me offer a word of encouragement. Even though we are a part of a religious culture and society that says, "Get over it!" I want you to feel – to feel deeply and wholly.

NAME TO TAME

Three months after experiencing what he called "a crisis of faith", Jonathan came to see me. He thought he needed to see a therapist because he felt sad all the time, lacked motivation, and felt anxious when he went to church. He told me he was a leader in his church and that many people looked up to him as a strong man of God. When he was with his staff and members of the congregation, he tried hard not to let people see the grief he was experiencing. I could tell, however, that he was in tremendous pain.

"I don't know what is wrong with me," he said as tears started rolling down his cheeks. "I am supposed to be strong, and God is

MARK GREGORY KARRIS

supposed to be my everything. Why am I feeling this way? Is there something wrong with me?"

I started to enter into his painful experience and compassionately empathize with him. "I can see you are in tremendous pain right now," I said. "This is really hard. Can we stay here with these feelings a minute?"

After allowing him to experience his full range of emotions and reveal his story, I wanted to normalize his struggle. I briefly shared how I went through a crisis of faith as a Christian leader and could attest to its disorientation. I helped him understand how, one by one, each emotion he felt had something valuable to tell him. As the session went on, I watched him take deep breaths and begin to calm down.

At the end of the session, he said, "Thank you. All these months I thought I was going crazy. What you said makes total sense. I thought that something was wrong with me and that God didn't love me. But you have helped me understand these crazy emotions I have been having. Deconstructing is hard. I am still hurting, but I do feel lighter and can breathe a little bit easier."

The hardest dynamic of the deconstruction process is the confusion that sets in because of your chaotic emotional experiences. Your level of anxiety and suffering is increased by your inability to understand what is going on. However, once you can better understand your emotions, and grow in your emotional intelligence (EQ), you can tranquilize your amygdala: the main area of your brain that triggers your emotional roller coaster in the first place. Research shows that when you can name your emotion and understand your experience, you can actually tame it and experience a greater sense of calm.[1] Matthew Lieberman, an esteemed researcher on this topic, wrote in the *New York Times,* "If the amygdala is like an alarm clock alerting us to potential threats, putting feelings into words is like hitting the snooze button."[2]

Many times, the chaos and confusion of our emotional experiences make them seem overwhelming. But when we can understand and even befriend our experiences, they become more bearable.

What Are Emotions?

Let's take a moment to examine the *purpose* of emotions. That way, we can better understand what we are going through in this season of deconstruction and reconstruction. In the end, we might feel less like we're riding on Montu and more like we're on the teacups at Disney World. We will still experience ups and downs, but they will be much more manageable.

Our core emotions exists as part of an inner GPS that allows us to know where we are, where we want to go, and how to get there.[3] All of our primary emotions convey powerful information and move us toward adaptive action. They may not always convey accurate, objective, truthful information, but they always point to a valuable subjective truth within the individual. Emotions do not have to lead to ultimate conclusions or definitively determine a person's course of action. However, when we listen mindfully to the way we feel, our emotions can help navigate the beautifully chaotic and wondrous world with greater skill and awareness.

Are you surprised to hear that your emotions can actually be helpful? I was when I heard that they were. For a long time, I preferred logic and reasoning over emotions, especially as vehicles to truth and living the Christian life. My early church experiences were filled with people who believed emotions were troublesome demons that needed to be quickly cast out of hurting people. And I conformed. I thought emotions were inferior, untruthful, unspiritual, and fleshly.

I will never forget one of my friends who was in the throes of grief. After weeks of being an absolute wreck, unbearably distressed because his girlfriend broke up with him, he decided to go to a weekend church service to find solace and community. After service, perceptive church members quickly gathered around him like bees and began to sting him with passionate and bold prayers, such as "I bind the spirit of sadness in the name of Jesus" and "You come out of him, you spirit of depression and anger." By ridding him of those nasty varmints (emotions), he would supposedly be restored and free again.

The bee-sting approach is at best unfounded and at worst extremely harmful. Don't get me wrong; praying for others is a sacred and beautiful experience, but it is *absurd* to try to "cast out" naturally occurring emotions and label them as "demons."

I don't believe emotions are bad, sinful, or demonic. There are, however, times when our emotions—our inner GPS—can go haywire as our healthy emotions quickly morph into unhealthy ones. What was meant to trigger healthy guilt, for example, can turn into unhealthy shame. Anger, for example, can serve as a defense mechanism against sadness. And fear can rise up when someone experiences the love and kindness of someone who cares deeply about them. Unable to decipher what is going on with our emotional experiences, or manage them appropriately, we are left confused, crushed, or carelessly controlled by them.

In reality, the emotions themselves are not the most common problem. Instead, it's the defenses and strategies we use to deal—or not deal—with them. For example, some people call a friend, pray to God, or read a good book when they feel sad and lonely. Others, on the other hand, isolate themselves, eat a gallon of ice cream, or go on wild shopping sprees. Some people petition for passage of better laws when they get angry about a serious injustice in the world while others get into fistfights. Strong emotions are not the problem. The issue may be what we do with them when they arise.

THE WISDOM OF EMOTIONS

Our ability to understand emotional experiences is vital to our ability to maintain sanity in this tumultuous time and engage in mindful reconstruction. So, I want to give you a peek into the power and wisdom of the most common emotions experienced during the D/R journey.

The following chart details the wisdom that our emotions can bring into our lives. As you read through the chart, make a note of the emotions you have experienced lately.

	COMMUNICATES INFORMATION	BUILT-IN PLEA FOR ACTION
SADNESS	Tells us there has been a loss	Moves us to seek solace, nurturing, and care from others
FEAR	Tells us there is danger	Moves us to fight, take flight, or freeze
DISGUST	Tells us something is toxic or foul	Moves us to turn away from and avoid it
JOY	Tells us a goal has been reached	Moves us to open up, stay engaged, or share with others
ANGER	Tells us a goal has been frustrated or something is unjust or unfair	Moves us to right the wrong and make a change
GUILT	Tells us our behaviors or thoughts are contrary to our values or those of our community	Moves us to reconcile, make amends, and restore relationships
UNHEALTHY SHAME	Tells us *we* are wrong for our behaviors or thoughts, which are contrary to our values or those of our community	Moves us to hide, attack ourselves or others, or engage in run-and-numb activities such as defenses or addictions

Now, let's take a deeper dive into anger, sadness, and shame to see how they can move and guide us, in their own unique ways, on the D/R journey.

ANGER

When the defense mechanisms of shock and denial stop working for those who are beginning their faith deconstruction, people often feel angry because they think they have been betrayed. They feel angry because they think the church let them down. They feel angry because they think God has abandoned them. And they also feel angry because of the injustice, incoherence, and downright oppressive nature of the doctrines they once believed. They may also feel angry at themselves. Why? Think about it for a second. If you think everyone is mad at you, including God, it is an easy leap to internalize and turn those messages on yourself. In self-directed anger, they blame themselves for the deconstructive mess in which they find themselves.

Anger is a completely natural emotion, rooted in our tribal evolutionary history, signaling that we (or those we care about) have experienced a wrongdoing or injustice of some kind. Anger has a strong physiological component to it. It tenses our muscles. It gets us ready to fight against or flee from our enemy. It raises our heart rate and increases adrenaline. Angry energy pulsates in our chest and our hands. When it's utilized for good, anger helps mobilize people to take action. For the dechurched, sometimes, that action is to change and help repair the broken religious system.

MY HOLY DISCONTENT

My holy discontent arises when I see Facebook posts or hear preachers talk about God hating people, sending folks to Hell, or God being repulsed by sinful people, I can feel the anger welling up in my bones. I start to think about all of the people who have suffered, and continue to suffer, because of those religious propositions. My feelings about the injustice of people turning away from the love of God because of toxic beliefs energize me to do something about it.

I recently had a conversation with a Christian who was adamant that humans were primarily evil. This person passionately informed me the Bible is proof that our hearts are always bent toward sinful actions and attitudes. With great zeal, he quoted Jeremiah 17:9: "The human heart is the most deceitful of all things, and desperately wicked. Who really knows how bad it is?" I immediately felt angry. I knew he had four children and was sad that at some point, most likely they would soak in that poisonous theology.

Many people who have grown up with religious parents espousing worm theology, and within religious communities who have done the same, have horrific views of themselves. I should know! I have seen many of them in my therapy office. Keeping those hurting people in mind, after he quoted Jeremiah to me, I could feel energy rise up within me. I knew, in that moment, I could either choose to respond calmly or impulsively react. I decided to use the fuel of anger by kindly sharing an alternative viewpoint.

I politely shared with him that the prophet Jeremiah's context was filled with persecution and trauma as he saw the oppression and enslavement of people that he loved all around him. Jeremiah was also surrounded by chaos, pain, lies, and misery. In his ancient world, he had to continually deal with the deceit of false prophets who led those he loved astray. In that context, God's statement to Jeremiah makes more sense, doesn't it? It's true, human beings can make choices that come from a place of pride, greed, and fear. At the same time, humans can do incredible things! Just a verse later, the text is about God rewarding those according to their deeds (v.10). And the fact that God rewards good deeds shows that people can indeed *do* good things, the kinds of things that deserve recognition from God. So, from God's perspective (or God's perspective as the writer understood it), people are obviously not wicked *all* the time.

If you haven't noticed, fewer things make me angrier than when people use the Bible out of context, like weapons, to hurt and sicken others. I think we *should* feel a sense of outrage when Bible verses are used as twisted, insidious viruses that cause people to feel terrible about themselves and fear an angry and violent-prone God. The Christian I talked to was single-handedly increasing shame in other people's lives, and potentially doing the same with his own kids. By increasing shame, he would be simultaneously increasing their propensity to engage in harmful behaviors toward themselves and others. That should be something that gets us heated!

So, what's the real point of Jeremiah's words? To point to the One who can understand the complexities and perversities of the human heart who, of course, is God (Jer. 17: 9b). Only God can truly know whether a person's deeds are born from a loving place or from a place of deceit. The author elevates the wise discernment of God and is not making a universal declarative statement on the primary nature of human beings. This is important because who we are matters. Our identity matters. The way we live, breath, and interact with the world is rooted in who we believe ourselves to be.

People should be really careful how they wield this verse (or any verse for that matter) and who they wield it toward. If mature adults want to talk about Jeremiah and his traumatic and chaotic context, then great. If they want to explore the wisdom of a God who can discern our deepest motivations, great! If they want to understand how both wonders and wickedness, selflessness and selfishness, can spring from the complex hearts of humanity, then wonderful! But you can be sure I will never, ever tell my young son that he has a wicked, sick, and evil heart. He has a good heart partly because he is my son but mostly because he carries within him the image of God and the Spirit of love. No matter what he does, *that* is his core identity. And I will remind him of that many times throughout his life.

ANGER CAN BE ADAPTIVE AND MALADAPTIVE

Anger empowers some of us to utilize our gifts as the antidote to toxic religion and motivates us to remain in Christian community to make a difference. For others, anger leads to an internal decision that they will no longer tolerate toxic religion—at all—moving them toward Station Seven: Farewell and Goodbye. It is like they are finally getting out of an abusive relationship and begin to shout, "Enough! You are a monster! I am leaving you for good!" Valerie Tarico, author of *Trusting Doubt: A Former Evangelical Looks at Old Beliefs in a New Light,* discusses how anger motivated her to make a change:

> My beliefs had become more and more idiosyncratic, as I tried to hold together the strange bundle of moral and rational contradictions that constitute born-again, Bible-believing Christianity. Now, finally, after two decades of warping my feelings, my perceptions, and my intellect to defend the absolute goodness of the biblical God, I got angry. I said to the god in my head: *"I'm not making excuses for you anymore ... I quit!* And just like that, "He" was gone. All that was left was the frame of tape and wire which once contained the empty excuses, rationalizations, and songs of worship that sounded oddly flat.[4]

Anger can initially be very adaptive and, if we listen to its wisdom, can illuminate what we don't want anymore. Anger also helps us to understand what we *do* want. Don't get me wrong, not all people feel angry in the midst of their D/R journey, especially if they casually decided religious life was not for them. But many people *do* get angry and prove this ancient proverb to be true: "An angry person stirs up conflict, and a hot-tempered person commits many sins."[5]

Early on in the disorientation and grief process, anger can be too wild to tame. This means that at times, we can easily be triggered and lash out at other people. The plus side of this heightened level of anger is that we start to get in touch with what we want and need. Unfortunately, if left unchecked, angry people can start hanging out in Station Six: Angstville, for too long. When that happens, what was originally adaptive becomes maladaptive. It is here where disorientated people can get stuck habitually reacting and hurting people like an abused porcupine with rabies. Reactive people tend to create reactive situations and, in their anger, can poke and hurt others. As an ancient spiritual writer wisely said, "Be angry but do not sin."[6] *Sin* is anything that distorts, fractures, or harms relationships with God, self, and others (including creation). It is okay to be angry. But let us also be mindful of how we tame and channel our emotions so that we do not sin against ourselves and others.

Anger can be a core, primary emotion. Interestingly enough, it can also be what psychologists call a *secondary* emotion. Secondary emotions are reactions against primary emotions. They mask and cover them up. Many times, the hard and hot emotion of anger is just a cover up, a deflection, a secondary emotion, for the soft and warm primary emotion of sadness. In many cases, someone who is angrily blaming and cursing God is a person who is deeply hurt and is feeling sad. The truth is that only when you acknowledge the anger, and sit and process the hurt and sadness, will you be able to move on to a place of acceptance and peace.

So, let's talk about another common emotion experienced during the D/R journey: sadness.

SADNESS

Sadness penetrates deep down to the core of who you are and reminds you that there has been a loss. In fact, the greater you have loved, the greater the sadness. The greater the intimacy in the connections you lost, the more you gave your heart to a God you once knew, and the zeal with which you believed old religious doctrines, the exponentially greater your sense of loss. Remember this: Experiencing sadness is a sign that your heart is alive and not dead, calloused, or cold. It is proof that you have loved fully and opened your heart and mind deeply.

Sadness tells us, during this difficult time, to move toward a comforting and caring connection with God and deep, supportive relationship with others. This is not a surprise considering our tribal-wired brains and our need to connect and belong. But this is why the D/R journey is so challenging—because the very thing we need (people) is the very thing we are separating ourselves from (people).

You can expect to be sad at the prospect of losing relationships you have had for so long in the church. You can expect that holding opposing beliefs about God or the Bible can become a wedge between you and those who were once closest to you. Losing people you ate with, engaged in communion with, prayed with, sang spiritual songs with, and did life with, warrants sadness. In discussing the emotional experiences of the de-churched, Packard and Hope wrote: "When they left, they experienced sadness at the loss of rituals, but they felt grief bordering on devastation at losing the connection with God that came through their church communities."[7] When considering the losses that can occur on the D/R journey, this all makes sense, but don't forget: you are not alone.

There is multiple events that can cause us to feel sad during this process. In the research paper, *The Resurrection of Self: How Deconversion from Religious Belief to Atheism Healed a History of Rejection, Trauma, and Shame,* one participant talked about her feelings of sadness when she thought about her sister's inability to appreciate where she was on her faith journey. She wrote: "When we were growing up we did believe in Hell. I'm assuming she still thinks that and she is just praying for us, which is kind of sad. I know that she is worrying about her husband and now she has to worry about me. But it is what it is."[8] It's incredibly sad when those we love can't join us in our newly emerging freedom, or worse, harshly judge us and condemn us for it.

SHAME

The last emotion I want to talk about, as it relates to our D/R journey, is shame. Brené Brown, a well-known author and speaker, says, "We all experience shame. We're all afraid to talk about it. And, the less we talk about it, the more we have it."[9] I think she's right and that those who come from religious backgrounds are more susceptible to this silent, joy-stealing emotion.

Shame is different from guilt. Guilt is an emotion experienced after a person has *done* something wrong whereas shame is an emotion that tells a person he or she *is* something wrong. After being rejected by their faith community, shame can send a person the message that they are unlovable, tainted, dirty, flawed, and no good. Lewis Smedes writes that shame is "a vague, undefined heaviness that presses on our spirit, dampens our gratitude for the goodness of life, and slackens the free flow of joy. Shame . . . seeps into and discolors all our other feelings, primarily about ourselves, but about almost everyone and everything else in our life as well."[10]

On many occasions, shame is guilt gone rogue. The ideal internal, emotional experience we have when we miss the mark (sin) with our actions, non-actions, and thoughts, is something I call *healthy guilt* (my version of the biblical phrase *godly sorrow*). *Unhealthy shame* (*worldly sorrow*) leads to death, but godly sorrow leads to life with no yucky residue (2 Cor. 7:10). Godly sorrow is good because it describes the remorse a person feels when their actions (or inactions) don't match up with their values and God's loving desires. It has a built-in plea for action, motivating a person to prioritize relationships, and moving them to right their wrongs.

Toxic shame is on a whole different level and, because it is such a debilitating emotion, it has no rightful place in the heart of a child of God. This kind of shame festers and darkens one's view of oneself, God, and others. It contributes to much of their suffering and catapults them into addictions, self-harm, and harming others. I know those are bold statements, but there is plenty of research to back them up.[11] Curt Thompson, a Christian psychiatrist, well-known speaker, and author of *The Soul of Shame: Retelling the Stories We Believe About Ourselves*, minces no words when it comes to the toxic and deleterious effects of shame. He writes:

> This phenomenon [shame] is the primary tool that evil leverages, out of which emerges everything that we would call sin. As such, it is actively, intentionally, at work both within and between individuals. Its goal is to disintegrate any and every system it targets, be that one's personal story, a family, marriage, friendship, church, school, community, business or political system. Its power lies in its subtlety and its silence, and it will not be satisfied until all hell breaks loose. Literally.[12]

I know from my own experience, and from the experiences of those I have counseled, that levels of shame can skyrocket when a person is deconstructing and reconstructing their faith. Why? Sincere people asking honest questions about life, God, and faith, who are turned away by their faith-community, will inevitably feel deserted and unwanted. As a result, they can often internalize that rejection and become shame-prone and self-critical. Here are some common shame statements people share during their season of disorientation and grief:

- I feel tainted. I deserve to be alone.

- I feel horrible about myself. People don't want me. God doesn't even want me.

- I feel like I did something wrong for this to happen. Truth is, there were a lot of sinful things I did in my life. God is probably right to punish me.

- Everyone else can be happy in their faith except for me.

- I am a leader in my church, so I should have it more together. I feel like a big loser.

- God loves everyone else but me.

- Why was I so dumb to not have seen the toxicity of these Christian beliefs before.

- I am sinful and no good. All the good that I have is like filthy rags.

- I am unloved. What is the point of living?

- I am a terrible person for telling my family about my doubts and causing them pain.

Deconstructing and reconstructing my faith has triggered shame countless times. This was especially true in the beginning of my D/R journey when people felt the need to tell me how terrible I was. Shame reared its ugly head with every "friend" who unfriended me on Facebook, every email that I received telling me I was a heretic and going to Hell, every religious family member who shared their obsessive worry and concern for me, and every time I would be denied a chance to use my gifts to serve in churches.

At first, I went into hiding and attacked myself with my own thoughts. After all, if I really was unlovable, why would anyone else want to be around me? And the more I isolated myself from others, the more I believed the message that I am not worthy of people's love. The less love I felt, the more my shame increased and the more I withdrew from other people. I found myself in the middle what Curt Thompson calls the "shame feedback loop." He writes:

> When we experience shame, we tend to turn away from others because the prospect of being seen or known by another carries the anticipation of shame being intensified or reactivated. However, the very act of turning away, while temporarily protecting and relieving us from our feeling (and the gaze of the "other"), ironically simultaneously reinforces the very shame we are attempting to avoid.[13]

Truth be told, I felt a lot of shame *before* this whole crazy faith-shift. There always existed a low-level hum of toxic shame in my life. It always creeped its way into the many thoughts I had about myself and about the way other people saw me. The rejection I received from Christians just magnified my deep-seated belief that I was unlovable and worthless and that no one would ever love me again. The thought of never having a tribe that would love me and believe in me, messy theology and all, threw me into the shame feedback loop long before I even knew what it was. Shame is a stealthy thief! It subtly robs us of life's goodness and beauty and keeps us from the crucial relationships that matter most. It also hinders us from our destiny and stunts our ability to freely love others. Here me on this: You are not alone and there is hope. I have experienced this journey firsthand. Hope is found in the embrace of loving and compassionate people. And it is also found in the love of Jesus.

Jesus manifests to us what God is like. Jesus touched and embraced the losers, lepers, liars, lunatics, loose-lovers, outcasts, and every other marginalized misfit. And he healed them and freed them from the grip of shame. Jesus loved and accepted every person, even when they ashamedly cried out:

- "No, you don't know who I am!"

- "You don't know what I've done!"

- "You don't know which disease I have!"

- "You won't be able to stand the smell!"

- "You don't know how many husbands I've had!"

- "You don't know how much I've stolen!"

Jesus said to them, in effect, "Yes, I do know who you are! I no longer remember what you've done! And there is no sin or stench that can keep me away from you!" He then proceeded to touch them, hold them, and heal them.

Jesus came to reveal what God is like. Through Jesus, we learn that God likes to remind us of our true identity. God wants you to know that even with your imperfections, failures, and frailty, you are loved. You are not worthless. Instead, you are priceless.

EMOTIONS ARE MESSY BUT VITAL

The Giver (2014), a movie based on a book of the same name, is about a community that made a decision to both eradicate suffering and maintain peace at any cost. To accomplish this, the community's authoritative elders forced people to take medication that removed their ability to feel deep emotions. As you can imagine, there were some serious side-effects of this medication: There were no more wars or murders. But love, passion, creativity, beauty, and the gift of music all disappeared. Before long, people could no longer distinguish between colors. Everything from an apple to the sky was the same bland hue. The messiness and mayhem of life were replaced by a safe, mundane and monotone existence.

The main character, Jonas, an inquisitive sixteen-year-old, came to realize, by experiencing the memories of an old man named "the Receiver of Memories," what his community was missing: emotion. As a result, Jonas became determined to restore the full gamut of human emotional experience to his community. In the end, Jonas was the hero, restoring things to the way they were before the elders prescribed their anti-emotion medication.

Perhaps there are times you can relate to the elders in *The Giver* who eradicated those bothersome emotions. The truth is without them your existence would be dull, boring, lifeless, and loveless. Emotions are vital to being human. They are the music to the un-choreographed dance of life. Knowing how to name and tame them will help you reign them in without inflaming them and aiming them at others.

No matter the degree to which one has experienced religious trauma, there is a psychological tactic—installing shock absorbers—we all utilize when dealing with our overwhelming emotions and negative thoughts. As we will see in the next chapter, these shock absorbers, commonly known as defense mechanisms, can be helpful in the short-term but destructive in the long-term.

QUESTIONS

1. What are the family, cultural, or church messages you have received about emotions?

2. What injustices in the church make you angry? How have you used anger to empower you toward solving the problems of the injustice that you see so clearly?

3. What is sin? Where did it come from? How does it affect us and the world we live in?

4. The emotion of sadness ideally moves us toward others for care and comfort. Do you find yourself moving toward or away from others when you are sad? What makes it easy or difficult to share your sadness with others?

5. In your own words, describe shame. How has shame affected you growing up, and in particular, in the midst of your faith shift?

6. What specific Christian beliefs or practices have caused you to feel shame?

7. How does the life, death, and resurrection of Jesus help us with our anger, sadness, pain, and shame?

8. How can a Christian community perpetuate or heal shame?

CHAPTER SIX

SHOCK ABSORBERS

"Mental pain is less dramatic than physical pain, but it is more common and also more hard to bear. The frequent attempt to conceal mental pain increases the burden: it is easier to say "My tooth is aching" than to say "My heart is broken."

— C. S. LEWIS, *THE PROBLEM OF PAIN*

In 1898, a French cyclist, J.M.M. Truffault, installed coil springs and a friction device that he claimed would "minimize vibrations." In that moment, he had unknowingly invented a piece of equipment that would revolutionize car manufacturing for the next century—the shock absorber. Then, in 1904, racecar driver Léon Théry won the Gordon Bennet Cup using this new invention on his car. And the rest is history. What makes the shock absorber so effective? It protects the car from dangerous energy caused by bumps and potholes in the road. The greater the energy, the more the shocks work to absorb it.

In the same way that shock absorbers minimize the vibrations caused by bumps in the road, our psyches have wired-in, emotional and psychological shock absorbers that have evolved to help us handle the bumps of life. These are known as "defense mechanisms." Defenses are innate gifts to vulnerable people like us who are unable to fully absorb debilitating and devastating blows to our souls. In the midst of a religious awakening, for example, a person can have difficulty absorbing the intensity of the experience into their consciousness. So, rather than coming into contact with a painful reality before them, and inevitable negative energy, that person's inner shock absorbers take the hit and redirect the energy somewhere else.

Defenses are automatic, unconscious strategies that help block and blunt reality for the benefit of our well-being. They happen without effort and help us to avoid uncomfortable feelings, unwanted desires, and undesirable thoughts that our unconscious finds to be anxiety-provoking. These unconscious shock absorbers make bad things look great, and yucky feelings go away, so we can feel better. Though defense mechanisms get a bad rap, they are actually a necessary form of self-deception, helping to maintain our psychological equilibrium so we can carry on in this labyrinthian journey called life.

DAVID, THE TRAUMA SURVIVOR

The Biblical character, King David, suffered some major traumatic experiences. Let's take a quick look at the significant, bumpy events in his life. He went through a huge change from being a humble shepherd to a warrior king in a relatively short period of time. Later in life, he fought numerous military campaigns and experienced firsthand the horror and savagery of war. There were also many times when he feared for his life as he hid from the jealous and murderous rage of King Saul, his royal predecessor. As he hid from Saul, some of David's own family members, and fellow soldiers, betrayed him. And as if that wasn't enough, God busted him for coercing a married woman, having sex with her, and murdering her husband in the process. Then, the biblical author implies that because of his sin, his dear child died.

Sounds like a made-for-tv movie, doesn't it? Needless to say, King David's life was chock full of drama, trauma, and pain.

Is it possible he suffered from PTSD? Could he have suffered emotionally to such an extent that he needed some shock absorbers? No doubt! He was a human being like us. Any person who has been through what David went through would have some seriously harsh memories they would want to block out. Honestly, I think David, known as "a man after God's own heart," used sex as a shock absorber to deal with his emotional pain. Don't believe me? Let's look more closely at snippets from his story.

In 2 Samuel chapter 6, we read about a time David danced naked through the streets in front of his slave girls. Sunday School teachers in churches everywhere have taught their students that they should be more like David: you should be so unashamed of your love for God that you're willing to dance joyfully through the streets! Although most commentators would say David's victory dance and disrobing in front of his slave girls (2 Sam. 6:20) was a sacred and pure act, I am a little suspicious. That event, at the very least, was a red flag that makes me think David struggled with managing the dynamics of holiness and horniness.

The real glaring evidence of his shock-absorbing tendencies is found in 2 Samuel 11:2–4. When he was lazily walking around one evening, he spotted Bathsheba and decided, in typical kingly fashion that he had to have her. It was lust at first sight. He had no idea what kind of person she was and could care less that she was a married woman. He had an insatiable urge to have sex with her. David had his messengers drag her from her home, and, the story goes that "she came to him, and he slept with her." If you're following along closely, the man after God's own heart abused his power, had a woman kidnapped, and then raped her. Let us be clear, David did not commit adultery. David committed rape. He then ordered Bathsheba's husband killed so he could hide what he had done and have her all to himself. I imagine what he did with Bathsheba was probably not David's first rodeo. After all, we *do* know that he had a bunch of other wives and concubines (glorified sex slaves).

What the heck?

You've got to be kidding me!

A man after God's own heart? No way!

According to the Bible, he was.

It makes sense to be cynical, but I suspect that being a man or woman "after God's own heart" never means perfection. It has to do with direction—where a person is headed, not where they've been—more than anything else. And David, no matter what sin he committed, always made his way back to God, falling down on his knees, longing for God's mercy and forgiveness.

To be fair, David lived in a very different time than we do. Ancient kings had many wives and concubines as a sign to the members of their empire that they were powerful and blessed by the divine. But lying, murder, and rape? Well, that is a different story. King David knew better. Sure, it is possible that God tried to nudge him toward love, truthfulness, honor, and respect during David's moments of prayer. But the truth is David's emotional pain from past experiences (remember that long list of traumatic events?) may have been so great that he regularly gave into his lustful shock absorber in order to cope.

The consequences of David's defense mechanism not only affected his own life but also the generations after him. He probably passed down his shock-absorbing tendency to his son, Solomon, who magnified it exponentially. We read in 1 Kings 11:3 that Solomon "had seven hundred wives of royal birth and three hundred concubines, and his wives led him astray." I can't even figure out how to be married to one person, let alone seven hundred!

Can you relate to David in some way? Maybe not with his extreme and atrocious behavior, but can you relate to how he dealt with his emotional pain? Haven't you ever tried to numb out and run away from your emotional pain in some way?

Here's a tweetable but profound truth: if we sow defenses we will eventually reap expenses. There is always a cost associated with maladaptive coping mechanisms. King David and King Solomon found that out the hard way, and eventually we will, too. So, let's look at some practical examples of defense mechanisms that we may see as we travel the D/R journey.

DENIAL

One of the most common shock absorbers is denial. It is the attempt to deny the reality that is right in front of our face. This tactic is clearly seen with any attempt to deny the reality of Cytotoxic splinters. For example, there was a time I read the Bible and came across scribal errors, conflicting messages between biblical writers, and additions to the original biblical text (e.g. 1 John 5:7-8). In that moment, I denied their existence and said to myself, "These aren't errors or contradictions. God's word is perfect and inerrant. I don't understand what I'm reading or how to make sense of it all simply because God's ways are higher than my ways. God has a reason for the text to say what it says." Why would I deny what was so obvious? Because the thought that the Bible was imperfect was too much to bear.

I naively believed that the Bible would no longer be sacred if it contained errors or contradictory messages. If it wasn't perfect, then it couldn't be trusted, and neither could God. And I had a scary thought that: "If the Bible is not true, I might as well just kill myself." Of course, that was an extreme reaction, but I felt that, without a divine roadmap, life was too big and complicated for me to navigate. Denial helped block the scary reality of an imperfect Bible, and an imperfect God, looming before me. Over time, I was finally able to handle the truth in small doses and eventually my unconscious no longer needed the shock absorber of denial.

SPLITTING

Splitting is a defense mechanism that causes people to label others as either "good" or "bad". Splitting enables people to steer away from complex feelings of ambivalence which are often uncomfortable. This shock absorber is wired inside of us because, let's be honest, it is sometimes easier to see the world as black or white than to see in shades of gray.

A great example of how this plays out is through angry totalizing statements such as "He is a sinner; I shouldn't listen to anything he says," or "How could they believe that; they are definitely not a Christian," or "Those Christians are just a bunch of ignorant, brainwashed idiots." These are all attempts to split people, labeling them as all bad in an attempt to soften complex reality and feel better about ourselves. If those *other* folks are all bad, then *we* are all good. Contrast this approach with a more balanced and truthful perspective through which a person sees the good in other folks and recognizes opportunities for growth in both themselves and others.

Those who walk away from the faith can split Christians as "all bad" to avoid their ambivalent feelings toward them. It is easier to hate church folk, or, at the very least, negatively evaluate them, than to be honest with themselves that they are conflicted— that they have both feelings of love and hate toward Christians. The very same thing happens to those who, in the midst of their deconstruction process, suddenly hate God, hate Christians, and hate the church. It is a form of splitting that paradoxically helps some grieve. There is research to suggest that those who harbor negative evaluations of their ex-part-ner directly after a breakup "show superior post-break-up emotional adjustment."[1] That also may apply to those who breakup with the church. Like each of our defense mechanisms, splitting serves an adaptive purpose, helping us cope with trauma. But that which is initially helpful can become a hindrance to our overall well-being later on. This usually occurs when people enter the Station of Angstville.

EXTERNAL SHOCK ABSORBERS

External—or what I call run-and-numb—shock absorbers are com-monly used by people experiencing excessive emotional pain. Many people, for example, run to drugs and alcohol to numb their pain. Others run to pornography to get a rush and distract themselves from loneliness, sadness, and grief. Still others run quickly into the arms of another lover to feel powerful or to receive assurance that someone finds them desirable or lovable. Some people become workaholics, laboring longer and harder hours. Others troll people on Facebook. And some read the Bible for hours a day, go on as many mission trips as they can, and hide their pain under the guise of religiosity, good works, and the piousness of being busy. These are all false intimacies and distractions that help people numb their pain and loss.

THE BLAME GAME

Another common shock absorber is blaming. This one is an oldie and is a defense mechanism with which we've all had experience. Remember Adam and Eve in the book of Genesis? They hid from God after eating the forbidden fruit because of their deep sense of shame. The only problem was that it was impossible to play hide-and-seek with the creator of the universe. When God found them, even though they *both* ate, Adam engaged the shock absorber of blame. Take a look at the account in Genesis 3:

And he [God] said ... "Have you eaten from the tree that I commanded you not to eat from?"

The man said, "The woman you put here with me—she gave me some fruit from the tree, and I ate it."

... The woman said, "The serpent deceived me." (Genesis 3:11–13)

Adam and Eve could not allow themselves to be fully exposed and take responsibility for what they had done. Perhaps their individual pain and shame were so intense that they chose to blame in order to get the loving, yet penetrating, gaze of God off of themselves and onto someone else.

This type of blaming is common for people during their D/R journey. Pastors say, "It's your fault you are a heretic! If only you hadn't read Rob Bell and ... " The other Christian in the room interrupts and yells, "Well, you're a fearmonger and a hypocrite ... And if only *you* hadn't ... " And around and around they go.

Blaming usually goes hand-in-hand with an attack. By attacking—cursing and slandering one another—we attempt to defend against the emotional pain by directing it elsewhere. Those of us on the D/R journey should be careful with this shock absorber because we can easily use it to distract ourselves from feelings of pain and loss; from grieving the loss of aspects of our faith and our existential need to reconstruct something in its wake.

Instead of blaming and attacking, it's important for us to understand the bigger, more complex picture. For example, with the exception of a few psychopaths, rarely is a person purely evil in the sense that every fiber of their being wants to control, coerce, manipulate, harm, and abuse others. I used to split my old pastor as all bad: "How dare that manipulative SOB take advantage of me," I would say to myself. "How dare he try to suppress my wild, creative mind and silly self. He's just power-hungry and insecure. He just wanted to control me. He made me fearful about whether or not God loves me. He ruined my faith and I hope he gets hit by a truck!"

In reality, I was blaming that pastor for all of my own spiritual struggles. I was labeling him as all bad and was engaged in a verbal attack. Of course, I still believe he is fully responsible for his controlling attitude toward me and for his fear-based sermons that caused me to doubt my faith every week. But *I* made the choice to go to church every week. He was looking to be worshipped and I obliged because I was desperate for a father figure. My yearning for security and answers to all of life's mysteries propelled me to cling to my pastor's every word. I needed life to be simple and he provided me with digestible, packaged answers that came from a supposed Gods-eye-view.

Don't get me wrong. I am in no way encouraging you to take the blame for severe abuse. No man, woman, or child should be blamed for what happened to them at the hands of their abuser. What I *am* saying, and I can only speak for myself, is that I had to acknowledge that there was an ache and a void in me that wanted the security of someone else taking charge of my life. I needed to admit that I longed for a controlling and coercive father-figure because that was exactly what I grew up with. Yes, it was toxic, but it also made me feel strangely at home.

Heinz Kohut, a psychoanalyst and the founder of a prominent model of psychotherapy wrote about the phenomenon I experienced firsthand. Kohut argued there is a difference between *mirror-hungry* leaders and *ideal-hungry* followers. Mirror-hungry leaders are those who need constant attention, admiration, and affirmation from those around them so that they can nourish their fractured, empty, and mirror-starved selves. For the mirror-hungry leaders to receive the attention they crave, they must be able to communicate "grandeur, omnipotence, and strength".[2] They are shame-filled narcissists whose drug is the admiring gaze of others. Honestly, this describes many of the fundamentalist leaders I've ever met. They are just like the wizard in the *Wizard of Oz.*

The Wizard is the unseen ruler of a land called Oz. He is known by the commoners to be wise, powerful, and capable of solving everyone's problems. He was godlike. In the movie, Dorothy, the troubled main character, was lost. So, she went on a journey to see the Wizard, believing that he could miraculously solve her problems and help her get back home. Unfortunately, he was no wizard. Instead, he was a conman from Omaha, Nebraska.

Many leaders are like the Wizard of Oz, putting on a show with great oratorical skills, Bible knowledge, gripping PowerPoints, and hip clothes. Behind all the apparent greatness is someone who is hiding behind their feelings of shame, low self-worth, and an insatiable need to be loved and valued. These pastors are child-emperors with no clothes.

In the crowd is a little boy or girl yearning to get the direction, love, and guidance he or she was deprived of as a child. They are folks who yearn for someone to put their clothes on for them. Ideal-hungry followers are those who long to merge with omnipotent figures to feel a sense of wholeness. These people are different from the "psychologically healthy follower rendered temporarily needy by societal stress… The ideal-hungry follower only feels whole when merged with the idealized other."[3] Ideal-hungry followers are easily wrapped up in fundamentalist groups and wrapped around the finger of omnipotent, mirror-hungry leaders in order to feel a sense of identity cohesion. Both the unhealthy leader and unhealthy follower are in a symbiotic relationship in which both need each other to keep from fragmenting and falling apart.

I can't fully blame my fundamentalist pastor for the messy, deconstructive state I was in. If I'm being honest, I have to admit that I was an ideal-hungry follower, desperate for a mirror-hungry leader. We were a perfect symbiotic match that brought some benefit, but eventually brought negative consequences into my life.

DISPLACEMENT

I remember it vividly. The food our mother prepared came out of the oven and was thrown violently down onto the kitchen floor by my father. Our mother, furious with rage, found a large knife in the kitchen drawer and pointed it at my father. They began yelling and cursing at each other, the venom of their callous words poisoning their already bruised hearts. They saw each other as enemies. Little did they know that their perpetual wars would leave lifelong wounds on innocent bystanders.

Our mom told my two brothers and me to go outside (which was great because we wanted nothing more than to get out of that room). So, we ran out of the front door. It wasn't the time to question. It was time to simply obey. As we listened to the sound of two angry monsters engaged in an epic battle, we looked at each other, silent with shock and disbelief. We were scared and didn't know what was going to happen. Then our mother, fierce and wielding that knife, chased our father out of the house. I was six when that happened and it's one of the only memories I have of my mother and father being together—if you can even call that "being together." Unfortunately, the death of my seemingly perfect family unit was not the only death I would experience.

As you could probably guess, my parents divorced after the incident with the knife. It's hard to come back from death-threats. The odds were stacked against them, anyway. They had twins when they were eighteen (I am one of them) and then a year later, they had my younger brother. That makes three kids at nineteen. Their marriage lasted six years which, in all honesty, was remarkable considering the circumstances. But their divorce was certainly was not a friendly one. The thing that boggles my mind is how in six short years, their deep love for one another quickly turned into a tenacious hatred.

Unfortunately, the greatest casualties of warring parents are usually the children. While my brothers have had their own perceptions of and reactions to our past (one of which has schizophrenia and life-imprisonment for murder), I can only share my own. I am not sure what I thought when I was six. I didn't have an adult brain, so my thoughts were certainly not integrated. But I do remember that fear was my predominant emotion during that period of my life. And I remember being divided. Whose side was I supposed to be on? Who was I supposed to love more? What did I do with my dad calling my mother every name in the book when he picked us up on the weekends? What did I do with my mom periodically keeping us from our dad just to spite him? I was afraid. I was confused. I felt divided. Just to survive, I had to shut down and hide my emotions. I had to placate whichever parent I was with because the potential loss of their love was too great to risk.

Not only was I divided within myself, but there was an even greater barrier between my parents and me. Their hate for one another blinded them, keeping them from seeing me as an innocent, formative child who needed help. I was desperate for affection and all I wanted was for them to compassionately listen to my hurting heart. But instead of seeing me as a person, they saw me as a canvas at which to throw their verbal vomit. My parents were so focused on hurting each other that they unintentionally diminished the already small presence they were able to offer to me and my brothers.

Their conflict was hardly the worst thing about my childhood. I had a mother who did the best she could, but she was addicted to drugs as far back as I could remember. She would eventually die from a drug overdose. I had a father who was mentally, emotionally, and physically abusive. He never told me he loved me, never told me he was proud of me, and never showed me affection. I can't tell you how many times I was told, "You're a fucking loser just like your mother," "You're a lazy piece of shit," "You're weak," and, "You're clueless," and other wonderful life-affirming phrases (note the sarcasm). I also had a step-father, a violent biker, who would eventually go to prison for decades. (Hmm. I wonder where my shame infestation and my suicidal tendencies came from?)

Okay. This isn't a Lifetime movie script, so I'll spare you the rest of the details. You get the point, right? My life was full of trauma long before my pastor and church experiences came along. And now, as I look back, I can see that while I was angry that the church profoundly hurt me and let me down, I was hurt and wounded way before that. The church was just a place where I displaced my enormous amounts of pain and anger. That is not to say the church, or more specifically people in the church, didn't threaten me, reject me, let me down, or seek to control me. Yes, they were responsible for their actions and the pain those actions caused me, but the pain and lostness I felt in the deep recesses of my heart pre-existed them.

Besides whining about the church and harshly judging Christians for being jerks (which I did a lot of), I found myself, as I traveled the D/R journey, reflecting on the deprivation of my early childhood. I realized I unconsciously wanted the church to become the parents I never had. I had unfairly projected my need for the love, acceptance, attunement, encouragement, and nurturing I never received from my parents onto a bunch of imperfect and wounded people.

Not only did I learn I was displacing my unresolved, negative emotions onto the church because of my parents, but I found there were other existential realities causing me pain. I was hurt by the unfairness of life. I was hurt about my brother rotting in a prison. I was hurt about the crappy decisions I made that caused heartache for me and other people. I was hurt about how hard I had to work just to inch my way through life. I was hurt that people in power marginalize and oppress others. I was hurt about my heart getting broken in failed romantic relationships. I was hurt that nothing lasts—that everything is fluid and changes repeatedly over time. I was just plain hurt, and someone had to pay. Someone, or some entity—specifically the church, had to be the scapegoat.

One of the most important moments in my life was when I realized I was dumping my own hurt onto the church. Some of that hurt was warranted, for sure. Some of it was not. I unconsciously expected the church to fix me or provide me with the idealized family I never had. The problem was I set the standards way too high. The payment for my hurt was more than the church could afford. The truth was that no one could fill the void that was left in the wake of neglectful and abusive parents and an unfair, ever-changing, and sometimes harsh existence—not even the church. Once I started realizing this truth, my heart shifted, and I began to feel compassion for the church and its people.

SHOCK ABSORBERS: THEY HINDER AND HELP

Let's pretend you are the mutant Multiple Man, a fictional character from the Marvel Universe who has the ability to duplicate himself (he appeared in *X-Men: The Last Stand* ... yes, I'm a nerd). You can split off into one, five, ten, or more carbon copies of yourself. Eventually, all of your duplicate selves will be absorbed back into one mutant, Multiple Man.

Humor me, and my love for the Marvel universe, for a second. Think of this scenario in light of our discussion about defense mechanisms and pretend that the duplicates are your shock absorbers. Let's say you're in an epic battle with an alien (the Church), who is shooting a harmful, large-diameter, radiation gun at you (trauma). So, you employ one of your duplicates (defenses) to jump in front of you and absorb the radiation. Even though the original "you" has been saved, your duplicate has heroically absorbed the energy. The problem is that after doing their jobs, the duplicates (defenses) return and inevitably contaminate you and anyone in relationship with you. Here's the deal: Defenses are necessary to protect you, but at some point along the way, they become hazardous to your health.

In many ways, shock absorbers are like overly helpful friends who mean well and try to look out for your best interests. While shock absorbers, like medications, can bring enormous benefits to your physical and emotional health, they can also produce disastrous side effects. They help you cope with the aftermath of trauma and loss—keeping your anxiety, emotions, and pain at bay—but they can also hinder the healing process, which, over time, can negatively affect you and those in relationship with you. Maybe we should call them "frenemies."

For example, let's say that you use the shock absorbers of excessive work and alcohol to deal with the emotional pain and anxiety caused by your D/R journey. Despite being maladaptive defenses, they *do* help you get by and not be overwhelmed and debilitated by negative emotions. The problem is that you can numb yourself with work and alcohol so often that you don't have time for meaningful relationships. As a result, you wind up pushing away those who really want to help you. Eventually, you will need to let go of the defenses so you can live and love in a healthier way.

Emotions communicate important information about ourselves and the world around us. So, if we distort reality with defenses, we can deprive ourselves of the very information our emotions are trying to convey. Sadness at the loss of an intimate relationship with God, is a great example. When we deny that we are sad, we don't allow ourselves to acknowledge loss and to follow the call to action—to move toward others for care and comfort. Instead, we isolate ourselves from others and feel depressed. If we deny that we are angry at the injustice of certain church policies or doctrines, and engage in the defense of rationalism or suppression, then we don't allow the wisdom of the adaptive anger to help us fix the problem.

If this whole discussion makes you feel overwhelmed about the D/R journey, take heart. Humans have been trying to cope with life in maladaptive ways for millennia. Like our ancient ancestors, Adam and Eve, we have all learned to sew fig leaves together to cover our fragile and hurting souls. It is a wired-in process that happens automatically, just like breathing. Even the best of sinning saints have used shock absorbers to deal with anxiety and emotional pain.

Using shock absorbers to cope with the turbulence of the D/R journey is completely normal. It is part of the grieving process and a necessary aspect of the path of reconstruction. I am *not* saying it is the ideal strategy to use with our emotional pain, but if we're honest, it is what we do as hurt and wounded human beings.

The point is that instead of using shock absorbers, we need to face the pain, our uncomfortable emotions, and distressing thoughts head-on and learn to use healthier coping strategies. By becoming more aware of our natural defense mechanisms, we can shed the old and put on something new.

I offer you sincere compassion during this trying time. I've been there before and I know how tough it can be. Suffering from religious disorientation is hard. I'm confident that through Love, who is always luring us toward shalom—peace—and through your daily commitment to be emotionally/spiritually healthy and move toward reconstruction, you will be less prone to using destructive defenses and learn valuable life lessons along the way.

QUESTIONS

1. In your own words, how would you describe the benefits of defense mechanisms?

2. What are your thoughts about King David having a craving for sex as a means to deal with potential trauma and PTSD?

3. Thinking about your faith journey, what ways have you used the defense mechanism of denial?

4. Thinking about your faith journey, what ways have you used the defense mechanism of splitting?

5. Thinking about your faith journey, what ways have you used the defense mechanism of blaming?

6. What are your thoughts about the synergistic connection between mirror-hungry leaders and ideal-hungry followers?

7. Thinking about your faith journey, what ways have you used the defense mechanism of displacement?

8. What external shock absorbers do you typically use to cope with your mental, emotional, and spiritual suffering?

PART III

THE WAY FORWARD

In Part I, we journeyed through the big picture of the de-churched and the stations frequently traveled. In Part II, we examined the inside-scoop of our internal mental, emotional, and spiritual processes that are common on the D/R journey. In Part III, we will take a look at specific, heavenly-minded but down-to-earth pathways, practices, and principles in which you can engage to help you heal and effectively participate in the fine art of reconstruction.

This section is founded on the idea that digesting information rarely results in transformation. Growth occurs, instead, at the point where knowledge and practical experience meet. That is why the Bible uses action words and phrases such as "do likewise" (Luke 10:37), "go and make" (Matt. 28:19), "put on" (Eph. 6:11; Col. 3:10), "put it into practice" (Phil. 4:9), "reflect" (2 Tim. 2:7), "meditate" and "consider" (Ps. 119:15), "follow" (Luke 9:23), and "clothe yourselves" (Col. 3:12; 1 Peter 5:5).

Some of these practices will be like life preservers for you while others may be thrown aside. The point is to find pathways, practices, and points of view that work for you. This is your way forward and you need to decide what brings life to your soul and what does not. The ultimate goal is to heal and reconstruct your life and faith one pathway, practice, and principle at a time.

CHAPTER SEVEN

THE BLESSING OF AN UNHOLY HUDDLE

"Anything that's human is mentionable, and anything that is mentionable can be more manageable. When we can talk about our feelings, they become less overwhelming, less upsetting, and less scary. The people we trust with that important talk can help us know that we are not alone."

— MR. FRED ROGERS

The historic Lorraine Cross has one vertical beam and, unlike the crosses we see in the West, two horizontal crossbeams. There are several interpretations of the design that point to the work of Christ on the cross, but for me it symbolizes the threefold relational pathway essential to a life worth living:

- The vertical pathway symbolizes the relationship we need with the Divine.

- The first horizontal pathway symbolizes the relationship we need with others and creation.

- The second horizontal pathway symbolizes the relationship we need with ourselves.

I believe the degree to which we are lovingly connected on the vertical and horizontal pathways is the degree to which we will experience emotional and spiritual health and vitality. One without the others will result in a lopsided journey and we will lose out on valuable relational resources for growth, healing, and transformative reconstruction. In this chapter, we will explore the first horizontal pathway: our crucial need for other people.

WE NEED OUR UNHOLY HUDDLE

In sports, players regularly form a tight circle, known as a huddle, to encourage one another and strategize about how to advance against their opponents. I believe you need a similar circle of people who are honest, real, and spur you along in your journey. Let's call this group of people an "unholy huddle." They are not the uptight holy rollers, who seethe with judgment, waiting to spew out of their mouths at the sight of an unchristian infraction. They are fellow journeyers who travel with you to the unholy abyss and embrace the so-called *unclean* aspects of who you are. They are a team of like-minded people who can listen to your story and encourage you through the struggles that lie ahead. Your unholy huddle will help you grieve losses, maintain your balance, and move forward to cross the goal line of healing and integration. With empathy and compassion, your teammates will help you strategize for success; extinguish harsh judgment, shaming, and criticism; and celebrate the victories along the way.

During my deconstruction process, I realized I was bleeding out and needed other people to come alongside me. The utter aloneness was excruciating. The occasional bouts of heaviness felt unbearable. The suffocating fear of the unknown was brutal. It was crucial for me to be around people seasoned in the areas of faith, deconstruction, reconstruction, loss, and life. I realized I could not deconstruct and reconstruct alone, so I became desperate to find community.

The first and greatest hurdle was overcoming my fear of letting others in. At first, I jumped over this obstacle with too much speed and shared my struggle with as many people as I could. I sought the wisdom and the listening ears of friends, professors, and even a couple of people I barely knew. Let's just say this wasn't the best strategy because not everyone had good advice or even the capacity to listen. And, if I'm honest, a lot of the people made the conversation about him or herself. The experience did help me learn to distinguish safe and comforting people from oblivious and cold ones. I started building a network of supportive friends which was beneficial not only for my season of disequilibrium, but for the rest of my life.

Because we can have so many thoughts—some of which are contradictory—and mixed emotions during our deconstructive process, our mind is on a mission to manage our mayhem and make sense of it all. Telling our story to others helps accomplish that mission. Our mind needs to tell the story after a distressing event just like the body needs to spike a fever during an infection. Just as our bodies seek to heal and restore themselves, so do our minds. Sharing with other people can even help us recalibrate our spirituality with who we feel God is calling us to be in the world.

Of course, being vulnerable with others is not always easy. We live in a society, and are part of a Christian culture, in which people tend to avoid difficult emotional, spiritual, and mental issues.

ANTI-GRAVITY

We live in an anti-gravity culture, both within the church and without. Here's what I mean: The prefix, *anti-*, means "against," and *gravity* comes from the Latin word, *gravitas*, which means "heavy or weighty." To live in an anti-gravity culture means to live where people are actively against dealing with the weightier matters of the heart such as grief, loss, fear, shame, pain, and other heavy experiences. They would much rather swim in the shallow waters than in the depths of each other's darker emotional experiences, difficult doubts, and thought-provoking questions.

Think about how our society, as well as some church cultures, has squelched natural and healthy expressions of emotion, doubt, and questions with anti-gravity messages like these:

- Don't cry.

- Are you sad? This pill or scripture verse will help you smile again.

- Suck it up.

- Don't be a sissy.

- Don't show weakness.

- Hey, be a man.

- Don't be so emotional, just lean into God's word.

- Just get over it, already.

- Stop dwelling on it and just trust in God.

- Put on your big-girl panties and deal with it.

- Girls don't get angry.

- Stop being anxious.

People who provide shallow responses, though they mean well, are implying you aren't supposed to feel the way you feel or that they simply don't have time or empathy to enter into your experience. We are probably all guilty of such communication. We might ask one another how we are doing on a regular basis, but seldom is it a real inquiry. Usually, it's merely a polite social greeting followed by the typical programmed response, "Good, thanks, how are you?" We don't realize we all need a listening ear and truth spoken out of a compassionate heart.

The problem is if we don't allow ourselves and others to feel, we split off and deny our emotional experience. When that happens, we then cease being congruent. A lack of congruence means we have to hide who we are and what we feel from others and, as a result, cannot truly be known by anyone. If we are not known, we feel isolated and alone. And to cope with our feelings of aloneness, we engage in defenses, making us feel more alone. And the cycle continues.

PERFECT(SHUN)

During the D/R journey, the defense mechanism of perfectionism is another factor that can keep us from connecting with other people. Hidden within the word *perfectionism*, at least phonetically, is the word *shun*, which is a constant reminder of the unfortunate consequence of trying to be perfect. I like to think of *perfectionism* as perfect-*shun*-ism.

When we shun somebody, we keep away from, hide from, or avoid that person. If we are affected by perfect*shun*ism, we tend to avoid or shun anything that appears to be broken, incomplete, raw, and imperfect. Perfect*shun*ism invariably keeps us from listening to the brokenness within ourselves and others and it keeps others from engaging with and listening to us. It stops us from intimately knowing each other and ourselves.

Perfect*shun*ism causes us to fear raw, unrefined inner experiences, along with the messy suffering of others, and to shun what our souls are really crying out for. So, we mask our imperfect pain with excessive activity, noise, programs, addictions, and the like. Can you relate? If you run away from your own pain, shame, and brokenness, you will most likely run away from hurting people who come to us in their time of need and desperation.

Perfect*shun*ism also causes us to look like someone we are not, putting a barrier between who we really are and other people. Since we will never be perfect, attempts at showing people a façade of perfection actually hides our inner selves from them. If we relate to people and God as we think we should (like an actor), then we keep others from listening and encountering the real us. At this point on the D/R journey, most of us are pretty tired of having to hide who we really are and what we really believe. While it is difficult, we know deep in our souls that we must come out of hiding in order to truly live and thrive. Yet, we must choose our friends, our unholy huddle, wisely.

EVERYONE NEEDS A WIT(H)NESS

Henri Nouwen, a spiritual mentor, author, and Christian teacher, identifies the qualities of a caring friend, the kind of person worthy of your unholy huddle. He writes that it should be full of people who "instead of giving advice, solutions, or cures, have chosen rather to share our pain and touch our wounds with a warm and tender hand … [who] can be silent with us in a moment of despair or confusion … [who] can stay with us in an hour of grief and bereavement … [who] can tolerate not knowing, not curing, not healing and face with us the reality of our powerlessness".[1]

Sarah Bessey calls her unholy huddle her *Somewheres*. She writes about those who are necessary for the deconstruction and reconstruction journey:

> Here are a few things you need to become Somewheres: An ability to welcome the contradictions in each other. Ferocious trust. Secret-keeping. A shared sense of humor. A fierce belief in the inherent goodness and holiness of each other. An equal amount of butt kicking and hair petting. Bravery. Silliness. A common core. The capacity to laugh through tears.[2]

STORY CATCHERS

Our unholy huddle needs to be comprised of *Story Catchers*. Story catchers are deep, empathic, compassionate listeners. They are intentional about catching the stories of others, about sincerely listening to the blessings and blunders of those they encounter. Story catchers embody acceptance, compassion, and grace. Why do we need these kinds of people in our lives? Story catching communicates messages such as You are loved; You are worth it; You are respected; and You are valued.

A story catchers' favorite life verse might be 1 Peter 3:8: "Finally, all of you, be like-minded, be sympathetic, love one another, be compassionate and humble." Story catchers believe like-mindedness, sympathy, compassion and humility are the route to deep, intimate relationships. They are serious about the biblical mandate to tune into the emotional and spiritual frequency of others (like-minded), to notice and enter into the pain and suffering of others (sympathy) with tender heartedness (compassion), and to acknowledge another person's inherent worth as a fellow journeyer who needs the grace of God as much as they do (humility).

I will never forget an episode of the show, *Hoarders*. It featured a hoarding therapist named Cory who wanted to experience what the hoarder experienced as a way of truly entering and understanding her world. So, Cory decided to sleep inside of a house packed to the rafters with clothes and garbage. Insects and rodents scurried over the heaps. And the home did not have heat. He certainly ended up with a frightening taste of what it was like to live as she did (spoiler alert, he didn't get a good night's sleep).

Cory's decision to enter into the multisensory experience of someone who was hurting is the best description of a story catcher. Story catchers proactively make a pact to cherish deep emotional, spiritual, and physical contact with those they encounter. They are willing to enter people's homes deep within their souls, no matter how messy, dark, or scary. Like Cory, they might feel nervous and uncomfortable at times, but they do the work courageously, knowing that through story catching they can literally love the hell out of people. Hell, in this case, signifying those things that torment or weigh heavily on the hearts of hurting people.

Story catchers do not believe deep connection can be found on the surface of people's thoughts, but in the place where emotions reside—where "deep calls to deep" (Ps. 42:7). They recognize that behind emotions—such as fear, sadness, loneliness, hurt, and shame—linger relational questions and longings, such as:

- Will you listen to me?

- Will you love me?

- Will you comfort me?

- Will you be there for me?

- Will you be proud of me?

- Will you hold me?

Emotions are a window through which story catchers are able to peer and access deeper parts of people's hearts and stories. By listening to the stories, accessing and acknowledging deeper emotions and longings, they often leave hurting people feeling profoundly understood. Those with a story catcher in their unholy huddle say they feel lighter, freer, and more connected to God, self, and others.

Somewheres, caring friends, and story catchers are the type of people that I needed on my journey. Thankfully, I found a few of them. Their witness—their *with*ness—changed my life for the better, and it continues to do so.

JESUS' UNHOLY HUDDLE

It is commonly known that Jesus had twelve disciples, but perhaps not so commonly known that, within those twelve, he had an intimate group of three: Peter, James, and John. Jesus was vulnerable with them, inviting them to see him at his best—and at his worst.

He showed his unholy huddle his best when he took them up a mountainside and revealed his glory to them. It is as if he was saying to them, "Hey guys, check this out. I want you to be the first to see this." The text says, "His face shone like the sun, and his clothes became as white as the light" (Matt. 17:2). He felt comfortable enough to show them his core self. Honestly, it sometimes takes more courage to show people the best side of you without fearing they will judge you or not be willing to appreciate your joy.

Jesus also needed his unholy huddle when he was at his worst. He took his three closest friends with him on his excruciating journey to Gethsemane. *Gethsemane*, ironically, means "olive oil press." Jesus was about to feel the weight and pressure of sorrow in his soul, as never before, and he didn't want to be alone. Mark 14:33–34 says, "He took Peter, James and John along with him, and he began to be deeply distressed and troubled. 'My soul is overwhelmed with sorrow to the point of death,' he said to them. 'Stay here and keep watch.'"

Jesus' unholy huddle was far from perfect, however. On one occasion, he told his disciples to stand watch, be alert, and engage in prayer themselves, but when he returned, he found them sleeping (Mark 14:37). Nevertheless, Jesus needed his imperfect friends for care, comfort, and support on his epic journey. And so will you.

THE NECESSITY OF RELATIONSHIPS

Relationships are the entire thrust of the Christian faith. The Hebraic Scriptures and New Testament are crammed with evidence that relationships are the very reason for our existence. God, who is inextricably relational, is always inviting humans to come into a profound awareness of that reality. Imagine the profound, parental pleasure God experiences when seeing us relate intimately and lovingly with each other.

While, ironically, people inflict wounds and cause our deepest pain, they also provide the most significant healing and growth. While we are healed directly through God's Spirit (the vertical pathway), God also heals us indirectly through the wit(h)ness of other people (the horizontal pathway). James 5:16 (AMP) says,

> Therefore, confess your sins to one another [your false steps, your offenses], and pray for one another, that you may be healed *and* restored. The heartfelt *and* persistent prayer of a righteous man (believer) can accomplish much [when put into action and made effective by God—it is dynamic and can have tremendous power].

Prioritizing the vertical relationship with God is vital, but you will also need to find a caring community in which you can be gut-wrenchingly open and honest about your spiritual journey. That can be very hard when the community you once thought was a safe place became a place where you were rejected and hurt. Author and spiritual director, Beth Allen Slevcove, discusses her own desperate need for community during seasons of grief. She writes,

> Grief, as we know, often feels like being held under water. Sometimes what we need is to buddy breathe. Buddy breathing happens when a scuba diver loses his or her air supply and another diver comes alongside and shares air, allowing both to breathe until they surface. I've done a lot of buddy breathing through my journeys of grief.[3]

Finding healing in community is not an alternative, or fallback plan, for those who do not have enough faith in God. It is a biological imperative and part of God's gold standard for successful healing and necessary for living life to its fullest. Finding people with whom you can share your story, and experiencing their authentic, loving wit(h)ness as a result, will allow you to grieve and reconstruct well.

There is plenty of research confirming the power of relationships. A research study of nine thousand people found that close friendships and marriage afforded people approximately one extra decade of life.[4] Another study of more than three hundred thousand people, who were followed for seven and a half years, showed they had a 50 percent greater chance of surviving and thriving than those who did not have close relationships.[5] In another interesting study, participants were asked to engage in an imagery task to estimate the steepness of a hill. Those who thought of a supportive friend during the task perceived the hill to be less steep than those who thought of someone neutral or whom they did not like.[6] Loving relationships are like super vitamins with potent probiotics that nurture us and prolong our days. When viewing the long and rugged hills of the D/R journey, supportive friends can help us perceive it as less daunting.

There is a reason for God's invitation to connection. The invitation to love wholeheartedly is one of those few timeless—forever-contemporary—truths and wisdom in the sacred text of the Bible that can contribute to an abundant life. Jesus' re-emphasis of "the greatest commandment" was for our good. Loving relationships with God, self, and others are key to spiritual and emotional health. And if we need them in the good times, imagine how much more we are going to need them when we are feeling stuck and hopeless.

Another way to understand the power of connection is to examine what happens when there is a lack of it.

LONELINESS KILLS

One of life's greatest tragedies is when we have to struggle alone. The problem is, we don't flourish when we're lonely. Loneliness is kryptonite for human beings and has holistically devastating consequences. Social researcher James House says, "The magnitude of risk associated with disconnection and social isolation is comparable with that of cigarette smoking."[7] John Cacioppo, one of the world's leading researchers of loneliness, says that loneliness causes an increase in suicide, lowers a person's immune system, and decreases the quality of sleep. He argues it also associated with an increased negative view of oneself and others.[8] Feeling alone and isolated has devastating consequences. Mother Theresa wrote, "The most terrible poverty is loneliness, and the feeling of being unloved." We are not meant to journey alone.

WE NEED RELATIONSHIPS

We will always walk with a "limp" if we fail to embrace the cross' paradigm of healing, wholeness, and vitality. In other words, we will miss out on vital relational pathways that are needed to grieve well, grow well, and live an expansive and epic life. We need both the vertical pathway (connection to God) and the first horizontal pathway (connection to community) from womb to tomb, from the cradle to the grave.[9] That is how we were created. Relationships with others need to be paramount on our D/R journey and for the rest of our lives.

For some people, the idea of being vulnerable in an unholy huddle conjures up memories of biting into a lime. They learned a long time ago that people are sour and hurtful, not sweet and safe, and it is better to try and comfort themselves than risk rejection from others. Brené Brown writes,

> As children we found ways to protect ourselves from vulnerability, from being hurt, diminished, and disappointed. We put on armor; we used our thoughts, emotions, and behaviors as weapons; and we learned how to make ourselves scarce, even to disappear. Now as adults we realize that to live with courage, purpose, and connection— to be the person whom we long to be—we must again be vulnerable. We must take off the armor, put down the weapons, show up, and let ourselves be seen.[10]

Perhaps at one point in your life, armor, walls, and shock absorbers were necessary. But I can promise you they are not going to bring you any lasting comfort or joy. If the thought of reaching out to other people causes you to cringe, I completely understand. Nevertheless, you are meant to be in community. You are biologically wired for intimacy—not meant to live life alone.

Richard Jacobson, an ex-pastor who had a crisis of faith and began to intently deconstruct and reconstruct what it means to do and be the church, wrote the book, *Unchurching: Christianity Without Churchianity*. Writing about community he states, "But if you are truly looking to apprehend what it means to become a genuine church community, it's not enough to simply leave behind the institutional church model; you must become intentional about creating some kind of authentic community with other believers."[11] One of the blessings of going to church is the intimate relational bond that is formed with other people. One of the consequences of leaving the institutional church is the loss of some of those bonds. In order to heal and reconstruct our faith, we are invited to find a few people to walk alongside us on our journey. Yes, it will be hard. Yet, it will take intention. But for some of us, it is a life or death issue. Aloneness kills. Intimacy heals and brings us back to life.

It might be time for you to be courageous, take a risk, and commit yourself to practicing vulnerability with the members of your carefully handpicked unholy huddle. If you are inclined to hammer a *Do Not Enter* sign on the front of your cave and shut yourself inside, practice reaching out to others. Don't travel the D/R road alone. Even if you think no one will understand you, it is better to take the risk, finding connection and support, so that you aren't alone when Montu takes off at full speed and you get sucked into the vortex of yucky emotions and obsessive negative thoughts.

Just like Frodo needed Samwise and Gandalf, Batman needed Superman (even though he tried to kill him in *Dawn of Justice*), and the apostle Paul needed Barnabas and Mark, we are also going to need journeying partners as we proceed through some of the painful and disorienting experiences that are inevitable in the deconstructive and reconstructive life.

Let me share a beautiful healing practice and process your unholy huddle can be a part of to help you on your D/R journey.

SPLINTER REMOVAL (DFRS)

Remember those Cytotoxic splinters, those rigid, outdated religious beliefs that wound up causing incredible emotional and mental suffering? They are those stubborn doctrines that seemed to take forever to get rid of. Well, we don't need to remove Cytotoxic splinters all by ourselves. Our unholy huddle can be instrumental in helping us remove them, heal the infected area of our mind and heart, and increase our capacity to love God, self, and others. They can be part of the splinter extraction process known as DFRS (*Deal, Feel, Reveal, Seal*).

DEAL

The first step in the extraction process is to make the choice to deal with your cognitive dissonance and aching heart. In John 5, Jesus was in Jerusalem at the pool of Bethesda, or pool of *mercy* as it is sometimes translated, surrounded by people with all kinds of ailments. As Jesus walked around the pool, he encountered a man who had been ill for thirty-eight years. The first question Jesus asked him was, "Do you want to get well?" In the midst of our mental, emotional, and spiritual suffering, I believe Jesus asks this question to all of us. Do you want to get well?

Whether we want to get well, and be congruent, may not always be an easy question to answer. Dealing can be costly. Healing is always better than remaining in inner turmoil, but there is always a cost to the ego—that part of us that likes to protect and hold on to the status quo for fear of losing our identity. Dealing with our Cytotoxic splinters causes us to feel things we don't want to feel, think about things we would much rather forget, or move in directions we may not be ready to travel.

The man from John 5, prompted by his own ego, could have said to Jesus, "Um, I have held to my beliefs about myself and this sickness for a long time; it is now a part of my identity. If I give it up, I will somehow lose all my friends who hang with me by the pool. I may lose my reputation and I care too deeply about how others view me. I prefer to keep things as they are. Thanks, but no thanks."

The first step toward jettisoning your Cytoxic baggage is choosing to deal with the religious beliefs that have been causing cognitive dissonance, and declaring you want to get well; declaring you want to be congruent. When *dealing*, you want to be specific in naming the actual splinters that are causing you distress. It is important to describe in detail the specific Cytotoxic and Theotoxic beliefs that you have been wrestling with.

FEEL

The second step is to allow yourself to feel. Although it is easier to use shock absorbers, this step calls you to be present with your anger, sadness, fear, anxiety, and any other overwhelming emotions you might experience because of the cognitive dissonance and disorientation.

Your major task in this step is to set aside time to face your feelings. Sometimes, sitting in meditation before God, the ultimate revealer of truth, can bring clarity to your experience. If God is not a safe attachment figure, then just sit in silence with yourself. Allow your body and your intuition to clue you into how you are feeling.

The authors of *How to Survive the Loss of a Love* encourage those in pain to feel deeply and fully embrace their inner experiences. They write: "Don't postpone, deny, cover, or run from your pain. Be with it now. Everything else can wait. An emotional wound requires the same priority treatment as a physical wound. Set aside time to mourn. The sooner you allow yourself to be with your pain, the sooner it will pass; the only way out is through. Feel the fear, pain, desolation, and anger. It's essential to the healing process. You are alive. You will survive."[12]

Although the use of shock absorbers may seem helpful at first, prolonged use will bring unwelcome side effects and you will, eventually, still have to come to terms with your emotional pain. Lysa TerKeurst, the author of *Unglued: Making Wise Choices in The Midst of Raw Emotions,* writes, "Stuffing means pushing emotions inward. We swallow hard and lock our hurt feelings inside, not in an effort to process and release them, but to wallow in the hurt. Much like an oyster deals with the irritation of a grain of sand, we coat the issue with more and more layers of hurt until it forms a hard rock of sorts." She continues, "But this rock is no pearl. It's a rock that we'll eventually use either to build a barrier or to hurl at someone else in retaliation."[13]

Suppressing your uncomfortable thoughts and feelings is like pushing an inflated beach ball underwater. Eventually it will burst back up with greater force than it took to push it down. If you're not careful, the ball will hit you or others in the face. Deal with your inner turmoil now so it won't forcefully and unexpectedly pop up, like the beach ball, somewhere else in your life.

Emotional pain you resist will persist and, over time, can become an unwelcome hindrance to experiencing life to the fullest. Allowing yourself to feel will be instrumental in grieving and reconstructing well and will be an invaluable skill that will benefit you for a lifetime. It will help you face the pain caused by toxic religion so that you can fully let go of it in the future.

REVEAL

The most powerful thing, yet admittedly the scariest thing to do, is to reveal your emotional experience and struggle with the beliefs you once held dear to a compassionate, empathic person—the third step. Yes, it takes risk and courage to be vulnerable and allow others into the inner sanctum of your heart, but the rewards completely outweigh the risks. It is healthier to reveal your emotions and troubling thoughts to the right person than to perpetually conceal them.

We can share our struggles with those we consider part of our unholy huddle. We can share them with a therapist or spiritual director. Or, we can share them with God. Though God may know our thoughts and how we feel, there is something sacred about putting words to our groans and expressing them. The key here is that, whatever it might look like for each of us, we muster up enough strength to share with others.

Throughout the ages, saints of old have laid bare their emotional landscapes before the Divine. In Psalm 31:9, the spiritual writer says, "Be merciful to me, LORD, for I am in *distress*; my eyes grow weak with *sorrow*, my soul and my body with *grief*" [emphasis added]. It was said of Hannah, "In her deep anguish Hannah prayed to the Lord, weeping bitterly" (1 Sam. 1:10). In Romans 9:2, the mystic Paul says, "I have great *sorrow* and unceasing *anguish* in my heart." Even Jesus was not afraid to be vulnerable. How can we forget his excruciating cry, "My God, My God, why have you forsaken me?" (Matt. 27:46). At some point, we will all feel pain, suffering, sorrow, anger, and grief. So give yourself permission to feel deeply. As the old adage says, "Keep it real."

Don't be afraid. God loves it when we are truthful, no matter how ugly we think our experiences may be. And God much prefers truthfulness than to see us wearing a mask—pretending and bearing false witness. God can't heal our masks because they are inanimate objects, but God can heal an authentic hurting soul that is laid bare before God's presence.

To whom can you choose to safely reveal your experience? God, a friend, a pastor, a therapist, a spiritual director? Any trustworthy person, with an empathetic ear and a wise and non-judgmental heart, is a good choice.

SEAL

The last step is to *seal*. Complete the practice of healing by giving yourself over to the seal of the compassionate, empathic response of your confidant.

Have you ever heard of a product called WoundSeal? Imagine someone, on a boating trip, accidentally cuts his hand while preparing fishing line and begins to bleed profusely. He desperately needs stitches, but the hospital is many miles away. WoundSeal to the rescue! WoundSeal is a special powder clinically proven to seal wounds and stop bleeding instantly. It has been a lifesaver for many. Compassionate and loving responses of others are similar to WoundSeal in that they cover emotional wounds and heal hurting people faster.

Seal—the last step of the DFRS process, occurs when you surrender to the loving response of another person. Whether they give you a touch, a hug, a word of encouragement, or a loving challenge, those to whom you reveal your pain can close the gaping wound allowing greater levels of healing to occur. Many times, the best seal someone can give is their presence where words fall away and compassion is still deeply felt.

Choosing to share my struggle with my Cytotoxic beliefs—"God is all you need and needing anything else is an idol" and "Every passage of Scripture must be taken literally, therefore a holy and just God does use violence to punish disobedience"—with people from my unholy huddle was liberating. I no longer had to hide. Talking with my Somewheres helped me feel less crazy. I shared where I thought God was leading me. They offered words of encouragement and affirmed my journey. They trusted that God would lead me where I needed to go. When I went too far adrift, folks believed in me and yet lovingly challenged me when necessary. They helped me remove my false, toxic beliefs and their kindness and words of wisdom sealed the wound.

Give yourself the gift of the compassionate, loving presence of another as many times as your wound opens up and oozes pain and discomfort. When your irritating phantom theologies sneak up on you, share your experience with someone. Dietrich Bonhoeffer wrote, "In confession the light of the Gospel breaks into the darkness and seclusion of the heart."[14] As we confess to others the toxic beliefs and associated pain lodged within us, the good news of God's love can break forth and speed up the healing process. Rarely is there a single-shot treatment for splinter removal. It is more of a process and journey than a one-stop shop. But the more we enter into the beauty of a safe and loving community, the better it will be for us in the long run.

Okay. Let's recap. We can choose to become aware of the splinter, *deal* with it, and name it. We can become aware and *feel* the discomforting effect of both old and new beliefs being juxtaposed with one another and the anxiety and emotional pain due to the consequences of potentially giving up those beliefs. We can then *reveal* our spiritual struggle with our newly emerging beliefs, as well as our difficult inner experiences, with the compassionate people in our lives. The love and compassion from sacred *with*nesses not only help the Cytotoxic splinters become extracted, but they become the *seal* that closes up the wound. This allows healing to take place and Theotoxic splinters to have their way in the soil of our hearts. The DFRS model allows for integration and full acceptance of our new core belief and values. Then, with incongruence, anxiety, and shame gone, we can have more sacred energy to love God, self, and others.

Allowing the deal, feel, reveal, and seal (DFRS) process to bring healing from your traumatic religious experiences can not only help you travel well through the D/R journey, but also help you traverse the rest of the valleys you will inevitably experience in life. May it be one practice, among many in your arsenal, that you use for your emotional and spiritual health.

MAKE A LIST

Pause now for a moment to ask yourself some questions. Where is safety? Who is willing to listen? Who can I call and ask:

"Can you come over? I need a hug."

"Hey, this D/R journey sucks. I am feeling a little lonely and sad. Can you keep me company on the phone for a little bit?"

"I am obsessing about God hating me again. Do you want to hang out and do something fun?"

Make a list of the trustworthy and compassionate people in your life, who you can call for help, and then work it. Find someone who is willing to commit to checking in on you. Find someone who is not afraid to go scuba diving with you in the deepest, murkiest emotional waters; someone you can count on to share his or her oxygen if you run out of your own.

If your list contains zero and a half people, or if it is difficult for you to take risks and connect with others, then pray that God will bring loving and safe people into your life that and you will be able to receive them when they come. The Divine cares for you and your wellbeing more than you care for yourself. God loves to bring people together to help one another. Psalm 68:6 says, "God sets the lonely in families," and my desire is that God does that for you.

QUESTIONS

1. Jesus reemphasized the commandment to love God, self, and others. What thoughts come to mind as you think about the greatest commandment being the path to the best possible life?

2. What are your experiences with an anti-gravity culture? What keeps us from sharing our aches, pains, doubts, and questions with other people?

3. Can you describe the characteristics of someone who is a safe confidant?

4. Can you share an experience that you had with a Somewhere or Story Catcher? What did you share? How did you feel after sharing it?

5. What are your experiences with perfect-*shun*-ism?

6. Why did Jesus need an unholy huddle to stay with him and keep watch with him at Gethsemane?

7. What implicit rules did you learn in your childhood about relationships? Are they safe? Are they unsafe? Do you tend to move toward others in distress? Do you tend to move away from others?

8. Do you see any similarities in how you relate to others, including God, with how you related to your primary caregivers as a child?

CHAPTER EIGHT

THE INVITATION TO LOVE THYSELF

"This is a moment of suffering. Suffering is part of life. May I be kind to myself in this moment. May I give myself the compassion I need."

— KRISTIN NEFF

Jim was a huge, intimidating military guy I met at church. One day he asked to meet for lunch and talk about some things that were bothering him. During lunch, he talked about how he was desperately "trying to be a Christian" after his recent breakup with his fiancée. He was also struggling spiritually. He didn't know why a loving God would allow him to go through such a painful experience. With his head down and his shoulders slumped, he told me he was struggling with smoking, pornography and "cursing up a storm." He said that while some weeks he was able to break free from the addictions, other weeks he was not. Jim, who was being really hard on himself and appeared to be filled with shame, couldn't understand why he was struggling so much.

I slowly pushed my chair toward him, looked straight into his troubled eyes and asked him a simple question. "Jim, do you love yourself?"

"Huh?" he said.

"Do you love yourself?"

For a split second, I thought he was going to give me a karate chop to the throat. I was grateful that didn't happen, but I became nervous that, because of his conservative Christian background, he might see me as a heretic for asking him that question.

Jim lowered his voice and said, "Mark, no one has ever asked me that question before." This was a thirty-five-year-old guy who was raised as a Christian, been in churches his entire life, and no one had ever asked him if he was following the latter part of the second greatest commandment, "Love your neighbor *as yourself*" [emphasis mine]. After I asked him my oddly provocative question, we had a candid conversation about him loving himself and how that would look practically in the midst of his grief. After our discussion, he came to a profound realization that he didn't have to hate, judge, or condemn himself in the midst of his current struggles (which, he confessed, he was doing plenty of). He later told me that our conversation over lunch was a pivotal shift in his spiritual journey. Learning how to love himself enabled him to reconstruct a faith in which he didn't have to loathe himself and experience so much tiresome shame.

LOVE THYSELF

Listen. You need to love yourself. Does that sound weak, weird, or sappy? Does that sound heretical? Like New Age sewage? Are we allowed to love ourselves as Christians? Isn't it sinful or selfish? Don't we love ourselves too much already, especially if we live in a spoiled, overly pleasure-focused, Western society?

Let me be clear: it is not sinful and selfish to love ourselves. It is, however, selfish, narcissistic, and contrary to the Divine aim if we elevate the love we have for ourselves while habitually neglecting others. But honestly, I don't think we love ourselves as much as we think we do. Think about America's daily consumption of drugs and alcohol; our dreadful diet of processed sugars that we eat while obsessively binge-watching oxymoronic, fake/reality TV. We also rob ourselves of human connection, anxiously tethered to our phones and gadgets with our haunted gazes firmly fixed on them. Engaging in such activities can actually be harmful and, in some instances, hateful toward ourselves. In other words, we don't love ourselves as much as we think we do.

Unfortunately, in my former work as a pastor and my current work as a therapist, I have found Christians to be some of the most self-deprecating people I have ever met. Not only do many of us not love ourselves, we do not even like ourselves. When was the last time you heard a sermon similar to "The Three Biblical Steps to Loving Yourself"? My guess is you never have heard anything even remotely close. I am tremendously saddened by this lack of self-love as I am sure it grieves the heart of God. And it is to our detriment. If anyone should be connoisseurs of a holistic love, it should be Christians whose God *is* love.

Granted, what the Jewish people meant by the latter part of the greatest commandment, and what Jesus meant by it, is not necessarily what those in today's society who champion self-love are referring to. We have a whole new research-based context in which to understand how powerful it is to be kind toward ourselves. However, we can use the idea embedded within "Loving your neighbor *as yourself*," which was a basic reminder to love our neighbors in the practical ways we would practically love ourselves, as a springboard to dive deeper into what it means to holistically love ourselves the way God would intend for us. Unfortunately, in the Christian Scriptures, verses that talk about self-love are pretty sparse. Those who value self-love and value the Bible will take as many springboards as we can get.

If Christians are in relationship with a God who is love, then why is it we often hate and despise ourselves? Why might Christians experience more toxic shame than those who do not believe in God? There are many reasons. But it may be due to what some consider to be one of the vilest of Christian doctrines vomited out from the toxic religious machine: the doctrine of *Original Sinful Hell-Bound People*.

ORIGINAL SINFUL HELL-BOUND PEOPLE

As the story goes, Satan and his minions fell from Heaven to Earth. So, there were literally thousands, or perhaps hundreds of thousands of demons on the Earth, along with Satan in the form of a serpent, hanging out with Adam and Eve, right? How that is considered "good" is beyond me. Wouldn't that be like a parent allowing their children to play in a neighborhood park that was infested with murderers, drug dealers, and pedophiles? Those parents would not receive the parent of the year award.

Yes, I know the argument. God is apparently so holy, pure, and powerful, that God doesn't owe humanity anything. I just figure that if God birthed humanity, God would watch over and supervise God's first two naïve, sinless, and very inexperienced children (Adam and Eve). It seems reasonable to assume that God, a loving parent, would make sure they were safe. Why would God, instead of watching over them, move his kids into a neighborhood to live around godless creepers and be influenced by such bad company? And come on, God knew, just like any parent, that when you tell a young child not to do something (i.e. "Don't touch this!"), they are going to want to do that very thing! The last zinger is that God foreknew all of this would take place. According to some Christians, this disastrous event, and the curses that followed, were all a part of God's creative plan and purpose.

The biblical account also suggests Adam and Eve had not sinned before all of this. Therefore, it seems logical to consider that perhaps they did not even know what sin was. Even if God explained it to them, we all know that it's a totally different experience to hear about something than to experience it firsthand. Did they know what death, lying, pride, coercion, and manipulation was? How would that be possible if they had never participated in, or were victims of those acts before?

The sad reality is that, according to the original-sinful-hell-bound-people story, two very sincere and gullible people, who had never sinned or experienced sin before, were deceived by an experienced, wise, manipulative, and savvy talking snake. Tellers of the toxic religious story say that when Adam and Eve ate of the forbidden fruit, a loving, wrath-filled, angry, and compassionate God (I know, confusing, right?), who knew it would happen and surrounded them with evil demons, harshly punished them. Sure, God lovingly covered them with fig leaves. But because they gave into temptation and were not perfect anymore, they were cursed, along with the rest of humanity, with eternal torment. God also threw in a few extra curses to make the journey on earth a living hell.

Let's recap for a moment. Based on the interpretation of the narrative found in Genesis, here is the story that has been spun and spewed to countless generations:

> Humans are sinful, evil, good for nothing delinquents who are deserving of the wrath of God and ought to be punished in Hell for eternity because of their wicked ways. God, like a vampire needing pure blood to be satiated and content, would be happy with human beings and remit their sins if God received a perfect meal of pure blood coming from a sinless person; so, God, who had pity on us, sent Himself. If

people believe on this perfect, sinless sacrifice, otherwise known as Jesus, then they can avoid their original fate of unending torture and blissfully go to a heavenly paradise for eternity.

As you may be able to tell, I am not a huge fan of the above reading of the Genesis account and the doctrine of Original Sinful Hell-Bound People. Sadly, this is how the Genesis account, and its consequences, are spun. While I admittedly presented a caricature of the doctrine, the problem is that people internalize caricatures and believe them to be true. I think if we are going to use the creation account to talk about who human beings are at their core, we need to start with Genesis 1—with the beauty, wonder, and goodness of human beings. We should *not* start with Genesis 3—the eternally cursed and the supposedly wretched creatures that humans became after the fall.

HELL?

There is no space to give a detailed exposition of Hell. So, I will be brief.[1] The words and concepts of "Hell" and "eternal damnation" are nowhere to be found in the Genesis account of God's punishments ("You will surely die" does not correlate to "You will spend eternity in Hell where you will be tormented forever"). If the story about the original transgression and the curses that followed never mentions ideas such as "Hell," "eternal damnation," and "torture for eternity," then violent-prone religious people must have made up that heinous and horrific punishing narrative along the vast theological road.

One last point. Jesus' use of the concept of Hell, in dialogue with people of his day, doesn't legitimize it as the official destination of the damned in the afterlife. It is widely known that Hell in Jesus' day, or more properly *Gehenna*, was a garbage dump of some kind in Jerusalem. Jesus regularly used parables and metaphors to discuss spiritual truths with folks, but that *doesn't* mean every one of his illustrations is meant to be taken hyper-literally. Jesus was referring to a place, that was known to his hearers, to evoke strong emotion and make a spiritual point. Does Gehenna point to a tormenting reality people can experience today? Absolutely! Does Gehenna point to a place that will exist for some in the afterlife? If love really does win, if God is luring all of creation toward the ultimate good, then it is highly unlikely such a place would exist in the manner, and for the eternal extent, that many suppose.

OSEP

While the creation account in Genesis is a valuable lens through which we can develop an anthropology, I think a theistic evolutionary perspective is another plausible lens—an alternative perspective to the story I just told. Although I am sure a cosmologist and quantum physicist could be more precise, I tentatively hold to what I call an *Ontology of Spatial Energetic Potentiality* (OSEP). What do I mean by that nerdy, esoteric, made-up phrase? The OSEP refers to the constant movement, change, and fluidity of matter. It encompasses the Divinely created spaces located within and throughout the fabric of all of reality (including the energy swirling within those spaces), that allow for potential events to occur. The OSEP opens up the possibility of phenomena such as growth, decay, movement, and creaturely experiences of choice, joy, despair, connection and disconnection to occur.

The OSEP assures that nothing remains the same; that everything is fluid. In the OSEP-based world, we are both paradoxically temporal and eternal, energetic beings, located in space and time, who are always being pushed forward toward future potentialities. Experiences of connection, beauty, and joy never last because life pulsates and thrusts us toward new moments of experiencing. A world created without an OSEP (which is an ontological oxymoron) would be a non-existent one or, at the very least, would lack life. It would be a one-dimensional world full of static, impassable forms, all of which would be without growth, movement, or fluidity. Imagine a beautifully dull, yet immortal and never-aging painting that forever sits in a dingy, forgotten attic. Like a world without an OSEP, it exists, but it is static and lifeless.

How does God fit into this alternative story? God lures all aspects of reality that are involved in evolutionary processes toward maximal experiences of beauty, goodness, and truth. Notice that God "lures" and does not unilaterally force or coerce. Creation didn't come about instantly when God snapped a finger, as some Christians suggest, but instead evolved over billions of years. Since creation evolves slowly over time, life and death, loss and gain, are perpetual dynamics in this type of processional existence. Nothing is wasted in God's economy. Each new moment for God, no matter how beautiful or ugly, is a springboard for God to create something new in the next moment.

Many falsely equate God's declaration that creation was "good" (Genesis 1:10, 12, 18, 25) and "very good" (Genesis 1:31), with a static state of "perfection". Yet, was there ever a moment in time when nothing was changing? Was there really a never-changing state of blissful original perfection without the hint of evolving processes? Was there really a time when the interdependency of decay, chaos, novelty, growth, life, and death never existed? Is it really possible that Adam and Eve did not have a bellybutton? Was there really no such thing as plants growing and dying before Adam and Eve sinned? Before the Fall, were there really no insects that were drowned by heavy rains or eaten by other hungry critters? Was childbirth originally created to be a painless experience full of pure physical and sensational delight? Could moments of joy, love, and peace exist without moments of loss, fear, and anxiety? The notion that Adam and Eve, before they were influenced by bad company on the playground, were living in some pristine paradise where pain, death, suffering, and sin were non-existent pre-Fall, just doesn't add up scientifically, philosophically, and—one can certainly make a case—biblically.

The idea of OSEP changes the theological game when it comes to our origin story and original sin. It helps us construct a compassionate anthropology rather than an overly judgmental one. We don't have to view humans as originally without sin, who became prideful, guilty sinners; godlike beings who defied God; and left a life of pure utopic perfection. A more compassionate approach is one in which we view ourselves as creatures who, through the ripple of time, have courageously fluttered, splashed, crawled, clawed, and slowly evolved into complex sentient beings through the moment-to-moment guidance and creative empowerment of a loving God. At a certain point in history, as we evolved to the point of experiencing meta-awareness, God invited us sentient creatures to participate in the image of God. We then became conscious enough to understand good and evil. Within this compassionate perspective, we could say that humanity's initial decision to willfully ignore God's lure toward love and goodness was the *original sin*. Even in that instance, though, God was not surprised and infuriated at us. God was patient and loving, ever inviting us into greater experiences of relational goodness, beauty, and truth.

I am not naïve. I don't think humans are all good and perpetually altruistic and unselfish. Leonard Sweet says we must "put on the spectacles of paradox and become a paradoxalist."[2] Just as light and matter can paradoxically display properties of both waves and particles, we are paradoxically both sinners and saints. We all have the capacity to be sinners. We can also be saintly. We can leave pesky particles of demonic dust in the wake of our un-Christlike actions. We can also send wild and wondrous waves of divine love toward others.

Thankfully, through Christ, and the power of the Spirit, we don't have to live like pre-sentient beings who live primarily according to

the most primitive part of our brain, what some evolutionary psychologists call *the reptilian brain*.[3] Our reptilian brain is the oldest part of
our brain and is mainly responsible for fighting, fleeing, fornicating,
and feeding (perhaps likened to *the flesh* in the Christian tradition).
As we surrender to God and deflect God's waves of light and love to
others, we can be followers and imitators of Jesus. We can be divinely
empowered and become fully human as God intended!

BAD THEOLOGY HAS NEGATIVE CONSEQUENCES

The Genesis account is a fascinating exploration into the Hebraic
creation narrative from which there is much sacred wisdom to gain.
However, developing a primarily grim and pessimistic anthropology around it, as well as storying a horrid, eternal destiny for human
beings from it, is unwise and detrimental to human flourishing. The
cost to our identity, as well as the cost to people's perception of the
character of God, is too great.

The idea that we are so sinful and good-for-nothing, only deserving of eternal torment, shows how little intrinsic worth we believe we
have in the eyes of our Creator. We are worth nothing more than an
old, worn-out rag doll being tossed in the fiery flames. We have zero
worth in and of ourselves. There is nothing good within us or about
us. We are objects deserving of wrath.

That eternal-torment-believing Christian might emphatically state,
"But God loves you so much that he sent his son to die for you!"

In my work with domestic abuse victims, I have heard that kind of
crazy making talk from abusive partners.

"You are a piece of garbage," the abuser would exclaim. "You ain't
worth nothing. Nobody would ever love you. You are nothing without me."

Then, moments later, the abuser would say, "I love you. I will do anything for you. Things can be different. Just listen to what I say, will you? If you would have just listened and done what I said, I wouldn't have to hurt you and we can be happy together."

Those who advocate for this type of "worm theology" would say God loves us. However, taking Original Sinful Hell-Bound People theology to its logical conclusion, it is not really *us* who God loves. As a result of God's holiness, God doesn't seem to love anything about us. God can't even look at us without wanting to vomit us into the pit of Hell. We are no good. We are evil (a common belief that even Jesus alluded to in Luke 11:13). We are so repugnant before a holy God, that God can only see us through the prism of Jesus. God's disgust and wrath toward us good-for-nothing rag dolls is held back and absorbed in Christ.

Worm theology makes it seem as though God is the ultimate gaslighter. He's a powerful figure who, through manipulation and abuse, makes us question our own reality, our own judgment, and our sanity. Worm theology tells us we are nothing; that we are worse than nothing. We are also intrinsically evil and nothing good dwells within us. Yet, somehow, we are valuable, and God loves us. Can you imagine a parent telling their child those contradictory messages growing up and what that would do to his or her mental and emotional health?

If we are so dispensable that we could, because of our sins, be thrown into an eternal fire by a wrathful God, we must be more exponentially evil and despicable than we are good, valuable, and precious. It seems like this kind of God wants to save us out of pity and *not* because we are intrinsically loveable. It is no surprise that Christians, who hear these indigestible messages, are prone to shame, self-hatred, and self-attack.

Here's where the real gaslighting and crazy-making kicks in. After being told such a contradictory and vulgar message, we are asked to ignore our cognitive dissonance and even to pretend it doesn't exist (e.g. "Don't question God's word!"). We are then manipulated into burying the dissonance deep down into our psyches, forcing ourselves to believe "that's just who we are and how God is." Unfortunately, there are emotional and spiritual consequences to this kind of religious gaslighting, consequences that are particularly heavy for those who have a sensitive temperament and are prone to shame.

Perpetuating the message of original sin and eternal torture, especially to children (granted, a less sarcastic and simplified version than my own), can bring grievous, monumental, pathological ramifications from which a person might take a lifetime to heal. Marlene Winell writes,

> In conservative Christianity you are told you are unacceptable. You are judged with regard to your relationship to God. Thus you can only be loved positionally, not essentially. And, contrary to any assumed ideal of Christian love, you cannot love others for their essence either. This is the horrible cost of the doctrine of original sin. Recovering from this unloving assumption is perhaps the core task when you leave the fold.[4]

In Amy Phillips' research study of 35 American Christians who de-converted and became atheists, the doctrine of original sin was reported as instrumental in their emotional and spiritual suffering. Most of the participants did have a history of abuse, some at the hands of their religious parents, making the picture even more complex. It was this combination of abuse and indoctrination with the notion of original sin that would cause their future feelings of toxic shame, guilt, depression, and anxiety. Phillips writes,

> It seems that childhood/adolescent rejection and trauma, combined with religious teachings such as Original Sin, led the respondents to see themselves as defective or bad in some way. When respondents experienced abuse or punishments from their parents or religious leaders, they may have believed that authority figures punished them

as a means to correct their defective or sinful nature. This shaming led the respondents to feel guilty for the bad or wrong that they had done. Based on the religious teaching of Original Sin, the respondents may have rationalized that this was due to their innately "defective" nature. Feelings of guilt then led the respondents to experience extreme anxiety.[5]

As many people can attest, even after de-converting and changing one's beliefs on original sin and Hell, the tenacious beliefs stick around long after they are thrown into the theological garbage disposal. Phillips observed this phenomenon in her participants when she wrote, "The fear of Hell was a concern that was so hard to overcome, that respondents experienced it throughout their deconversion and even after loss of belief had occurred."[6] Why do these dastardly, stubborn doctrines refuse to leave us?

These types of doctrines stick around so much not because they are true, but because they are so vile and horrific that they leave a traumatic imprint on our brains and bodies. Our brains, in particular our amygdala, carries the anxious message, "Even though I don't believe it now, I don't want to forget it, just in case it is true." Remember, the primitive part of our brain does not always care about what is objectively accurate. It cares about keeping us alive and seeks to protect us from pain at all costs.

No longer believing in original sin and Hell is like telling the brain after a lion attack that happened years ago, "Yeah, you remember that ferocious lion? That really wasn't a lion (even though you have scars to suggest otherwise)." We were told by those with spiritual authority that God, the Creator and Ruler of the universe, thinks we are depraved sinners deserving of eternal torture in Hell. It is hard to forget those instances and the absolute electric, traumatic shock of fear that initially rippled through our nervous system.

Christians who continually remind us of those doctrines with their hate and hell-filled picket signs, or angry preachers preaching hellfire and brimstone sermons on television and movies, don't help either. They are perfect examples of *triggers*—any word, person, or behavior that sets off an immediate and overwhelming emotional reaction. While the newer, more rational and logical part of the brain (the neocortex) thinks the doctrine of Original Sinful Hell-Bound People is rubbish, the older part of the brain, where fear memories are stored (the amygdala and dorsal hippocampus), gets triggered and believes those perceived, God-created nightmares are true. Since the amygdala doesn't have a sense of time, triggers feel today just like the first time your brain experienced the electric shock of the fear-based teaching.

FUEL LINE CLOGS

Unhealthy shame is one of the harshest negative consequences of bad theology. It is one of the biggest obstacles in the way of people's ability to overcome maladaptive patterns in the midst of spiritual struggles and to walk in freedom and intimacy with the Divine. The doctrine of *Original Sinful Hell-Bound People* definitely contributes to incessant shame. Since we discussed shame already, I will add a few comments. Researchers Ronda Dearing and June Tangney, who have spent a considerable amount of time studying shame, write:

> Experiences of shame tend to be intense and overpowering because they evoke a sense of being bad, worthless, or contemptible. Shame is frequently associated with a sense of powerlessness, as well as sensations of shrinking, feeling small, being exposed, and wanting to disappear. People experiencing shame evaluate the eliciting mistake or transgression as being indicative of a self that is fundamentally flawed.[7]

Unhealthy shame reminds me of clogged-up fuel injectors. In cars, fuel injectors are tiny valves that open and close in response to electrical signals from the car's computer. They open and release fuel to the engine. Sometimes, though, grime and dirt build up in the valves, a problem which causes the car not to accelerate or even start. In the same way that valves can be clogged up by grime and dirt, shame, condemnation, and harshness toward yourself can clog your spiritual and emotional fuel injectors. They can prevent the divine fuel of freedom and joy from running smoothly through your heart, keeping you bound and joyless and unable to reconstruct well. Shame and condemnation have no place in your life and are contrary to Jesus' life-message and redemptive work on your behalf.

Jeff Turner, author of *The Atheistic Theist*, writes, "Heartbreakingly, the most original of human sins, that is, the sin we're most likely to first engage in or be engaged by, is that of self-hatred, and it is all too often reinforced by religious teaching. Jesus called such teaching stumbling blocks, and condemned those who peddled them, but we've called them gospel, and embraced them as orthodox."[8] What is an antidote to self-hatred, fear, shame, and the ripple effects of the doctrine of *Original Sinful Hell-Bound People* and other toxic doctrines? What is one of the most powerful attitudes and practices we can adopt on the D/R journey? Self-love in the form of self-compassion. Self-compassion has drastically changed my life and I absolutely think it can do the same for you.

LOVE YOURSELF AS GOD LOVES YOU

The mission of Jerry and Denise Basel, co-directors of *The Father's Heart*, a global care and intensive Christian counseling ministry, is to encourage people to love themselves. This is a practice they dub "the missing commandment." Denise writes, "I have walked many people over to a large mirror outside my office, had them look themselves straight in the eyes, and then encouraged them to verbalize a love for themselves that agrees with God's own deep love for them. This prayer of declaring our love for ourselves is one of the hardest and most powerful prayers we can pray to break lies and strongholds and to free our hearts to love."[9]

Ministers like Jerry and Denise, from all over the United States, are beginning to see the enormous gap between current Christian teaching and the need to be kind and loving toward oneself. Champions of self-compassion and self-love want people not just to love themselves as an end in itself, but to treat themselves the way God would treat them. As a result of this self-love, their fear and shame starts to dissipate, and they become freer to love God and others.

Tania Bright, the Christian author of *Don't Beat Yourself Up: Learning the Wisdom of Kindsight,* writes about the power of self-compassion. She says, "With true kindsight, instead of beating ourselves up, or—worse still—judging others, the greatest gift we can give is compassion. Compassion will have a far greater chance of combating a negative coping mechanism than condemnation ever will."[10] Self-compassion, birthed from the heart of God and sadly missing from today's Christian spiritual practices, is finally making its way into the church's consciousness.

As you read this book, it's possible that you're in one of the most difficult and confusing times of your life. You may feel as though you've been beat up by Christians and even by yourself. Maybe you're in an addictive loop—coping with your spiritual confusion and religious trauma in destructive ways to forget about your pain. You engage in more destructive activities to cover up your shame only to feel more shame in return. Round and round you go.

If that describes you in any way, let me share something really important. It's a truth about you and about God that was helpful to me when I was finding my way along the D/R journey. In the midst of your hellacious journey, you have the option to relate to yourself as the Father of love (1 John 4:16) relates to you, or as the Father of lies (John 8:44) relates to you. Do I need to tell you which option is best?

The Father of lies is another way of describing the internalized harsh and critical *Other* we have within us that daily whispers, "You're not good enough and your future is doomed!" It is the internal and oppressive wagging finger. The Other can have deep roots in being raised by cold, distant, perfectionistic parents. The authoritarian critical Other can also form out of larger systemic, oppressive, and dehumanizing cultural dynamics. It can even be the result of church leaders passing down a deformed image of a critical and punishing God that should never have been taught in the first place. Relating to yourself like the Father of lies means you internalize negative external messages and believe them as though they were your original thoughts.

Relating to yourself like the Father of love in the midst of spiritual, emotional, and everyday struggles is the ultimate goal. Kim Fredrickson, the author of *Give Yourself a Break: Turning Your Inner Critic into a Compassionate Friend*, writes, "We are to model ourselves after God in the way he relates to us. His way is to be drawn to vulnerability and struggle, to respond with compassion and guidance, and to also correct whatever sins or mistakes we've made with grace and truth."[11] In the midst of the D/R journey, imitate the relational style of the Father of love (or *Mother of love*, if you prefer), exterminate the relational style of the father of lies. In the midst of your struggles, you're either treating yourself with compassion or condemnation, with relenting hope or a negative nope, with tender forgiveness or toxic bitterness.

SELF-COMPASSION

You may be reading this and thinking to yourself, "Okay. I get it. Relate to myself in the same way that the Father of love relates to me. But what in the world does that mean?" I'm glad you asked! In recent years, some of the world's leading scholars have done incredible research on self-compassion, the fruits from which are ideal and practical ways to relate to and love yourself in the midst of life's struggles.

Kristin Neff is one of the world's leading self-compassion researchers. She describes self-compassion in a very practical way: Respond to yourself in the midst of struggle as you would a dear friend.[12] She has shown that self-compassion increases motivation, forgiveness, happiness, hopefulness, positivity, wisdom, curiosity, engagement in new experiences, agreeableness, extroversion, and conscientiousness, while also decreasing shame and depression. In her study, participants ranked their partner's level of self-compassion and then listed the characteristics that influenced their ranking. Participants who scored higher in self-compassion were described as significantly more warm, considerate, and affectionate. In contrast, participants who ranked lower in self-compassion were described as more self-absorbed, detached, and controlling. Self-compassion is revolutionary!

Neff argues that there are three main practices of a self-compassionate person who is in the midst of suffering or personal failure: self-kindness, common humanity, and mindfulness. Self-kindness is treating yourself as you would a loving friend who is in the midst of pain and suffering—with kindness, warmth, and genuine care. Rather than engaging in self-hatred, harshness, judgment, and criticism, self-kindness is when people to treat themselves gently and compassionately despite their own flaws and foibles.

Common humanity, a central component of self-compassion, is the recognition that all human beings are imperfect, wounded, and prone to making mistakes. The opposite of common humanity is the tendency people have to isolate themselves when in distress. They might neglect this important piece of self-compassion and say "I'm alone on this journey. I am the only one having these doubts about God and faith." Isolation breeds self-judgment and leads to disconnection from other human beings. On the other hand, understanding their common humanity, when they're in the middle of personal failure or mental and emotional suffering, is an invitation for people to bring compassion into their experience.

Mindfulness, the last component of self-compassion, is an awareness and acceptance of the present moment. It's the ability of a person to experience and observe thoughts and feelings in a way that makes them external. In other words, when you practice mindfulness, you understand that thoughts and feelings are not *you*; instead, it *is you* who are having thoughts. The opposite is overidentification in which people identify and fuse themselves together with negative thoughts and feelings. Mindfulness, however, allows people to view negative emotions and experiences realistically while cultivating an open and flexible perspective.

If you're thinking to yourself again, "That's a great concept. But what does mindfulness look like in real life?" Well, here's a practical application of mindfulness, along the D/R journey, in the beginning of the disorientation phase. If you're like most people, it's easy to have thoughts such as: "God doesn't love me," "I'm spiritually dead," or "I'm a sinner deserving of punishment." Instead of taking a step back and recognizing that your brain is just doing what it does best—spitting out thoughts—you can end up believing that those thoughts and feelings describe who you are as a person.

The alternative is to be *mindful,* or *aware*, of those thoughts when they occur. The phrase, "God doesn't love me" morphs into "I'm having the thought that God doesn't love me." The gist is that mindfulness creates space around thoughts so you can choose to believe them or not; to identify with them or not. It not only increases your free-will, but it also increases your "free-won't"—the ability to choose *not* to believe or act in a particular manner.

SELF-COMPASSION AND THE BIBLE

Even though self-compassion is rarely emphasized in Christian circles, all of Neff's components of self-compassion can be found in the Bible. Self-kindness, for example, is an implicit biblical principle and, contrary to what our fundamentalist friends might say, is neither narcissistic nor evil. Remember what we just discussed: in the midst of our suffering we can either relate to ourselves like the Father of love or like the Father of lies. If we want to be like God, whose nature is to be comforting and compassionate toward people when they are suffering, then we should be comforting and compassionate toward ourselves.

I'll be honest. I wish self-kindness was more explicitly taught within the pages of the Bible. My sense is that when you think God hates imperfection and can only tolerate sinless perfection, you can easily believe that humans must beg God to be loved and forgiven. After all, why should we believe we have intrinsic worth in spite of our frailty if our Creator doesn't believe it?

While the mystic psalmists caught glimpses of and wrote about God's compassion toward humanity (Psalm 103 is a perfect example), there are too many stories of God violently punishing people for their sins, imperfections, and rebellion. These mixed messages make it difficult for anyone to develop a robust theology of self-love and self-kindness. In this respect, we have much to learn from the nuanced and direct teachings on self-compassion from our Buddhist brothers and sisters.

The idea of common humanity is more evident in the Bible than self-kindness and teaches us that we are not alone in our experiences and in our imperfections. It is the acknowledgment that we are all playing on a level playing field, that "no test or temptation that comes your way is beyond the course of what others have had to face" (1 Cor. 10:13 MSG). The biblical approach to common humanity reminds us that we all fall short of perfectly loving ourselves, others, and God (Rom. 3:23). Henri Nouwen writes about the importance of recognizing our common humanity. He says, "the way we let go of our losses and sorrows is by connecting our personal pain to the great suffering of humanity, by understanding our own grief and loss as part of the larger picture of the world. For we are not the only ones who suffer in the world. Nor are we all alone."[13] We are never alone when we suffer. We have a brave cloud of faithful witnesses, from the past and present, who have walked the same road and whose tears join ours in the vast sea of human suffering.

The last of Neff's components, *mindfulness*, is an aspect of self-compassion that the Bible does, in fact, call us to practice. The author of Psalm 4:4 challenges us to "tremble and do not sin; when you are on your beds, search your hearts and be silent." Paul, in Colossians 4:2 says, "Devote yourselves to prayer, being watchful and thankful." These phrases: search your hearts, be watchful, and be silent are just biblical words for *awareness*. The Bible calls us to live wide-eyed and open-hearted with unblocked ears and an uncluttered heart. As ambassadors of Christ, we are encouraged to be hyper-aware of how we engage with God, ourselves, and the world around us.

Secular mindfulness, in contrast, involves moment-to-moment awareness of thoughts. In other words, the task is to notice thoughts floating by like they're a leaf floating down a river. The beautiful thing about being in relationship with the Divine, is that while we are invited to be mindfully aware, we also seek to "take captive every thought to make it obedient to Christ" (2 Cor. 10:5). As Christians, we notice the thoughts as they arise, but then we surrender them to the universal Christ so that love will replace the lies with liberating truth.

There's one more concept that we need to understand if we're going to fully grasp the importance of mindfulness. When we include God in the process, God guides us and convicts us to let go of the lies we've embraced and allows us to distinguish between truth and lies. If you're anything like me, the word "conviction" can make you break out in hives because it sounds like the opposite of compassion and acceptance. I can assure you it's a good thing.

Contrary to what many people think, the word *convict* doesn't have anything to do with making people feel bad. It comes from the Greek word *"elegcho"* meaning "to expose, reveal, or bring to light." And that's exactly what the conviction of God is all about: revealing and bringing to light, with a loving Spirit, what is really going on in a person's heart and life. Ephesians 5:13 says, "But everything exposed [*elegcho*] by the light becomes visible—and everything that is illuminated becomes a light." As Christians, we don't merely *let go*, as in the case of secular mindfulness. Rather, we are called to *let God* (Yes, I just said, "let go and let God."). To experience truth-based awareness, we need the light of God's Spirit to expose what is hidden in the dark recesses of our hearts. Then, we can then hear God's loving, compassionate truth spoken into our inner most being, reminding us of our true identity that we are forgiven and unconditionally loved.

SELF-COMPASSION IN ACTION

Jennine came to see me for counseling after she'd left the church she had attended for nine years. Even though she intended to move on and valiantly reconstruct her faith, her Montu-like experience occasionally threw her into bouts of depression. By the time she came to see me, she had been struggling in her relationship with God and felt God was silent. She lacked motivation to do things that once brought her joy. Although she was suffering, she had several friends who checked in with her weekly because they knew about her crisis of faith. In our counseling sessions, we worked through her grief, shame, and self-criticism through the practice of contemplative prayer and self-compassion.

One day when she was alone, she noticed her anxiety level was high and that she was having a lot of negative thoughts toward herself. She wrote them in her journal and shared some of them with me:

- This is too hard. Why do I have to go through this when everyone else is happy and in their relationship with God?

- I don't like how I look today. I look freakin' ugly!

- I hate judgmental Christians. Why can't they just accept me the way I am?

- I just feel really stuck right now. What is the point.

- Why does everyone on Facebook seems so happy but me?

When Jennine finally realized her ruminative thinking and untamable emotions were starting to snowball, she immediately practiced self-compassion. First, she sat down in silence and became mindful (or aware) of her thoughts and experiences, being careful not to pass judgment on herself. Her train of negative thoughts ran wild and, as a result, she felt anxiety in her stomach and sadness weighing her down. In that moment of distress, she reminded herself of her common humanity, that she was not alone in her suffering, and that many people, even Christians who are loved by God, struggle with negative thoughts and emotional pain.

She read Philippians 4:8 to herself: "whatever is true, whatever is noble, whatever is right, whatever is pure, whatever is lovely, whatever is admirable—if anything is excellent or praiseworthy—think about such things." She placed her warm hand over her heart and offered herself compassion. She spoke cherished truths over herself out loud: "You are a beloved daughter of God. You are forgiven and loved. Your sadness is normal and is a sign that you are grieving many losses. You will get through this." After this self-compassion exercise, she felt peace and was able to continue on with the rest of her day.

People who prioritize and practice self-compassion discover optimum spiritual and relational health. It is a sacred virtue. Think for a moment about the fierce and compassionate motivation of a firefighter that thrusts him or her into a burning building to save people from suffering. That is the same motivation we should have when we feel the singe of suffering rise up within ourselves. So, next time you are called a heretic, blocked on Facebook, triggered by what a Christian friend or pastor said, or you become sad due to grief, be kind toward yourself. Be kind toward yourself with the zeal of a firefighter.

If you experience suffering, close your eyes and allow yourself to feel the pain. Make note of the primary emotion that arises when you think about your suffering. And then be mindful of your body's physical response to that emotion. Remind yourself, in that very moment, that you are not alone in this type of hurt and that even Jesus may have felt the very same feelings. Place your warm hands on your tender heart and gently repeat to yourself at least three times,

"I feel the sharp arrow of this deep hurt. May I be kind to myself in this moment. May I be loved. May I be at peace. May I press on toward becoming who the Divine has called me to be in this world."

This simple practice can tap into your inner drug store and release oxytocin, the neurochemical that triggers feelings of warmth, calm, trust, and safety.

COMPASSIONATE SELF-TALK

Another practical way to love yourself is to speak to yourself the way compassionate others would speak to you. Paul, the ancient Christian mystic, writes, "Do not let any unwholesome talk come out of your mouths, but only what is helpful for building others up according to their needs, that it may benefit those who listen" (Eph. 4:29). While this verse refers specifically to how we speak to one another, it makes sense to apply the concept when speaking to ourselves.

You've probably realized by now that it's easy to be hard on yourself in the middle of the D/R journey. You might speak to yourself the way the Father of lies speaks to you by criticizing your own emotional condition, judging your level of stupidity, bashing yourself for your lack of spiritual vitality—and the list goes on. Paul, however, encourages us to not let "unwholesome" talk come out of our mouths. That word, *unwholesome*, comes from a Greek word that can mean "rotten or bad." In other words, Paul is saying, "stop trash-talking yourself!" Instead, say things to yourself that are encouraging, that are going to build you up, and will not tear you down. If you can't picture a loving and compassionate God saying it, or if it isn't something you would say to your dearest friend, then don't say the words to yourself!

Whenever we think about the fruit of the Spirit and its characteristics, we usually think of how we demonstrate them toward others. But how powerful would it be to demonstrate them toward ourselves? It is a good thing to pray for more love, joy, peace, forbearance, kindness, goodness, faithfulness, gentleness, and self-control toward ourselves during our time of deconstruction and reconstruction.[14] I can assure you, relating to yourself the way the Divine relates to you is a life-changing experience.

THEY ARE ALL CONNECTED

Loving yourself through self-compassion is not a separate concept from loving God and loving your neighbor. Each one is connected and interdependent.

This interconnectedness is beautifully demonstrated by a recent study into a person's emotional health after a traumatic event, specifically PTSD, generalized anxiety disorder (GAD), and depression. The researchers studied individuals who had recently experienced a traumatic event by measuring their degree of social support and self-compassion with various evidence-based, self-reported assessments. They found that people with a greater degree of social support (via family, friends, and significant others) had a greater degree of self-compassion and a decrease in symptoms of PTSD, GAD, and depression. The researchers believed that self-compassion and relationships were interrelated. They concluded that "social support may reduce symptoms of PTSD, GAD, and depression through increased self-compassion in those who experienced a trauma."[15] In other words, love from others increases our ability to love ourselves.

You might have heard the expression, "You can't love others until you love yourself." I think it goes deeper than that. It becomes easier to love yourself when you allow yourself to be loved by others; especially by God. The author of 1 John 4:19 reminds us, "We love because he first loved us."

When we are loved by others, it is God—with whom we live, move, and have our being—who is loving us through them. Of course, God can love us apart from others as God is within us. But ultimately, until we can accept that we are loved by God, whether through the love of other people or God, we will never be able to wholeheartedly love ourselves. As we experience that love, we internalize it and we increase our capacity to love ourselves. Why is this so important? The more we love ourselves, the less shame we have. The less shame we have, the more freely we can love others and reach out to God. Loving God, others, and ourselves are all intertwined. They cannot be separated and are indispensable for the spiritual journey.

QUESTIONS

1. What messages have your received from the church about loving yourself?

2. What are the differences between healthy self-love and unhealthy narcissistic self-love?

3. If God did not curse Adam and Eve with eternal torment in Hell, then where did the curse of Hell come from? What is Hell? Should the reality of Hell be preached today?

4. What do you think of OSEP? What is your anthropology? How would you describe the core of human beings? Sinful, evil, good, etc.?

5. What are the consequences of telling children that they are sinners and they are in need of the grace of God to go to Heaven?

6. Why do old doctrines stick around and haunt people?

7. What is your experience of the components of self-compassion and their opposites: Common humanity/Isolation, Mindfulness/Overidentification, and Self-kindness/Self-attack?

8. Why do you think it is easier to speak compassionately to someone else who is struggling, but it is more common to speak harshly toward yourself?

CHAPTER NINE

THE BLOCKS AND PATHWAYS TO DIVINE INTIMACY

"You, God, are my God, earnestly I seek you; I thirst for you, my whole being longs for you, in a dry and parched land where there is no water."

— PSALM 63:1

Let's do an exercise. Note any thoughts or emotions that arise within you when you read these next few sentences. Ready? Here we go.

God loves you.

No really. God really, really does love you.

God wants to tenderly hold you and comfort you during this difficult time.

God is good, and you can trust God with all your heart.

What is your gut reaction? Can you take those words in? Do they bring comfort? Do they make you angry? Do you feel indifferent? Do you have thoughts like, *Amen, I am so grateful that God does?* Or do you have thoughts like, *Yeah, right. God is the one who did this to me.*

Perhaps you're wondering, *God holding me, comforting me—what the hell does that look or feel like?*

There are many different types of responses people have to the above questions. There are no right or wrong answers. It is an exercise that allows you to gauge where your conflicted heart is with God in the midst of your D/R journey. After having their hearts and minds twisted by religion some people angrily move further away from God, while some draw closer for loving comfort. Some people wrestle with guilt because it feels as if God has abandoned them, so they no longer feel free to tell others how wonderful and amazing God is. And, while others don't feel that God has abandoned them, praying seems like a monumental enterprise. Once you know how you feel toward God, it provides a clue to the areas in your life to which God can bring growth and healing.

I admit that I am biased. I want your answers to point toward a dynamic relationship with *God*, the *Divine*, the *Creator*, the *Spirit*, the *universal Christ*, the *Ground of All Being*, *Father*, *Mother*, or whatever title you want to give to the revealed mystery of the One who is love. It saddens me, and I am sure it also saddens God, that we run *from* God in the midst of adversity, brokenness, and pain, instead of running *to* God. I also understand that life is messy, our faith gets tested, and the best of saints have dark nights of the soul. Wherever you are with God, the key is to be honest about it and to be open to experiencing God's tenderness, love, and affirmation in a profoundly tangible way during your journey of deconstruction, healing, and reconstruction.

"How can I be open to a God I don't really know and who cannot be fully known?"

I understand you may be a little cautious to open your heart to embrace and be embraced by God. Your holding back, even if slightly, makes sense. I mean, what the heck does that spiritual, mumbo jumbo of opening up our hearts to God even mean? God who?

The descriptive words we use of God are not God. They are place-holders, and imperfect ones at that. They are fingers pointing to that which cannot be fully pointed to or named. I could tell you that God looks like Jesus. And, that is an incredible place to start. Jesus is God fully manifest in the flesh. But, even our conceptions of Jesus are diverse. Our minds, which are our filters that are conditioned by a great number of factors, such as the time and place in which we live, cannot even fully and perfectly conceptualize or reflect him. A messianic Jew in Israel's version of Jesus is going to be different that an African's view of Jesus, an American's view of Jesus, and a Korean's view of Jesus. Just as a seed may grow differently depending on the soil in which it is planted, so does Jesus bloom differently in the unique soil of our hearts and minds. But, imperfectly name and call out we must.

I am cautious as I write about a chapter inviting you to intimacy with God. Being in this perplexing journey of taking apart our faith and putting it back together is such a tender and circumspect time. Many of us have given ourselves to God, only to find out the version of God we were believing in is not real. It may have been a counter-feit God that was spoon-fed to us by those who have gone before us (which was spoon-fed to them too). So, which version of God do we trust? Which version of God do we surrender our hearts to? Then some of us are still asking, "Do I want to even worship a fictitious God anymore?"

I can't tell you definitively who God is. A part of me doesn't even want to try. I don't want to be guilty of giving you my version of God to believe in. I don't want to be like all the other evangelists out there with perfect versions of their gods, including Jesus.

"Believe in this Jesus!"

"No, believe in this Jesus! I have the right version!"

I am more interested in you figuring out who God is for you. That being said, there is another part of me that wants to share who God is for *me*; how God has grown in the soil of my heart. I want to invite you into my imperfect and cloudy perspective born out of study, experience, prayer, communal wrestling, and deep reflection. Perhaps in doing so, it may tweak your image of God for the better and increase your intimacy with the Divine.

OBSTACLES TO GOD

Although we logically know how vitally important it is to stay connected to God during this topsy-turvy journey, sometimes debris can block our paths toward reconstructing our view of God. There are two important obstacles that typically keep people from a loving relationship with God during the shifting sands of the D/R journey. One has to do with overwhelming emotions, and the other has to do with a person's "soul wear," or internal image of God.

OVERWHELMING EMOTIONS

My nieces and nephews are adorable. Normally, they are well mannered and well behaved, but they also have moments when they are out of control. Some days when I visit my brother, they are running wildly around the house, shrieking loudly, throwing things at their siblings, and refusing to listen to reason. During these times, I ask my brother, half-jokingly, if they have had a mound of candy. He usually says yes.

The kids are having what is called a sugar rush. Although some researchers claim the phenomenon is bogus, anecdotally, it definitely seems real in my nieces and nephews. They eat some delicious candy and the sugar rushes through their bloodstreams; then their cells start doing the happy dance and they can't sit still. Even when my brother or I tell them to settle down and sit on the couch like good little boys and girls, they continue to squirm and make weird animal noises, and one of them invariably gets in trouble for hitting another.

One reason that people on the D/R journey find it difficult to sit still and pray is that they are flooded with a rush of swirling emotions—much like my nieces and nephews when they're experiencing the wacky effects of sugar in the bloodstream. From a brain-science perspective, the bomb of the faith crisis has exploded and activated the disoriented person's *sympathetic* threat system, putting him or her in fight-or-flight mode. The person is flooded with intense emotion that propels them to move and take action. That emotional energy can cause a person to feel anxious, making it extremely difficult to sit still and pray.

The person not only can't sit still because of their emotional energy, but a part of them doesn't want to sit still. A part of them is unconsciously afraid that the difficult emotions and negative thoughts will rise to the surface and become unbearable. In other words, sitting still means facing the anger, shame, sadness, and existential dread brought on by the D/R journey, and many people would prefer a rain check instead, or even better, to lose the receipt.

Others, however, have a secure attachment (a safe, emotionally-connected relationship) with God and can discipline and regulate their emotions and unwanted thoughts enough to sit and be soothed by God's presence. In turn, through prayer, they can feel the delight of their triggered *parasympathetic* nervous system—the God-designed calming system of the body. More specifically, they are stimulating their vagus nerve, which activates the inner chillax response and tells the stress response part of the mind-body to shut down because the coast is clear of danger. Usually, these people have prayed through emotional pain often enough in the past that it has become an ingrained, automatic spiritual discipline. Thus, the habitual act of prayer has a conditioned response of calm and relaxation.

I totally get it if you struggle to pray during extremely emotional and difficult times. Your intense emotions and activated sympathetic nervous system—the part of you that wakes you up, energizes you, and prepares you to fight or flee—kicks into high gear. It then seems impossible for you to sit in silence. Practicing little by little may help. Try it for thirty seconds for one day, then one minute, then five minutes, then back to three minutes if it gets too difficult. Adjust accordingly until you are able to pray for longer periods of time with ease. If you can't do it at all, then don't. Relationships shouldn't be forced or coerced. There is a time and season for all things. Talking with God (prayer) is an invitation, not a demand.

I had an insecure attachment style of relating to God (and other people), which in simple terms means I had a hard time trusting that God is good and cares deeply for me. Initially, when I experienced a radical shift in my faith, I had to distract myself with work, movies, hanging out with friends, getting into another relationship, and even doing busy leadership work for God. Most of those things were positive coping strategies. Stillness was scary for me though. Being quiet with God was like looking into an ultra-clear and streak-free glass mirror; it was terrifying. In God's presence, my brokenness with all its painful emotions and pessimistic thoughts about myself and the future became crystal clear, but at the time I was not ready for the intensity.

Over time, I learned the practice of being in the beautifully dangerous presence of God. And, when I use the term God, I don't mean I have God figured out. It is a knowing that transcends words. It is Spirit to spirit. It is an embrace of mystery or a quiet assurance that Mystery has embraced me.

Remaining in the silence of prayer was risky. There was no telling what dark, painful, or challenging experience would be revealed and encountered in the light of God's love. It was also beautiful because the God I was running from was far more loving, gentle, and supportive than I ever imagined. God's ability to tenderly show truth without overwhelming me helped me trust God more as time passed. It also helped me move from an insecure attachment to a secure attachment; an experience of love, safety, acceptance, and belonging.

If you are struggling to experience a relational pathway with God because of overwhelming emotions, know that others are in the same boat. Even Jesus' disciples struggled with praying, which is why they asked Jesus to teach them how (Luke 11:1). When you ask the same from an earnest and tender heart, God will beckon you into deeper waters of intimacy.

Intense emotions are not the only obstacle that can keep heartbroken people in pain and feeling separated from the presence of a loving God. The biggest obstacle I have encountered in pastoral ministry and in counseling clients experiencing disorienting grief is their *soul wear*—their internalized image of who they think God is. If we can adjust our image of God, then it becomes easier to be vulnerable with God in prayer.

SOUL WEAR

Eyewear comes in all shapes and sizes, with radical and colorful lens and frame choices, and in a variety of prescriptions. Some dramatically affect how you see the world. There are glasses you can wear to see the world in a reddish or bluish tint. You can put on glasses that give you a glimpse of how a person who is nearly blind sees the world, or you can experience a virtual tour through the eyes of a person with dementia. There are even glasses that you can wear to see how bees see the world. I and countless others would be unable to see the world in all its beautiful complexity without glasses. They are truly a godsend.

Just as we have eyewear, we have what I call soul wear, the unique lens through which our soul views God, the world, and ourselves. Some people wear darkly tinted soul wear. To them the world appears unsafe, neither God nor people can be trusted. Some people wear rose-colored soul wear and perceive reality as better than it really is. Each person's soul wear is uniquely shaped by the primacy of early experiences when we were younger. They are also formed by other poignant experiences we have had over the years.

Although research shows that our relationships with caregivers in our first few years of development are the most important, other crucial dynamics shape how we see the world as well.[1] A person's place of birth, ethnicity, culture, temperament, and socioeconomic background, along with national crises, such as war, financial collapse, or racial or ethnic instability—all play a part in forming his or her soul wear. That is why there are so many unique perspectives about God and the world we live in.

The blessing of soul wear is that there are so many fun, creative, and exciting ways to see the world. The curse is that our soul wear can be shaped in such a way that it distorts reality, becomes an obstacle, and negatively affects how we relate to God, others, and ourselves.

Do you struggle to trust God? If I asked you whether God is primarily angry, sad, or glad toward you, what would be your core response? Is your perception of God laced with criticism, harshness, or judgment? When was the last time you believed and felt deeply that God loves you or is proud of you? In the midst of this unpredictable spiritual journey, are you more prone to worship God with your intellect, yet find your heart and emotions cut off or cold toward God? Or do you feel God's presence, enjoy Divine holy hugs, and hold onto God for dear life?

Your responses to these questions are directly related to your soul wear (your overall internal image of God). Soul wear makes it either quite easy or extremely difficult to love God and to allow God to love you. Let me share a couple of examples.

MARIAH'S SOUL WEAR

Mariah was a spunky young woman at my church. She grew up in an urban neighborhood with safe, hardworking, and loving parents. They were not rich, but they seldom had to worry about affording rent or food. They were far from perfect, but Mariah always felt safe enough to confide in them and seek advice when she was in trouble. If she got hurt, she knew her parents would provide a listening ear along with empathy, comfort, safety, and encouragement.

Mariah's soul wear was largely shaped by her relationship with her amazing parents. For her it was a no-brainer to go to God with the grief she experienced when she broke up with her fiancé, because her parents had always loved and comforted her. Mariah internalized that care and comfort, which shaped her soul wear, so she saw God as the loving, comforting, healing God that God is. Even though going through the D/R journey was definitely one of the worst times of her life, she was able to grieve well and find tremendous strength and comfort in God's presence because she experienced God as a safe haven. Unfortunately, not everyone is as privileged as Mariah.

MY SOUL WEAR

My soul wear was quite different from Mariah's, though also largely shaped by my family environment and social relationships. I think most families are dysfunctional to some degree, but my family's level of dysfunction was off the charts. Although I am greatly appreciative of some loving aunts, uncles, and grandparents, being surrounded by chaos, drugs, abuse, violence, and neglect did not help my ability to connect wholeheartedly with God and others.

Relationships with my peers were also very important in shaping my lenses. My peers made fun of and picked on me incessantly for wearing "coke-bottle" glasses. They called me a *nerd* before the word came to mean someone smart who could, potentially, make millions of dollars, like Bill Gates. I was always the last kid picked for gym class team activities. In addition to having difficult relationships, I was a sensitive young kid by nature (temperament) and someone who internalized all my pain, abuse, neglect, and abandonment.

My inner lenses had a darker tint, and I looked at the world in a less trusting way than Mariah did. I had acute abandonment issues, along with powerful, ingrained, lie-based inner beliefs etched on my soul. I believed, mostly on an unconscious level, that I couldn't count on anyone—that no one would ever really love me for who I was, and that men in authority disliked me and were always angry with me. And guess what? I projected all those distortions onto God.

Now don't get me wrong. I loved and had a relationship with God, but at times, deep pain triggered some lie-based emotional perspectives and kept me from experiencing God's love and comfort when I really needed God the most. Then, the fact that God, at least initially, seemed to be like my earthly dad on steroids, raging violently at people who disobeyed him, didn't help my projections. At that point there was a fine line between the projections of my dad and the harsh reality I saw of God in the Bible. Trying to figure out who God actually was, apart from my projections, has been extremely difficult. Though, I am suspicious if we can ever fully do so at all.

Because I saw God similarly to how I saw my dad, I didn't want to hang out with God. Why would I want to spend time with a God who didn't like me, who criticized me, and who was too masculine to show me compassion, affection, and tenderness. I was in desperate need of new lenses. Thankfully, that radically shifted when I didn't have to read the Bible like a hyperliteral history textbook.

IT'S NOT YOUR FAULT, BUT . . .

I now realize that my experiences were valid, and my inability to come to God with the open-armed, simple faith of a child made sense. To a large extent, I didn't fashion or design my soul wear. On top of my early childhood experiences, the lies that I gobbled up were fed to me by the church and only distorted my lenses even further. Therefore, my impaired vision was not my fault. My lenses looked an awful lot like those worn by previous generations of my family members. They also looked a lot like those inside the church.

It is not your fault if you have painful hurts and traumas from childhood that get in the way of your intimacy with God and with confidently relating to other people. It is not your fault that you were told that you are not loved and accepted by God as you are. It is also not your fault that people taught you that every violent portrayal of God in the Bible was an accurate description of reality, rather than seeing biblical authors who were just like you and me—imperfect folks trying to figure out who the heck God is and how that mysterious God calls us to live, move, and breathe in the world.

It can also be difficult when you *believe* God loves you if it doesn't *feel* like God does. Research from cutting-edge neuroscience (science that looks at the nervous system and brain) now shows that *head* knowledge (explicit knowledge), which is based in one part of the brain, is different than *heart* knowledge (implicit knowledge), based in another part of the brain.[2] In other words, it makes sense that we can sing, "Jesus loves me—this I know, for the Bible tells me so" from our heads, yet sing contradictory lie-based lines like, "Jesus loves them, but not me, because I am so dirty" from our hearts.

If it seems you have multiple personalities when it comes to your faith, rest assured, you are not crazy. Science validates our experience. We can have contradictory feelings and thoughts. We can have different parts of ourselves vying for their unique positions. The hope is that we can combine and integrate our head knowledge with our heart knowledge and align them with the truth of who God says we are and move a few degrees closer to who God really is. Through hard work (engagement in spiritual disciplines), allowing ourselves to be loved in community, and God's grace (compassionate and active, moment-to-moment love), it can be done. Thankfully, over time, we can receive a new prescription for our shoddy lenses.

As adults, it is our responsibility to do something about the pair of lenses we were given as children. It is also our responsibility to do something about the lenses that have been shaped by experiences in later life by religious trauma. We can either go to SoulCrafters and allow God, the skilled Ophthalmologist, to craft some corrective lenses or stick with our own fogged-up pair that has been shaped by earlier painful experiences. While we need to acknowledge our past, we do not have to allow it to dictate our present and future. We can either remain victims of our circumstances or become victors who take hold of all the Divine desires for us.

LASIK

LASIK is an amazing surgery that uses a laser to reshape a person's cornea, allowing light to enter in just the right way to help correct someone's vision. In this section, I want to share powerful images of God from Scripture that may help correct your vision of who God is. A spiritual LASIK procedure, if you will. I hope to offer images that may modify your soul wear and remove unnecessary obstacles to allow your heart's eye to more readily recognize the God of love. I also want to offer some healthy images that, when embraced, can help you transition into talking to God with greater ease during this difficult time of your life. I don't think I can get you to 20/20, but I do think I can sharpen your heart's vision by a few degrees.

IMAGES OF GOD

What is your internal image of God during your D/R journey? When you feel beaten up by the effects of sin, whether someone else's or your own, or when you are tired, dirty, lost, confused, scared, hungry, and desperate, how do you picture God's view of you? What do you think God wants to do or say to you in those moments?

Is God like a tough drill sergeant, demanding that you do twenty push-ups for failing at an illusory and idyllic version of what it means to be a Christian? Is God a wise Yoda, teaching you lessons for your journey? Is God a prosecutor, pointing out every mistake you made along the way? Is God a distant uncle who loves you even though you haven't heard from him or seen him in a while? Humans have many unhelpful ways of relating to God that don't paint a full or accurate picture of who God is.

While the ancient contemplatives, such as the psalmists, had a more intimate picture of God, the Israelites' primary view of God emphasized that God is *holy*—God is totally separated from sin and completely different from everything that exists. The Hebrews never wrote the name of God in the Scriptures. They used only the sacred letters YHWH, in an attempt to preserve the "otherness" of the living God, and any Israelite caught pronouncing this name of God was stoned to death. It was whispered only once a year when the high priest, with incense and candles, went into the Holy of Holies and lay prostrate on the ground.

At the time Jesus walked the earth, the Greek philosophers—the most prominent of whom were the Stoics—greatly affected the mindset of people all over Europe and the Roman Empire. They saw God as unemotional, incapable of feeling or relating to emotion. This idea of God was very important during that time, because a God who had feelings could easily be subdued by them, and the Stoics considered this to be too vulnerable and belittling to be true of a holy God. Unfortunately, tainted and defective soul wear greatly affected many people's view of God at the time.

GOD AS ABBA

Jesus was familiar with the many different metaphors and images used to describe God in the surrounding culture and Scripture. In Exodus 15:3, Moses wrote, "The LORD is a warrior." Other Old Testament writers described God as Healer, Lord, Rock, Fortress, Lover, Stronghold, Lion, Leopard, Shepherd, Groom, Potter, Judge, Pillar of Cloud, Wind, Fire, Ancient of Days, and Bridegroom. And while all of these may depict an aspect of the God of the universe, in the midst of all of the metaphors Jesus could have emphasized to describe God, Jesus gives us a profoundly simple way of relating to God—as a parent, as Abba or Father. Can you imagine Jesus' listeners hearing him address God so intimately? Jesus could have prioritized any number of metaphors to relate to God, and yet, he chose Abba, Father.

Jesus was totally Abba-centered. In John 5:19, he says, "Very truly I tell you, the Son can do nothing by himself; he can do only what he sees his Father doing, because whatever the Father does the Son also does." In John 4:34, it says, "'My food,' said Jesus, 'is to do the will of him who sent me and to finish his work.'" Jesus prayed in the garden of Gethsemane during one of the most emotionally difficult times of his life. Mark 14:36 says, "'*Abba*, Father,' he said, 'everything is possible for you. Take this cup from me. Yet not what I will, but what you will.'" If being Christlike is a Christian's priority, and if Christ related to God mainly as a Father, then perhaps we should learn something valuable from his image of and his relationship with God.

THE PRODIGAL FATHER

Back to the question of how God would relate to you in the midst of your confusion, grief, and journey toward reconstruction. I think God would demonstrate God's love toward you the same way a father did to a young man Jesus spoke about in the parable of the prodigal son, or as I like to call it, the parable of the prodigal father (Luke 15:11–32). *Prodigal* can be defined as "rashly wasteful or extravagant."[3] The son was certainly prodigal in his *wild living*, but the father was prodigal in his *wild loving*. Granted, you might not have sinned like the prodigal son, so it might not be a homecoming moment for you. Nonetheless, the parable uses a motherly father figure to symbolize God, giving us some striking insights into God's wildly loving and compassionate nature.

In this parable, Jesus gives us his internal image of God as a powerful, compassionate, and loving motherly Father who embodied the best of both masculine and feminine traits. Yes, the father in the parable is a strong, wealthy, authoritative male, and yet, I think Jesus' image of the Father defies the norms of what many in our society—or in Jesus' own society—consider masculine.

The father in the prodigal story is a concerned dad who obsesses over his wayward son and who is constantly longing and looking for him. He is a dad who defied cultural gender norms as he picked up his robe, ran toward his son, and then firmly hugs and warmly kisses him. Instead of giving his son a history lesson on what he has done wrong or scolding him in public, which would invariably have pushed the son further down into a pit of shame and despair, the father reminds him of his true identity. The father gives him royal garb and proclaims boldly, "For this *son* of mine" (v. 24, emphasis mine). Lastly, the father knows intuitively that his son needs a coat, slippers, and a ring. I know it is stereotypical, but from my perspective, the father, in part, seems like a modern-day, annoyingly loving and compassionate Jewish mother.

The primary metaphor Jesus gives us for God is that of a father. Premier New Testament scholar and historian John Dominic Crossan writes, "Despite its male-oriented prejudice, the biblical term 'father' is often simply a shorthand term for 'father and mother.'"[4] And that makes sense. Genesis 1:27 says, "So God created humankind in his image, in the image of God he created them; male and female he created them" (NRSV). In other words, male and female together demonstrate a complete picture of the image of God; at the very least *a more mature* image of God.

God desires to be *otherworldly extravagant* (prodigal) toward you when you are rejected, cast out or forced out of your tribe, feel beaten up, and hurt deeply. God wants to run passionately toward you, throw big, strong, gentle arms around you, and kiss you with compassion and tenderness. Not only that, but God longs to clothe you with the finest of robes, place decked-out shoes on your feet, and slide the most extravagant ring on your finger. God longs to do all of this to remind you that no matter who else wanted or didn't want you, you are God's cherished and loved child. As 1 John 3:1 proclaims, "See what great love the Father has lavished on us, that we should be called children of God!"

The Spirit of God wants to perform spiritual LASIK surgery on you so you can see afresh that God wants to be the perfect, complete parent to you. As you embrace a clearer picture of who God is, perhaps you will have a greater desire to spend more time keepin' it real with God in prayer.

THE DOG LOVER

Let's look at the concept of soul wear from a different perspective. Imagine you are a kind-hearted dog lover. You love dogs. You love to pet them. You love to feed and take care of them. You even give money to local dog shelters.

As you are walking down the road eating your leftover sandwich, you see a dog on the side of the road. It looks dirty, hungry, and even a little hurt. You get the sense that the dog might have been abused.

Your heart melts, and you cautiously try to approach it. You want to pet it and offer it some comfort, or at the very least, give it some of the food you were eating. And as you begin to go near it, the dog lowers his mangy head and shrinks back in fear, trying to distance itself from you. You begin to approach it again, and this time it struggles to get behind some brush, away from your gaze and presence.

How sad is that? The dog is deeply afraid of you and wants nothing to do with you—and it has never even met you. It wants nothing to do with you, not because of who you are but because of experiences it has had with other people. If it only knew how loving, kind, and compassionate you really are, it would quickly limp into your arms and experience the joy of being held, fed, and loved back to health.

I think the dog's sad and fearful experience is similar to the way some people experience God. There are countless wounded and hungry people who do not run into the loving arms of God because of a false perception of who God is. Instead of basing their perceptions on the revelation of God's character as shown in the parable of the prodigal Father or in the compassionate life of Jesus, people base their perception of God primarily on their own past experiences. These are typically painful and traumatic experiences they have had with other people, especially early relationships with their own father or mother, or lack thereof. They are also suffered by people in the church and by the sub-Christlike portrayals of God that were taught to us.

Such misperceptions must cause the Divine great sadness. If those who were suffering only knew how loving, kind, and compassionate God really was, they would limp into God's arms and experience, perhaps for the very first time, what pure, compassionate, and healing love truly feels like.

God is not mad at you or seeking to pulverize you with a baseball bat. God is not counting the days until you pass away, hoping you will be sizzling in Hell like a juicy ribeye for all eternity. God loves you more than you and I will ever know.

I am convinced that the more our internalized image of God is in line with who God really is, the more our intimacy with God will become vibrant and consistent.

GOD WANTS TO PARENT YOU

I have counseled many struggling people who have difficulty in prayer because of a sub-Christlike image of who God is. God is not an emotionless, ubermasculine, authoritarian military-style God or a busy absentee landlord. God doesn't want to harm you, condemn you, snub you, or ridicule you. God wants to lovingly parent you through the spiritual maze you are navigating through. God wants to be the most amazing Father, as well as the most amazing Mother, to you during your D/R journey so you can be comforted, grow, and reconstruct well.

I understand if you are angry with God and don't want much to do with God right now. Sometimes, the nature of pain and extreme hurt keeps us balled up, not wanting to open up and risk vulnerability. I am thankful, though, that no matter how you feel, God's loving and graceful grip on you is a whole lot tighter than your grip on God.

I picture God saying to you what Jesus said to the people of the holy city of Jerusalem who felt lost and confused in the midst of calamity and chaos, and who were therefore keeping God at a distance. In Matthew 23:37, Jesus says, "How often I have longed to gather your children together, as a hen gathers her chicks under her wings, but you were not willing." There goes God, being motherly again, a merciful mother hen to be exact, wanting and longing to protect, comfort, guide, and parent God's people.

Speaking of mercy, did you know that *mercy* in the Hebrew Bible many times comes from the Hebrew word meaning "womb"? The psalmist had this meaning in mind when he cried out in Psalm 40:11, "Do not withhold your mercy from me, LORD; may your love and faithfulness always protect me."

Psalm 103:13–14 says, "As a father has compassion on his children, so the LORD has compassion on those who fear him; for he knows how we are formed, he remembers that we are dust." God understands your frail and wounded heart, and he wants to hold your hand through this oftentimes chaotic journey of life, not harm you. "'For I know the plans I have for you,' declares the LORD, 'plans to prosper you and not to harm you, plans to give you hope and a future'" (Jer. 29:11). I think these mystics are on to something. They received revelation through profound intimacy with God, rather than the myriad number of rules and man-made doctrines that were floating all around them. They knew that God is good. God is compassionate. God is love. And, God desires to prosper us and instill hope in us.

God knows you feel confused, ambivalent, and maybe even apathetic. God is not about to snuff you out. On the contrary, God knows you might be barely holding on, trying to make sense of your D/R journey. God wants you to reconstruct your image of who God is. God also wants to reinvigorate the relationship you have with God, parent you compassionately, and restore you.

Talking about blocks to intimacy with God and offering an image that is dear to countless people's hearts can be helpful. Engaging in experiential practices is even better. To conclude, I will map out a neuroscience-informed practice and pathway that can help you reshape your soul wear to experience a loving God more fully.

MEMORY RECONSOLIDATION

Our experiences, especially those that are full of intensity and emotion, in time become *consolidated* and hardwired together into the membranes of the brain at the synaptic level. Here they each reside as an ingrained memory, holding their place in our life-history like a completed document on a computer disk.

Scientists had previously thought this *consolidation* was a way of "locking" memories in so that they remained stable and fixed throughout life. Contemporary research in neuroscience, however, has demonstrated that this is an oversimplification of what actually happens.

We now know that whenever we recall or retrieve a memory, it has the potential to become malleable within our bandwidth of "open files" again. At this point, we have the ability to update the memory with new information and thus alter the content, especially the way the memory makes us feel. The first kiss of *my girlfriend* takes on new, richer emotions and meanings once that same event is now updated with information about the first kiss of *my wife*.

Scientists have coined this memory revision process *memory reconsolidation*. Memory reconsolidation allows for the possibility of erasing the "sucky" feelings and negative thoughts surrounding difficult past events as we update, reframe, or rewrite them from a new, more experienced perspective.

Memory reconsolidation is a remarkable discovery within the field of neuroscience. In fact, memories are not *fixed*. Every time we bring a memory to mind, or open it, we have the potential to change it. Memory reconsolidation is the brain's natural mechanism for overriding the negative baggage that comes with painful or traumatic memories. In some cases, the memory itself may change, as new details emerge through the reconsolidation process. In other cases, the details of an event may remain the same, but the painful, overwhelming emotions and negative thoughts associated with it disappear. In our case, this means that even past religious traumas or memories of them, including destructive images of God, can be recast and reshaped in order to promote healthy, permanent transformation in our lives.

Research scientist, therapist, and author Bruce Ecker has brought the practical application of memory reconsolidation to communities all over the world. In his workshops and publications, Ecker notes that the *transformational change sequence*, which is at the root of clinical symptoms, is a "theory-independent, universal meta-process."[5] In other words, if transformational and permanent change has taken place, whether inside a therapy room or inside a church building, then memory reconsolidation has most likely occurred. If a person is in therapy or is receiving healing prayer and afterwards no longer suffers from anxiety, depression, or debilitating self-doubt, memory reconsolidation has taken place. Based on the synthesis of memory reconsolidation research to date, Ecker has identified a three-step sequence that promotes the transformational process.

THE 3-STEP MEMORY RECONSOLIDATION TRANSFORMATIONAL CHANGE SEQUENCE

How does memory reconsolidation unlock memories at the synaptic level and bring about healing and transformation? Though there are actually three *preparatory* steps that occur before the main process begins, for simplicity I will only describe the three main steps of memory reconsolidation itself. These three steps allow your brain to "unlearn and erase" targeted emotional learning (the emotionally-laden beliefs we developed based on emotionally-powerful experiences).

The first step is to re-evoke and reactivate the problematic memory. It is this memory, or to be more precise, the emotional and mental baggage associated with the memory, that is continually generating the negative symptoms and keeping you stuck. In a therapy context, the therapist would guide the client into the specific memory they conjecture might be the source of the distorted beliefs and painful emotions that limits the clients capacity to love and be loved.

Here is a simple example. As a therapist, I was helping Sarah, a Christian client who is shy, anxious, and seldom speaks her mind with her friends. Sarah wants to speak up more and be involved in conversations with her friends, but her anxiety gets the best of her. During conversations, she is usually frozen with fear and keeps quiet.

Through our work together, especially the exploration of past memories, we have discovered the subconscious emotionally-laden belief that may be evoking her symptoms:

> "If my parents got angry with me when I wanted to express myself, then expressing myself with others will make them angry, too. I am deficient, and my voice is not worth listening to. So, it is better to keep my mouth shut."

Sometimes these beliefs sound really crazy, or childlike, when said aloud, but they ring true to the client on an emotional level because, when believed, they explain a clear rational pattern of otherwise irrational behavior.

Sarah shared one memory in particular. When she was younger, she tried talking to her parents about how she couldn't believe God would send people to hell. Her parents immediately yelled at her.

Dismissing her thoughts, they told her that she was being argumentative. Not only that, they said she must be listening to Satan, who likes to question God's Word. Her parents then sent Sarah to her room.

That was a pivotal moment for her. The event formed a key memory in her mind and registered a life-changing emotional lesson, teaching her that her voice was not worth listening to and that it could, in fact, be harmful. It became the basis and distorted lens for how she viewed talking with others in every subsequent conversation that took place following that "teaching moment."

Psychologists call that lens or viewpoint from which we see the world a *schema*. In a Christian tradition, we would just call it a *lie*. In any case, the schemas that shape our view of the world and of ourselves are often outside of our own awareness. For Sarah, the unconscious lie or schema embedded in her memory long ago prevented her from sharing her voice and opinions with confidence, even today. Our work was to re-evoke, reactivate, and add new truth to the embedded schema that contained a powerful lie in order to allow for the possibility of reconsolidation transformation and the release of unwanted behavioral symptoms.

The second step necessary to promote lasting change is to re-activate, in a deeply experiential manner, a completely different memory—one that contradicts the conclusions a person has been drawing from the painful memory. This step is the key to unlocking the synapses of the original memory and emotional learning that keeps a person stuck. It seeks the proverbial "truth that will set you free."

Retrieving the original memory in juxtaposition with the new, contradictory memory, renders the original memory open, plastic, and changeable for about five hours. Within that timeframe, not only the memory but the entire lie that used to flow from it can be altered. This crucial step of entering into and experiencing a contradictory memory in juxtaposition with the original one, supplies the new information our brains can use to transform a lie-based memory and put it in its rightful place, the past, where it no longer controls our behavior on a subliminal level.

In Sarah's case, she had shared with we me a fairly recent example of progress: an incidence where she actually took a risk and spoke out in a Bible study with her friends. By being an empathic listener, Sarah was able to help her friend find a solution to a difficult spiritual problem she was facing. With a smile on her face, Sarah related how her friend was extremely grateful for her words and gave her a hug. Sarah reported feeling excited, loved, and special after this event. This is precisely the type of divergent and contradictory experience we are looking for in Step 2!

Step 3 is where the magic finally happens; with the erasure or revision of the lie-based memory and/or of the negative emotional learning. Here there is a simultaneous experience of the original memory, and most importantly the *feelings* and *thoughts* that came from the original memory, alongside a vivid, concurrent experience of the new and contradictory memory. The task is to go back and forth between them, in a side-by-side process of experiencing two incompatible truths. As the two opposing memories challenge one another in this "synaptic duel," the malleable brain, now open to updates and reframes, will embed and encode the information contained in the positive, "truthful" memory into the original memory, with its lies and deceit. Sometimes we have to experience the juxtaposition between the original, painful memory, along with the facts from the new, contradictory memory, multiple times, for permanent change to occur on a synaptic level.

I could begin by reminding her of the painful memory when she shared her thoughts with her parents, only to be rejected and condemned, and of the false conclusion that her young mind had drawn from that experience ("I am deficient, and my voice is not worth listening to.") With that experience fresh in Sarah's mind, in a compassionate and empathic manner, I could then bring up her more recent, joy-filled, and empowering memory: the recent event when Sarah shared her voice with her friend in a way that genuinely helped her.

However, just focusing on a positive, contradictory memory is not enough. It is important that both memories are brought to mind side-by-side, in a deeply experiential manner, with all the feelings, thoughts, and bodily sensations accompanying both of them that a person can muster. Remember, it is the *juxtaposition of both experiences* from the memory banks that prompts the synapses to unlock and become open, ready for change. Viewing both experiences simultaneously helped Sarah to question, on a deep neural level, the absolute and rigid authority of her parents in the first situation, allowing her to add *new* information that contains more truth and greater personal freedom for her now.

As a child, it was natural for Sarah to assign greater authority to her parents at the time, but with *new* information experienced on a deep neuronal level, Sarah could now recognize that her parents don't have to have the last word in her psyche. She could now also see that the youthful conclusion her mind drew from that experience didn't have to have the last word, either. The reaction of her parents was harsh, and the lie she believed because of it was actually *not* true. The truth was that her voice was valuable, and that she could share it with confidence today in a way that could demonstrably help those she cared about. In this way, the original memory and the painful emotional learning buried in her unconscious lost much of its power to control her behavior.

The true test of whether this process worked or not is in Sarah's own life. *Is Sarah still anxious about sharing her voice and unable to express herself freely with her friends?* Her actions reveal whether she still believes, "I am deficient, and my voice is not worth listening to." If indeed Sarah is *still* fearful in group situations and cannot muster up enough courage to share, there is no reason to despair. In some cases, the same memory needs more work. In other cases, there are a collection of memories that work in concert to produce the distorted lens that she looks at life through. In any case, with each problematic or painful memory that we are able to reconsolidate, we move that much closer to freedom from the chains that have bound us.

MEMORY RECONSOLIDATION IN PRACTICE

The transformational change sequence of memory reconsolidation can help us deconstruct traumatic images of God, and reconstruct new, life-giving images. We don't have to be held hostage to a traumatized brain that can't rid itself of haunting images of God. Practices that can bring healing and transformation are now at our fingertips. Tim Desmond, a well-known speaker and therapist who uses memory reconsolidation practices in his work with his clients writes, "This [memory reconsolidation] is the neurological recipe for emotional healing."[6] I would also add it is the neurological recipe for spiritual healing as well.

Frequently one of the most difficult images to delete from our minds is the "God of Judgment," the One who is ready to pounce on us for doing something...*anything*...wrong. It could be an image of a God who is cruel, judgmental, harsh, critical—who always seems to be displeased with us. Thankfully, we can take advantage of memory reconsolidation to help delete old, toxic images of God and begin to experience the "God of Love" more fully and naturally. Set some time aside in a safe, nurturing environment to try this exercise out for yourself. Follow its unique steps and get a feel for the process that takes advantage of the possibilities available to you in the memory reconsolidation transformational change sequence process.

MEMORY RECONSOLIDATION CHANGE SEQUENCE EXERCISE

Step 1: Think about an old image of God that you've carried, which still causes you some mental and emotional pain. For example, it could be the image of an angry old man in the sky with a beard and a fuming scowl...a God who is bent on criticizing and punishing people. When you have an image in mind, get in touch with sounds (including tone of voice), touch sensations, tastes, or smells associated with this image.

Step 2: When the disturbing image of God is clear, become aware of tension or uncomfortable sensations in your body. Notice where you feel them. Stay with those sensations, without trying to change them. Notice also your feelings. *Do you feel sad? Angry? Shame? Fearful?* If you get distracted, bring your attention back to the image, and your remembered experience. Practice this, mindfully staying with it, for at least three-to-five minutes. If it becomes too overwhelming, be kind to yourself, take a break, and if and when you are ready, try again.

Step 3: Now, move to an image of God you find comforting. For some, you may consider using the image of God found in the parable of the Prodigal Motherly Father. If the father metaphor doesn't work for you, change it to the Divine figure that resonates with you most. If your relationship with God is too complicated, you can bring to mind a loving and accepting animal, relative, or friend. You can also create your own ideal compassionate image.

Step 4: For those who have found a comforting image of God, picture God sending you love. Imagine God running toward you with compassion. Imagine God holding you tenderly and loving and accepting you as you are. Picture God saying kind words to you like, "You are my beloved child, in whom I am well-pleased." Use whatever expression of love that is meaningful to you. Pay particular attention to the compassionate feelings this image generates. Feel what it is like to receive this love from God. If there's another figure you find comforting, then imagine love being sent forth to you from that image.

We humans have a primal *fight or flight* response to stress or danger. We also have a *tend and befriend* or *care-circuit*. The care-circuit is that part of our nervous system that gives us the warm fuzzies and feel-good feelings. The key in this step is to really feel the love and care in your body. Practice this for at least three-to-five minutes.

Step 5: Repeat steps 1–4 one more time. The key is the juxtaposition between the *negative* image of God with the *positive* image of God or other compassionate image, and to repeat that process a few times. Picture them side by side, almost as if you can have an experiential awareness of both at the same time.

After completing the process, the original image as a memory will hopefully be *reconsolidated* in a less distressing form. And, after practicing the sequence, there should be less emotional baggage associated with it when you revisit the original image in the future. Tim Desmond encapsulated the memory reconsolidation process very simply:

"Distressing Memory + Care Circuit = Less Distressing Memory."[7]

We can seldom think our way out of religious trauma. Rather, to move beyond its distressing effects in our lives, we must engage in practices that rewire our brains for the better. Rewiring our brains rarely comes from receiving new information; it comes from *experiencing* new information. The benefits of memory reconsolidation and practicing the steps to open the brain up for synaptic change *can* help. Old emotional learning that contains traumatic neural sequences, when re-evoked and re-fired together with new, more positive neural experiences, can wire together in a miraculous, healing manner, and create a whole new reality for us. Whether it is new experiences with our unholy huddle, or new experiences with novel images of God, or experiential practices like forgiveness, self-compassion, and serving others (as we'll discuss more in later chapters), we can tap into the wondrous nature of the human mind to reconstruct and re-story our future religious and spiritual selves.

QUESTIONS

1. What is your reaction to the exercise on p.223? Could you take those words in? Did they bring comfort? Did they make you angry? Did you feel indifferent?

2. What is your main metaphor for your relationship with God? Describe why it is important to you. (Some examples of relating to God may be experiencing God as: Lover, Father, Mother, Protector, etc.)

3. How would you respond if someone came up to you and asked you, "Who is God?"

4. Is it easy or hard to talk to God when you are hurting? Explain.

5. What makes it easier to share your hurts, fears, joy, and other feelings with God rather than with people? Or is it easier the other way around? Or is it hard to do both?

6. What experiences have you had when it comes to head knowledge and heart knowledge? For example, have you ever believed God loved you logically but felt something different in your emotional experience?

7. What are your thoughts on Jesus' emphasis of God as Abba? What is your connection to God as Abba like?

8. What are your thoughts about memory reconsolidation? What was it like to engage in the memory reconsolidation practice at the end of the chapter?

CHAPTER TEN

THE ANCHOR OF GOD'S UNCONVENTIONAL LOVE

"An uncontrolling God neither creates us as robots nor temporarily roboticizes us. From God's special incarnation in Jesus to activity in the smallest creatures, God acts without controlling. And this lack of control—at all levels of existence—makes loving relationships possible."

— THOMAS JAY OORD

Michael is a highly intelligent guy, passionate about God. For a long time, he would set aside a period of quiet-time when he would diligently pray and read his Bible. He would excitedly read every apologetic book he could find, was an avid evangelist passionate about defending his faith, and a faithful attendee at his church. All Michael ever talked about were the great things God was doing in his life.

He went to a church that preached what is infamously called *the prosperity gospel*. With the right amount of faith and obedience, so he was told, Michael and others could have it all: healing from sickness, financial prosperity, a family with beautiful children and a white picket fence, and confidence that God would provide them with highly successful careers (all with the right donation, of course).

Then, one day, tragedy struck. Michael's sister, who went to the same church, got into a terrible car accident and died. This tragic event would eventually lead him into the wild disorienting vortex of the deconstruction and reconstruction journey.

Like many who are on the D/R journey, Michael struggles with understanding how God could allow people to experience terrible accidents, evils, abuses, and religious traumas. This is the age-old theodicy question. Theodicy refers to the attempt by humans to make sense of how a good, loving, and omnipotent God promotes, or prevents, the harsh evils and suffering in the world.

There are others who—once the veil of Christian clichés, platitudes, puritanical doctrines, and preposterous prosperity teachings are lifted—become confused as to the true nature of God. The theodicy question is then connected to other questions like, "Where was God when I was being taught, and while I was believing, abusive and abysmal doctrines?" or "Why was God silent while I was in the midst of believing false images about who God is?" They wonder how prayer and miracles work in the midst of suffering. And, many wondered if they could ever love God after being deceived, especially after believing they had an accurate depiction of who God was.

The reality of suffering, especially evil, has turned countless people away from God. It has created such enormous cognitive dissonance for folks, that some end up in a cold and distant relationship with God. I am convinced that to reconstruct our faith, we must have a theology of suffering anchored in the unconventional love of God. This is especially important in a world full of pain, suffering, confusion, sorrow, and death. I believe that the unconventional love of God is shown in God's perfect, moment-to-moment, uncontrolling, and co-operative love.

MY CLOUDY OFFERING

I hesitate to offer a theology of suffering and an overall theodicy that can help us make sense of the nature, or working, of God in the world. I do it out of reverence, knowing I am walking on sacred, blood-stained ground. Treading carefully, I am trying to make sense of where and how God fits in with real people's everyday trauma, abuses of various kinds, social injustices, and the unspeakable evil that surrounds us all. I don't take these situations lightly.

People who advocate for an anti-theodicy position resonate with me. I mean, humans trying to understand God are like an intelligent monkey trying to understand the mechanics of spaceflight. There is an absurdity to anyone saying, "Let me give you a God's-eye view of who God is and exactly how God works in the world." In offering a theodicy, I am also mindful that I don't want to fully take God off the hook. I don't want to absolve God of all of the brutality of human existence or the tragic fate of all other forms of life. I don't want to rob people of the natural experiences and expressions of lament and protest in the face of such appalling realities.

Yet, as I shared earlier, when talking about God, I must give it a shot. The risk of giving the main stage to theodicies that are based on a controlling, all-powerful, autocratic, and authoritarian God is too great. The countless victims of *God is in control of everything* theodicies are too much to bear. I cannot sit idly by while mumbling, "Well, it *is* a mystery. Who can really know?"

I can relate to that great mystic, the apostle Paul, who wrote: "Ever since the creation of the world his eternal power and divine nature, invisible though they are, have been understood and seen through the things he has made" (Romans 1:20, NRSV). He's right. We can understand aspects of God's nature by reflecting on our experiences of creation and life itself. All of the complexity, richness, diversity, beauty, and grotesqueness of life says something about God. We are not in *total* darkness. But we "see only a reflection as in a mirror" and "know in part" (1 Cor. 13:12) when it comes to truth in general. I admit, when it comes to understanding the mysteries of free will, suffering, and God's sovereignty, the mirror is a bit foggier than normal, making it difficult to flesh out a perfectly accurate reflection.

Despite the difficulties of seeing perfectly and clearly, I am compelled to share my imperfect monkey truth. Being that this is only a chapter, I assure you it will bring up more questions than answers. However, I offer it in the hopes that it removes a few unnecessary obstacles to your relationship with the Divine. My desire for this chapter is to help you reconstruct an image of God that is saturated in God's love, without making you leave your brain at the door.

The remainder of this chapter will briefly explore God's perfect, moment-to-moment, uncontrolling, and co-operative love through the lens of constructive theology, philosophy, the biblical witness, and my experience. Also included is a brief examination of what God's love means for important topics such as our soul wear, evil, petitionary prayer and justice, trust, and miracles.[1]

GOD'S PERFECT, MOMENT-TO-MOMENT LOVE

In the book of Matthew, Jesus says to his disciples "Be perfect, therefore, as your heavenly Father is perfect."[2]

Okay. If we are to be perfect like God, we must ask ourselves in what way is God perfect?

Some think that perfection is all about not sinning. "Stop being so worldly, Christian! Be perfect as God is perfect!" shouts the angry preacher.

Jesus' plea for perfection has caused some Christians to feel an enormous amount of guilt and shame. They feel they have to be perfect and never sin. If they do sin, they think God will be furious at them. However, the context of the verse reveals that perfection has nothing to do with sin management. Rather, it has everything to do with how we are called to love others. The invitation is to *love* as God perfectly *loves*.

So, how does God perfectly love? Let's look at the immediate context. God "causes his sun to rise on the evil and the good, and sends rain on the righteous and the unrighteous" (Matthew 5:45b). Did you catch that? We are called to emulate God's perfect, unconditional, all-inclusive love—even with people on our naughty list. This is why Jesus says in the previous verse, "Love your enemies and pray for those who persecute you, that you may be children of your Father in heaven" (Matthew 5:44–45). In telling his listeners to love their enemies, Jesus is asking them to love like God does. How does one do that? Recognizing that God demonstrates perfect prodigal love by loving those who do not love God back: prayer-less, disobedient, and God-ignoring enemies.

We do not wish, pray, or beg God's nature into existence. God is perfect love. God loves. That is who God is and what God does. God's perfect love extends to all. The birds do not pray, but a loving God takes care of them (Matthew 6:26). The lilies do not intercede, yet God is mindful of them (Matthew 6:28). Enemies and persecutors of God's children do not pray, but God loves them (Matthew 5:43–48; Luke 6:27). The ungrateful and wicked do not pray, yet God is kind to them (Luke 6:35). God "so loved the world" without the prompting of prayer (John 3:16). God exists as who God is: a God of love. God's attributes—God's holiness, justice, mercy, and power—are funneled through that love.

God's love is perfect and active. Moment-to-moment, in every creature's life, God seeks to maximize goodness, beauty, truth, love, and healing while minimizing evil. God never sits on the bench, or on the sidelines, excitedly waiting to be called upon to venture into the game of life. God is not casually hanging out, sitting on his blinged-out chair made by the purest and most reverent of carpenter angels. God isn't good some of the time; God is good all the time. Right now, in this very moment, God is up to something. In each moment, we can become grace catchers, those who are aware of what Divine love is up to and enter into that grace-filled love adventure.

GOD'S UNCONTROLLING AND CO-OPERATIVE LOVE

There are things God cannot do. God cannot lie (Hebrews 6:18); God cannot be tempted (James 1:13); God cannot be prejudiced (Acts 10:34–35); God cannot sin (Deuteronomy 32:4); and God cannot get tired (Isaiah 40:28). Due to the nature of God's uncontrolling love, it is not that God can control creatures and chooses not to do so, but perhaps God cannot control creatures due to God's very loving nature. Simply put, love does not control. Therefore, God does not singlehandedly control others. That's why we call it *uncontrolling love*.[3]

God is doing all God can do to maximize good and to minimize evil, but God is constrained by God's love. Love must preserve the sanctity of free will even at the cost of what people with free will choose. To disregard and usurp free will is to cease being loving.

Suggesting God *cannot* unilaterally control people or events, and manipulate them as God sees fit, is of huge theological significance. Many Christians do not hold to this idea because it implies God is not all powerful. For some, the idea that God is not all powerful, implies that God is weak. For example, the Christian philosopher, William Hasker, describes one common perspective: "God's capacity to control the detailed course of events is limited only by his self-restraint, not by any inability to do so."[4] He reiterates what I said before: many Christians believe God can control but chooses not to. It is a complete paradigm shift (a heretical shift for some) to suggest that God simply *cannot* control because of God's uncontrolling, loving nature.

Just because God does not *unilateral* control, however, does not mean God is unable to exercise any kind of control at all. God is not passive and powerless. God's control is a different kind of control. God's power is a different kind of power. According to the Oxford dictionary, the word *control* can mean "the power to influence or direct people's behavior or the course of events."[5] I suggest God lovingly and powerfully influences us by inviting, empowering, inspiring, filling, convicting, leading, comforting, healing, and challenging us toward ever-increasing experiences of shalom. And God does this without coercion or force.

It is not enough to say that God's love is uncontrolling. It's a negative statement about what God *can't* do (God can't control others). We need to also talk positively about what God's love *can* do. God's love is *co-operative*, meaning God requires mutual assistance and collaboration to accomplish God's purposes. An idea that Thomas Oord so eloquently reminds us in his book, *The Uncontrolling Love of God*, is that God never intervenes in the world unilaterally; God never acts alone, of God's own accord, disregarding lawlike regularities (a.k.a. the laws of nature) and the free will of people. On the contrary, God always works through willing cooperation.

Let's explore what the unconventional love of God—God's perfect, moment-to-moment, uncontrolling, and co-operative love—looks like in our everyday lives, especially as it relates to our D/R journey.

GOD'S UNCONVENTIONAL LOVE AND SOUL WEAR

God's silence in the midst of my yearning for truth has pained me more times than I can remember. I can recall countless times, humbly lying in my bed with tears in my eyes, crying to God, begging God to reveal God's self to me.

"Why, God, are you silent?! I just want the truth! I am confused. I don't know what to believe. Just tell me what the hell I should believe, and I will believe it! Please, I beg you, speak to me."

I was desperate to hear God's voice. I wanted God to set the record straight. The God who created the universe should surely be able to talk to me as if I was talking to a friend. Right? Sadly, the crickets amidst the silence of God's voice was deafening. The existential aloneness in those eternal moments filled me with crushing agony.

How did we get thrown into the deconstruction and reconstruction journey and become so disoriented? How did people's soul wear, and people's soul wear before them, get God so wrong? Why did our soul wear and our internal beliefs of God become so distorted? Why didn't God simply stop people from teaching and believing heresy? Why does God continue to allow us to be in a constant state of confusion?

THE UNFOLDING PROCESS

God, whose love is uncontrolling, is not forcefully in control of history. So, keeping God's unconventional love in mind, it makes sense that human beings are in an ever-unfolding process of physical, spiritual, and emotional growth. God is moment-to-moment and noncoercively luring creatures toward the Divine aim of evolving experiences of love, goodness, beauty, and truth. God's co-operative love invites simple and complex organisms to cooperate and to dance together toward evolving organismic artistry.

It is hard to believe that we went from wiggly, single-cell organisms to sentient human beings over billions of years. And it is wild to imagine that we were once sacredly drawing on cave walls, looking up at the moon in deferential awe as if it were a god. Now we are drawing on advanced computer systems and have stepped onto the moon, symbolically declaring that we are gods. All of life is in process, including our image of God.

It is very apparent, with thousands of different religions out there—and over 30,000 different Christian sects and denominations—that humans are a creative and diverse bunch. We love to create and imagine and then arrogantly think our creative imaginations are *the* truth.

What is also apparent is that God doesn't have a pattern of materializing into human form to declaratively and definitively tell us who is right and who is wrong. Referring to God's inspiration in our lives and those of the biblical writers, pastor and theologian Gregory Boyd writes, "God refuses to undermine the personhood and freedom of people by lobotomizing them so that they perfectly conform to his will…God respects the integrity of a mutually impacting relationship, which is what a relationship of love requires."[6]

Our views of goodness, beauty, and truth—including our image of who God is—cannot be forcefully manipulated to correspond completely to God's truth. The truth God is trying to convey to us can't be instantly and coercively downloaded. Even being in love with Jesus doesn't completely solve the issue of perfect knowledge.

I could say that Christ is the definitive revelation of God and that he solves all the answers to our questions of who God is. The problem is that there is no Christian consensus on the exact details of who God is through Jesus, what Jesus came to do, and what Jesus meant when he sought to describe the life to come.

While the Spirit is in all, while all creatures manifest and reveal the Spirit, and as Jesus reveals God in an unmatched fullness, God is continually revealing deeper levels of revelation of God's wonder, beauty, truth, and nature as if through faint radio waves. We are constantly tuning into the frequency of the Divine, never arriving at a destination, but always learning and evolving (and sometimes, devolving). The problem is that we like to think we have arrived. We are terrifically creative, tragically tribal, and commonly prone to thinking we have all the right answers.

Case in point: I find it utterly fascinating that whether people are Calvinist, Arminian, Essential Kenosist, Universalist, Hopeful Universalist, Process Theologian, PSA Enthusiast, Proponent for a Non-Violent God, Premillennial, Amillennial, Cessationist, Inerrantist, Exclusivist, Inclusivist, Creationist, Dispensationalist, Covenantalist, or Open Theist, rarely do they admit to obvious contradictions in their esteemed doctrine. No one ever says, "I've read all 31,000 biblical verses and there are some that contradict my position." They say the exact opposite and engage in incredible hermeneutical gymnastics to prove the flawlessness of their biblically superior viewpoint.

Not only does the above phenomenon show the incredibly creative mental feats involved in maintaining a homogenous theological position, it also demonstrates the epitome of cognitive bias and pride. It also shows us that God, whose love is uncontrolling, lets non-coercive love take its course alongside the imaginations of humankind. Since God, as a spirit, doesn't have vocal cords, God cannot shout loud enough for people to hear what is absolutely true. So, theologies continue to multiply—with no end in sight.

TRUST THE GOD IN YOU

It can be scary for those of us on the D/R journey to trust God again. I get it. How could we jump in with both feet after we've been burned before by false theologies? The best encouragement I can give you is an invitation to sit at the feet of Christ, who is love. Sit in silence. Embrace mystery. Allow the mystery that is Love, to guide you into all truth. Then, do the unthinkable. As you are in community with God and others, trust in your experience. I know that *experience* gets such a bad rap. But, unfortunately, the alternative is to trust everyone else's experience and how *they* interpret the scriptures, God, and reality. My hope for you is that, just like the Apostle Paul did, you will allow God's perfect, moment-to-moment, uncontrolling, and co-operative love to lead you into truth.

PAUL'S EXAMPLE

It is incredible that Paul wrote about 50,000 words, or 28%, of the New Testament (more or less, depending on which books you believe he authored). Do you know what percentage of those words Paul explicitly used to quote Jesus' sayings from the gospels? Probably 2% or less. That's right. Not much! What does that mean? I am sure it could mean many things, but for me, it points to the liberating invitation to be who we are in God and to value our own experiences. That's exactly what the Apostle Paul did!

Paul was obviously familiar with the oral tradition, and the incredible stories passed down to him concerning Jesus. He was an exquisite teacher of the law and knew the Hebrew scriptures very well (he quoted about 100 of them in the NT). Most importantly, Paul was also head over heels in love with Christ. He was completely Christ-centered. All things were rubbish, he said, apart from Christ.

Still, rather than memorizing and quoting what others said about Jesus, or what others said Jesus said, Paul spoke from his own experience. It seemed, that out of the deep, intimate relationship he had with Jesus, Paul spoke his truth. And his truth, as he marinated himself in the presence of God, now constitutes much of the New Testament.

Paul did not just settle for others' experiences of Jesus. He did not feel the need to quote Jesus secondhand to share powerful and provocative spiritual truths. He did not say, "Well, since I can't find what I am saying explicitly in the scriptures, or verbatim from Jesus' words as quoted by others, it must not be worthy of sharing. Out of his profound mystical relationship with Jesus, he began to connect the dots between love and law—between his newly found captivation with Jesus and the religious-saturated Hebraic world he thought he knew and understood.

Paul lived in Christ, through Christ, with Christ, and for Christ. He was bold and courageous enough to be congruent with how Jesus was leading and guiding him. Despite the nay-saying of religious heresy hunters, he took creative risks and liberties to convey how he understood the world around him, including the sacred Hebrew Scriptures. And, don't miss this: he also did it in community with other people struck by the fierce arrow of Jesus' love.

I encourage you to be free, to live and speak out of that intimate place you have with Christ. Be courageous to share what God has placed in your heart and mind. You are not less spiritual if you don't quote five of Jesus' sayings before and after you share your truth. Share and wrestle in community (including the community of saints and sinners found in the Hebrew Bible and New Testament), so that their divinely inspired truths can either validate your experience, expand your vision, or temper it. Sometimes, you may even need to be a pyro-theological trendsetter, setting ablaze what has come before you. Other times, in humility, you may have to admit you went too far.

Will your truth be perfect? Definitely not. Whose is? Will your truth be revised? I am sure it will change over time. Sarah Bessey writes,

> The more I tried to keep God contained, the more God insisted on escaping from my fetters. Every time I build a box for God, God transcended that box ... while still somehow often abiding within it to meet me there. Every time I think I have it figured out—*this is*

how God acts, this is who God is, this is what God will do, this is what God expects—that reorienting, bracing, dangerous Love becomes and unbecomes again. And so I have been made and remade and unmade over and over again in response to the ancient one.[7]

All of us are in process. Sometimes we get it right, sometimes we get it wrong, but oftentimes it is a mix of both. All of us will have theological truths that are likened to wood, hay, and straw that will eventually be burned in the refining fire of God's love. But we need to accept that this is where we are now. If we wait until our truths are viewed perfectly through shiny and transparent glass that peers into the heavenlies, then we will be waiting for quite some time. Until then, you have permission to be congruent, to be authentic, and to share *your* embodied truth, through *your* unique soul wear, with the world!

GOD'S UNCONVENTIONAL LOVE, EVIL, AND SUFFERING

No doubt the theodicy question, in relation to evil and suffering, is one of the most perplexing questions to wrestle with. It is also one of the main reasons people either ditch God, stay distant roommates with God, or never want to introduce themselves to God in the first place. Well-known author and pastor Timothy Keller writes, "As I took up life as a minister, I tried to understand why so many people resisted and rejected God. I soon realized that perhaps the main reason was affliction and suffering."[8]

Evil, loss, and suffering are common to all people, in all places, regions, and socioeconomic statuses. No one can escape the effects of suffering, no matter how rich or poor they are, or where they live on earth. The truth is that if you don't have an adequate understanding of God's role in the midst of the chaos of life, the weight of evil, loss, and suffering can crush you. Your theology can either deepen your suffering or bring deep consolation during your D/R journey.

When people think about the concept of evil, they typically think of heinous and morally reprehensible acts like murder, rape, and genocide. While all of these acts are evil, the biblical concept of evil is much broader. Simply put, evil is anything contrary to the will of God, such as thoughts (Gen. 6:5), deeds (Prov. 5:22), desires (Rom. 6:12), spirits (Mark 3:11), etc.

Thomas Oord writes about useless pain and suffering, calling it *genuine evil.* Oord writes, "Genuine evil events cause more harm than the good that could have occurred."[9] A child being sexually assaulted is a genuine evil. A pastor stealing money from his congregants is a genuine evil. A person commanding genocide is a genuine evil. Suffering is an inner, cognitive/emotional reaction to these kinds of experiences.

Where there is evil, suffering is usually not far behind; however, where there is suffering, evil is not always present. For example, a child who is told by his parents to go to bed early may experience suffering while the event of going to bed early is not necessarily an evil act.

So, what does God's perfect, moment-to-moment, uncontrolling, and co-operative love have to do with the conundrum of the reality of evil? Everything!

Thomas Oord, probably the most articulate theologian championing God's uncontrolling love, writes: "To be transformed, we must reform our beliefs ... reconstructing requires changing our view of God's power. We should not blame God for evil because God cannot prevent it singlehandedly. God neither causes nor allows suffering but always expresses uncontrolling love."[10]

Due to God's love, God doesn't force God's way into people's lives; that would be contradictory to God's nature. So, evil exists, to the extent that it does, because a loving and uncontrolling God, by God's very nature, cannot forcefully stop people from choosing to commit evil acts.

Think about the alternative. Do we really want to believe that God has the power to singlehandedly stop evil from occurring, but simply chooses not to?

What would we think of a man, watching a child be sexually assaulted, having the power to stop the event from happening, but simply choosing not to help? Our inner spirit captivated by love and justice would passionately rise up and object to the unjust and immoral actions of that man. In the same way, our spirit would also rise up against a view of God as someone with full ability to intervene in horrific events, but who simply chooses not to help (but unfairly decides to help others).

As much as we yearn for God to unilaterally control people and forcefully stop individuals from committing acts of evil, like *The Dark Phoenix* of the Marvel Universe, God simply cannot. We wish God, on occasion, would ignore free will and knock a rapist unconscious before he engages in a violent transgression, but it is simply outside the bounds of what God can do. God can't stop evil like a divine Whack-A-Mole. God also can't disregard lawlike regularities and stop a tsunami from killing hundreds of thousands of innocent people.

Those who are angry at God because of the world we live in, want an altogether different world than the one we have. When asked what the world would look like if a loving, uncontrolling, and non-coercive God actually exists, people struggle to articulate another possibility. Given that love takes risks and doesn't force, coerce, control, or manipulate, how would that kind of God work in this world? It seems that if we took God's unconventional love seriously, we would end up with precisely the world we find ourselves in—a world where free creatures, randomness, and lawlike regularities can run amok, sometimes in the direction of beauty, other times in the direction of destruction.

GOD'S UNCONVENTIONAL LOVE, PRAYER, AND JUSTICE

Amidst all of the topics of deconstruction, the effectiveness and coherency of petitionary prayer, especially to battle rampant evil and injustice, or to bring solace and healing to hurting and sick people, is definitely on the top of many people's lists. I will only scratch the surface of the conversation here.

Once the fantasy of a controlling God, and an "everything happens for a reason" philosophy goes out the window, people start wondering about petitionary prayer. They may ask questions, such as:

- Does prayer work?

- What exactly happens after the words leave our lips or after we speak them silently? Does God instantly hear them? Or do they first move through the traffic of heaven where angels and demons are engaged in an epic battle?

- Does a person who prays for God to heal their ill father give God extra power, energy, or motivation to do so?

- Is persistent petitionary prayer performed simply to annoy God, so that God will eventually, although begrudgingly, do the right thing and answer those prayers, as in the parable of the persistent widow and uncaring judge (Luke 18:1–18)?

- Is more prayer better? Does God increase his active love because a larger number of people pray? Does God say, "Well, just twenty of you prayed. If thirty of you had prayed, I would definitely have healed him"?

- If an all-powerful God could single-handedly save and deliver loved ones, but allows them to get into fatal accidents, become sick, be raped, or experience other tragedies because people did not pray for them, is that consistent with what a loving God would do?

- Does petitionary prayer only change us—the ones who are praying—or does it change God in some way?

Petitionary prayers are requests to God for answers to life's questions and concerns. They are also pleas for God to be the sole responsible agent to act on behalf of the one who is praying. I define the traditional understanding of the typical petitionary prayer as *talking to God and asking God to love in a specific manner in which God was not doing so beforehand.* Here is the bottom line: the perfect, moment-to-moment, uncontrolling, and co-operative love of God drastically changes the ballgame of the intersection between petitionary prayer and issues of justice and moral responsibility. Our petitionary prayers can either increase the severity of injustice or they can increase the level of shalom. Let me explain.

- Every 10 seconds, a child dies from hunger.

- Every 98 seconds another American is sexually assaulted

- Every 33.5 minutes, someone is murdered.

- Over 52,000 will die from drug overdoses this year

- On a single night in January 2015, 564,708 people experienced homelessness.

For me, if the traditional understanding of petitionary prayer doesn't work as we suppose, then these statistics are evidence that the stakes are *too high to ignore*. If we believe that by simply talking to God (or begging God), that God can singlehandedly force God's will to occur in situations and in people's lives, then we are engaging in an immature form of petitionary prayer, and ultimately, a superstitious practice. We cannot engage in spiritual activities that cause us to feel good, thinking we are accomplishing great things, but ultimately not achieving the good we set out to accomplish, or worse: contributing to the evil and suffering in the world.

THE BYSTANDER EFFECT

"The bystander effect" is a term used by social psychologists to describe what happens when individuals fail to intervene during crises or emergencies when they perceive others are present and aware of the event. Preeminent social psychologist Elliot Aronson writes in his classic book, *The Social Animal*, "If people are aware that an event is being witnessed by others, the responsibility felt by any individual is diffused".[11] I became familiar with the term after reading A. M. Rosenthal's, *Thirty-Eight Witnesses: The Kitty Genovese Case*. The book is an account of the brutal rape and murder of Kitty Genovese, which occurred on March 13, 1964. It was reported there were thirty-eight people who were aware that the horrific event was occurring but did nothing to stop it. In a more recent occurrence in 2009, Dominik Brunner was murdered by two 18-year-olds. Dominik was trying to stop the violent teens from attacking other children. Unfortunately, his sacrificial gesture led to his death. Like the Genovese case, people witnessed Brunner being attacked, but no one adequately intervened to stop it.

Of course, all is not so grim for humanity. There are plenty of stories demonstrating heroic acts by bystanders. The research shows the bystander effect lessens when there are perceived real emergencies, when perpetrators are present, and when physical harm is imminent.[12] Nonetheless, the bystander effect is a genuine social phenomenon.

Have you ever witnessed violence, unethical practices, a crime, a beating, theft, bullying, or other harmful acts and done nothing about it? Sadly, I know I have.

Why am I talking about the bystander effect?

It has been my contention that the traditional practice of petitionary prayer contributes to further evil and suffering in the world. I know; it is quite the claim. I suggest the bystander effect may be one dynamic among many behind this problem.

If people believe an all-powerful and controlling God is aware of the person or situation being prayed for, then it is easy for them to become passive bystanders. When praying, it is easy to believe, "Well, God is powerful. God has a plan. God is in control. And God is going to take care of it." Unfortunately, that is exactly the kind of thinking some bystanders have when horrific violence is occurring: "Well, there are plenty of people watching. Surely, there are more competent people than me who are going to take care of it. I am sure someone has called 911 by now."

When someone engages in the typical petitionary prayer, God becomes the competent, grand Witness who diffuses human responsibility; the bystander effect is on full display. The problem is the bystander effect can have terrible consequences. Suffering increases exponentially. Death can be a result. If I believe the most loving and powerful divine agent is on the scene, then there is a natural easing of the direness of the situation. If God is taking care of it, then perhaps I don't have to. I can lift my prayers up and then go about business as usual.

Let's say there are immigrant children who are taken from their parents and forced to be confined in subpar conditions to anxiously be with people they do not know. They are suffering physically, emotionally, and spiritually. After hearing about this heartbreaking news, a well-meaning church comes together and prays:

"God, pour out your love on those children."

"God, comfort those children."

"God, bring justice swiftly."

"God, I bind the enemy in Jesus's name."

"God, change the leaders' hearts."

"God, change the policies that are in place so this does not continue to happen."

The prayers above are coming from sincere hearts. But, in this case, sincerity without action can perpetuate further harm and suffering. You see, we already know God's stance on the issue. God hates when children are mistreated (just read Luke 17:1–4). It is not God's will for children to suffer such anguish. God already loves the children. God is already seeking to comfort the children to the extent they are able to receive God's comfort. God already desires to bring swift justice. God already wants the enemy to be bound. God already wants policies changed. God already wants leaders' hearts changed. God's love transcends ours. If we want the wellbeing of those children, don't you think God wants it exponentially more? The problem is God cannot singlehandedly bring all of this about. Due to God's uncontrolling love, God is constrained from forcefully changing hearts, manipulating people's wills, and coercing people to change policies. God is not a puppeteer. Don't you think that if God could instantly change the outcome, God would? Does God really need to be begged to do what God does best, which is to love? What kind of God has the power to do something about those innocent, suffering children, but simply chooses not to?

It is one thing if our primary goal is sharing our heart and desires passionately with God. That is a beautiful and intimate endeavor. It is another to believe those energetic prayers somehow equip, move, inspire, or empower God to single-handedly change a person or circumstance. If people believe that praying to God in a certain manner, at a certain volume, and with certain words will convince God to single-handedly root out prejudice, abolish dehumanizing policies, reduce hate crimes, solve the problem of homelessness, heal drug addicts, stop people from committing arson, stop rapes from occurring, and so on, they are engaging in magical thinking and superstition of the worst kind.

Petitionary prayers can become an ironic gesture. Their intent may be to increase God's loving activity and shalom in the world. But prayer becomes problematic when we unknowingly and inadvertently pass the responsibility of shalom solely to God ("God, *you* fix the problem!"). We thereby avoid God's primary method through which God achieves shalom: humans, filled and led by the Spirit of God, fulfilling their vocation as God's empowered emissaries.

PRAYING FOR THE HOMELESS

In New York City, a congregation gathered for a prayer meeting. A winter storm was expected the following day, so they took time to pray for a group of homeless people who frequented an area not too far from the church: "God, pour out your love on the homeless people downtown. Help them find shelter. Protect them from the cold and from illness. Show them the salvation of your dear Son, Jesus Christ."

Perhaps those church members were the ones who needed to be saved from the pitfalls of petitionary prayer. They may have meant well, but their prayers stemmed from a belief that talking to God (which is what prayer is) would absolve them of any responsibility to do something about the problem and, instead, placed all responsibility upon God. Ironically, instead of being beneficial, their prayers got in the way of God being able to use that congregation as his Spirit-led and empowered emissaries to love, help, and save those homeless people. God is not the one who needs to be coaxed, persuaded, or reminded in any way to love the homeless. God longs for them to be holistically saved and grieves that some will suffer in the freezing cold. If prayer in its simplest form is an act of talking, then perhaps God whispered to that congregation: "Church, pour out your love on the homeless people downtown. Help them to find shelter. Protect them from the cold and from illness. Show them the salvation of my dear Son, Jesus."

CONSPIRING PRAYER

Keeping in mind God's perfect, moment-to-moment, uncontrolling, and cooperative love, I have proposed and detailed a model of petitionary prayer, in my book *Divine Echoes,* called "conspiring prayer." In today's world, the word "conspire" has a negative connotation: to plot with someone to do something wrong or evil. However, the English word *conspire* comes from the Latin word *conspirare,* which literally means "to breathe together" and "to act in harmony toward a common end." I combine both definitions to express what I mean by conspiring prayer.

Conspiring prayer is performed *with* God rather than *to* God. Conspiring prayer is a form of prayer where we create space in our busy lives to align our hearts with God's heart, where our spirit and God's Spirit breathe harmoniously together, and where we plot together to subversively overcome evil with acts of love and goodness (Romans 12:21). This subversive sacred practice calls forth thankful, open-hearted listeners who humbly petition and partner with God to become divine echoes, committed to bringing forth shalom in the world.

God always seeks to lovingly decrease the injustice in the world and meet the basic needs of humanity and the rest of his creation. Basic needs are needs for God to love, heal, save, and deliver from the most fundamental obstacles in the way of human flourishing. For example, a basic need is to be free from poverty. God never desires that people, deprived of sustenance, starve to death. Another basic need is to be free from racism and oppression. It is never God's will for people to suffer discrimination because of the way they look, their gender, or because of their race (and so on). Other basic needs include a world without violence and genocide and a world in which healing from devastating injuries and accidents can occur. A basic spiritual need is one of salvation. God always desires people to be saved and to know God's love intimately.

God's primary medium for providing basic needs is through people. God has an open-door policy. God continually looks for open-hearted faith on the earth and seeks the cooperation of human beings to co-steward creation toward shalom. While the motivation to pray common, petitionary prayers for the basic needs of others is derived from a pure inner spirit, we need to recognize that God is already actively seeking to meet those needs. God isn't keeping us from shalom, but *we* are.

At the writing of this, we are experiencing a pandemic. As the millions and millions of earnest prayers have gone up to the hazy sky to beg a controlling God to snap His fingers to make this pandemic go away, at the end of this devastation, we will not have found such an omnipotent and unilateral gesture. There will have been thousands and thousands of people cooperating with the love of God to see the coronavirus slowly become eradicated from our everyday lives. There will have been countless doctors, nurses, and other health care workers who heeded the call to love and who sacrificially gave their lives for the sake of others. There will have been thousands of hours of research, testing, and the manufacturing of mitigating products by those who are using their God-given faculties and who cooperate with a God who values human flourishing. There will have been people like you and me—those who cooperated with Love and made sure we were keeping ourselves, our loved ones, and our neighbors healthy, safe, and well-resourced.

If we are caught in flooding from a dangerous hurricane, and are about to drown in a car, do we really want to rely on some saints' "thoughts and prayers?" Or, do we want to rely on thoughtful and prayerful people who take courageous action? I am sure you would desire the latter. The same goes for how we respond to the basic needs of others and issues of social justice. God always loves us and is willing to provide for our needs. Moment to moment, God also offers pathways for us to share with those in need. We can prayerfully join in on what God is doing or we can choose not to.

GOD'S UNCONVENTIONAL LOVE AND MIRACLES

I can't tell you how many times I've heard, "I can't hold to your view of God's perfect, moment-to-moment, uncontrolling, and co-operative love because I believe in miracles." There is absolutely nothing inherent in a view of God's unconventional love that implies a belief that God can't perform miracles.

I do believe in miracles, but I do so without believing God single-handedly and forcefully intervenes to bring them about. Certainly, I can affirm that breathing, sunrises, and the body's ability to heal itself are miracles, but the more mysterious miracles that jolt the senses, and wow our hearts and minds, can also occur.

God is never coercive and is always working toward greater experiences of shalom on the earth. So, I have to imagine that miracles are synergistic encounters between God and cooperative agencies, cells, elements, quarks, and many other variables. Imagine a person who has cancer and experiences the "miracle" of healing. When God's loving power + a faith-filled and humble heart + cooperative cells and organs of a body + the right temperature + loving and compassionate others + the right nutrients + a myriad of other variables come together, it could = a healing miracle.

Yes, miracles can happen. However, since God cannot coerce or control others or situations, God requires cooperation for miracles to occur. Thomas Oord, in his book *The Uncontrolling Love of God*, writes: "God's self-giving love invites creaturely cooperation for radically surprising actions that promote overall well-being. For this reason, miracles are neither coercive interventions nor the result of natural causes alone. Miracles occur when creatures, organisms, or entities of various size and complexity cooperate with God's initiating and empowering love."[13]

I can't imagine the lack of miracles we see around us has anything to do with God's willingness. That is what the alternative view suggests. In the alternative, traditional view of miracles, God picks and chooses who to heal and who not to heal. God can do what God wants to do, when God wants to do it, and how God wants to do it. God can perform miracles apart from any cooperation from humans, cells, and laws of regularity. Apparently, within this understanding, God appears much of the time *not* to want to perform miracles and heal those who are suffering, to stop people from raping and killing others, or to prevent kids from brutally suffering and suddenly dying from cancer.

In my understanding of miracles, because God's nature is love—and love doesn't force, coerce, or unilaterally control—God cannot always heal. One view says God *can* but chooses *not* to heal. Another says God *wants* to heal, but simply *can't*.

The view of God's uncontrolling love and a "God Can't" approach is not in contradiction with "God Can." When we say, "God Can't," we are just saying "God can't perform miracles singlehandedly without any cooperation from people, laws of regularity, and other dynamics." When folks say, "I can't get on board with the 'God Can't' model because I have seen weird stuff or miracles happen," I get confused as to why they imagine the two ideas are mutually exclusive?

Those who hold to a view of an uncontrolling, loving God would never say God can't perform miracles in people's lives. They would say it is not the case that God intentionally chooses to heal some and not others. Rather, miracles happen when God and other variables synergistically align and work together with one another. Because of that, some get healed while many others do not.

So, where does the mystery really lie? Does the mystery have to lie with whether or not God can heal but chooses not to? Is that who God is? The kind of God who has the power to instantly heal anyone, but unfairly heals some while allowing others to suffer? Does God say, "I will instantly heal five-year old Suzy from leukemia, but I will not heal five-year old Maria with leukemia?" Isn't it more plausible that God doesn't singlehandedly and coercively heal people? Perhaps it is better to suggest that "The mystery does not lie in whether God can but chooses not to; instead it lies in not knowing what variables came together and cooperated with God to cause this miracle to occur."

A view of God's uncontrolling love, in the context of a world in which miracles and healings do not happen, provides a compassionate framework for Christians. There are, I believe, too many Christians who are bogged down by the weight of shame because they look at others who are healed and ask, "Why not me?" They conclude something is wrong with their faith, their prayer life, or themselves. Lack of healing should never be blamed on a lack of faith; that would be cruel. It's important to understand that God is in relationship with more than just human agency. There are other doors that need to be open for God to accomplish creative, relational endeavors, such as miracles.

GOD'S UNCONVENTIONAL LOVE AND TRUSTING GOD

Everyone has heard the phrase "trust in God!" It is a powerful phrase that is often used by people who suppose God is in control of all things. In some circles, it encourages listeners to surrender to an all-powerful God who—it's implied—can snap Divine fingers and instantly give them their heart's desires, making their circumstances right again. I question the accuracy of that view. Keeping in mind God's perfect, moment-to-moment, uncontrolling, and co-operative love, is there another way to understand "trust in God"? I think there is.

If we are encouraged to "trust in God," a good question to ask is: "What can we trust God for?" If we trust in God, does that mean we will never get into a terrible accident and lose both of our legs? Does that phrase mean we will never die in a horrific bombing? Does that phrase mean we will never be betrayed by a good friend or by an unfaithful partner? Does it mean we can trust that our children would not be harmed, murdered, get cancer, or die a painful death?

I know mine is not the most uplifting and traditionally pastoral sentiment, but I have come to the stark realization that I can't trust God to single-handedly stop any of the above events from happening. I don't think anyone can. Truth is, bad things can happen to anyone, at any moment. No one is promised their next second of life. No one is promised a life free from harm. Why? Bad stuff happens in this world, including vicious evil, precisely because God is not in control of all things. What else would we expect in a world where love and freedom are at the core of reality?

Today, we are bombarded with horrific stories and shocking images all day long. And this overwhelming evidence of evil creates an enormous amount of cognitive dissonance that demands a verdict. The idea of a Blueprint God, sovereignly in control of all things like a Grand Puppet Master, is untenable. Anyone who claims that God is in control of all things is implicitly stating that God is the Grand purveyor of evil. In other words, they are implying that God plans and wills everything that happens. Thankfully, that is not the case. Even if one believes God is powerful in the traditional sense of having the power to unilaterally control any outcome—but that God has chosen not to control free creatures and is bound by God's own self-binding decision—the reality remains the same: Because God is love, God doesn't control people or events, whether by volition, or due to God's uncontrolling loving nature.

Those events mentioned above can happen to any one of us, even if we are fully surrendered, God-lovers. Any view that implies God is in control of all things and can instantly change our circumstances (or keep us from future pain and suffering)—if we trust God enough— is, while comforting, simply not true.

While God is in relationship to all creatures big and small, the only thing that God is in complete control of is God's self. That's it. So, while God can always be trusted, the same cannot necessarily be said to be true of human beings. Creatures big and small, laws of regularity, and spooky quantum anomalies cannot always be trusted to have our well-being in mind. Horrific events occur because randomness, law-like regularities, and human choices collide.

Here is the problem: If I told you that you could trust God to get what you desperately wanted or needed, and all you had to do was continue to trust and pray, I would be lying to you. The truth of our reality outweighs the consequences of the fantasy we desire. Why? First, we are invited to put away childish fantasies, to grow up, and see reality for what it is. We don't live in a Disney movie. The truth, as harsh as it can be at times, will set us free. Secondly, if people trust the finger-snapping genie God, who some preachers and teachers suggest God is, and they do not get the things for which they trusted God, they often blame and distrust God. They feel like God has let them down, and their hearts grow cold. Some even abandon God altogether!

"Alrighty, Mark. You are making me depressed. What is the good news then? Can we trust God for anything?"

Abso-freakin-lutely!

Whether a loved one dies by the hands of a terrorist, our limbs are cut off due to an accident, our children are killed by a sick maniac, someone we know gets sexually assaulted, or someone dies from a random rock falling off of a cliff, we can trust that God is always good, loving, and trustworthy.

"Trustworthy? How?!"

We can trust that while God won't (or can't) always give us pristine circumstances, devoid of suffering and heartache, God's loving character and commitment to shalom remains constant. We can know that a loving God does everything possible to stop evil from occurring, but simply cannot forcefully stop every terrible event from happening. We can trust that God is the smartest, wisest, most loving, and most personable agent in the room—at all times. We can trust that God is an expert of healing love, a virtuoso who is, moment-to-moment, serenading the universe through God's Spirit and captivating those who lend an ear.

We can trust that God's love is trustworthy and that it never fails. However, there is a paradox here. God's love does fail at accomplishing God's will in our lives precisely because God's love is uncontrolling. The very fact that we can "grieve the Holy Spirit" (Ephesians 4:30), shows us that God doesn't always get what God wants. However, God never fails at loving us, moment-to-moment. Just as when I go to lovingly save someone from jumping off a bridge, and they jump anyway, and it is appropriate to say, "I failed in my attempt to save them," when God is not able to achieve God's goals of increasing love, beauty, healing, and truth in our lives and in the world, God fails. God fails all the time at getting what God wants. *And,* God's love never fails.

God is good all the time, and all the time God is good. Every moment pulsates with the love of God. If my relative is sick, I can trust that God is lovingly and compassionately doing the best God can to heal them within an array of vast complexities and agencies. If we need a miracle in our lives, we can trust that God loves to show up in creative and unexpected ways while working alongside other people and creaturely elements.

Sometimes, when we fully trust and surrender our hearts to God, amazing things can happen. But there are no guarantees. The most beautiful gift that can be received, when one fully trusts God, is the peace of God that even in the midst of the storms of life—which transcends all understanding—can guard our hearts and minds in the beauty of God's perfect, moment-to-moment, uncontrolling, and co-operative love.

I understand that coming to believe that God is not in control, and that God does not dictate every action, reaction, or happening on this planet, can provide discomfort for some and veer into emotional chaos for others. For many, believing that God is not in control is an existential slap in the face that brings an enormous amount of anxiety. There is a reason why the "God is in control of everything" theology has stuck around as long as it has. It can be quite comforting to know that we don't have to worry because God is on top of things down here. What happens is said to happen because God wants it to happen as part of God's mysterious plan. Things happen for a reason. Things are the way they are supposed to be. It all sounds good, but it just ain't so.

As you travel this D/R journey, you can trust in God's goodness. God did not desire for you to be taught hideous doctrines and for you to believe them. God did not want or allow that evil to happen to you or a loved one. I want you to know and wholeheartedly believe that.

Speaking of the phrase, "God Allowed," let's examine it. The 9/11 attack was a terrible tragedy in America's history. I was in New York at the time and was vicariously traumatized watching the terrible events unfold. How could God be thanked in the midst of such a horrific event? Many people said God shouldn't be.

They are right in their logic. If God intentionally allowed 9/11 to occur, it would be hard to be thankful toward God. Saying God allowed 9/11 suggests that God could have *dis*allowed it. Saying, "God allowed," suggests God could have stopped the evil event from happening. This, however, makes God out to be a voyeur who arbitrarily jumps into time, willfully intervening to stop some tragedies but not others. "God allows" suggests that through God's inaction, God intentionally consents to each horrific or tragic event that occurs. Is that the sort of view of God, we want to promote?

I propose that we Christians need to get rid of the phrase "God allows." If we did, I suspect fewer people would be confused about God's role or, worse, blame God for the horrific events that occur. Eliminating "God allows" could remove an unnecessary, cognitive, and emotional obstacle that prevents many from having a loving and grateful connection with their Creator.

We can trust that God is not allowing and disallowing specific forms of abuse and evil to occur. God always desires that we pray and conspire with God to thwart and eradicate injustice and evil. God is always seeking to do the miraculous. God is with you. God is for you. God can always be trusted to be, and remain, what God is: love. God's unconventional love—God's perfect, moment-to-moment, uncontrolling, and co-operative love—is captivating!

QUESTIONS

1. Why do traumatic events cause some to lose their faith or distance themselves from God?

2. What is your theodicy? How have you come to make sense of why there is evil and suffering in the world?

3. The author believes that, "Moment-to-moment, in every creature's life, God is seeking to maximize goodness, beauty, truth, love, and healing, while minimizing evil." What are your thoughts about such a theological claim?

4. Do you believe God *can* stop evil from occurring but chooses not to, or do you believe that God can't do so because God's nature is love? What are the differences? What is at stake believing either option?

5. If praying to God moves God to action, would God refuse to act and allow people to suffer or even die because people did not pray? If an ailing dad did not have any prayers offered to God on his behalf, would God simply allow him to die because of this?

6. Why does God not perform more miracles? Do you think it is because God chooses not to perform more miracles, or is it because God can't due to God's uncontrolling love?

7. What are your thoughts about the idea that God is not in control and does not dictate every action, reaction, or happening on this planet? Does such a notion provide comfort, anxiety, or both?

8. Trusting God is an important element of our faith. What do you believe we can trust God for? What thoughts and feelings come up for you as you reflect on trusting God?

CHAPTER ELEVEN

THE SACRED ART OF UNCOMMON PRAYER

....

"The Word lies hidden in the soul, unnoticed and unheard unless room is made for it in the ground of hearing, otherwise it is not heard; but all voices and all sounds must cease and perfect stillness must reign there, a still silence."

— MEISTER ECKHART

....

When I was deconstructing my faith, I got tired of prayer. It seemed illogical, monotonous, and silly to quote passages of scripture to a God who knew them better than I did. Was I trying to convince God of their veracity or myself? Day after day I would go through my prayer list. But, why? God already knew the situation of those for whom I was praying for. If God loved them, and God's love far exceeds my own love, doesn't God want shalom for them too?

Was God being stingy with God's love? Would God only release love, comfort, and healing for ourselves and others if we begged and pleaded? My unconscious understanding was that the more I cajoled God with prayer, the more likely God would cease being passive, get off the throne, and engage in the loving action desired. After some reflection, I realized God had to be more loving than what the form of my prayers suggested. I began to search for other ways to pray and to reconstruct my repertoire of intimate practices with God.

In this chapter, I want to talk about a few uncommon but wonderful prayer practices that can help you connect to the vertical pathway (relationship with God), namely centering prayer, weeping and crying out, and imaginative meditative prayer. I use the word *uncommon* because Christians may or may not engage in these types of prayers very often, although some engage in a few of them without even knowing it. These practices are rooted firmly in the Scriptures and the Christian tradition. May you find them helpful for enabling you to reconstruct well and become closer to God, not only during this D/R journey, but throughout the rest of your life.

CENTERING PRAYER

There are dozens of ways and places to pray. You can pray prayers of thanksgiving, intercession, consecration, exaltation, and request. You can also pray angry prayers (protest), sad prayers (lament), buckshot prayers (praying for a million things at once), bullet prayers (very focused and specific), and the list goes on. You can pray in the wilderness, in the bathroom, on the beach, at work, or really anywhere you want because God is everywhere. You can also engage in centering prayer.

Centering prayer can be one of the most difficult prayers to engage in because it requires stillness and silence, which are completely countercultural and counter-ego. Stillness and silence are countercultural to our drive-thru, drive-by, and driven society that fosters a jittery nervous system and type A(DHD) personalities. Many people, therefore, think of stillness, silence, and solitude as alien planets too far outside their solar system to explore. Additionally, the notion of sitting still—doing nothing in many people's minds—is not going to skyrocket one's career and win the esteem of a culture that values and honors the doers, go-getters, and the fast and furious.

Centering prayer is also counter-ego because, when the brightness of God's loving floodlight shines on our wounded souls, it can disrupt what we believe we know to be true about God, ourselves, and the world. And, since the ego likes sameness and status quo, it tends to run away from the brightness of God's floodlight the way little bugs scurry away when someone lifts a rock and exposes them to the sun. The ego is deathly afraid of change because it sends a person into the unknown. Even if the change God invites us into is beautiful, good, and liberating, our self-protective ego tends to prefer what is familiar, even if it is ugly, sinful, and binding.

For the most part, centering, or contemplative prayer is meant to be *wordless* yet *full* of the *Word*. Thomas Merton, a well-known Catholic writer, contemplative, and Trappist monk, reminds us of the wordless level of prayer. He writes, "The deepest level of communication is not communication, but communion. It is wordless … beyond speech … beyond concept."[1] In this type of prayer, words, which are humanly constructed, are not as important as communication coming straight from one's spirit directly to the Holy Spirit. The sacred word that is used in contemplative prayer, which we will explore shortly, is mostly a reminder to be present in this wordless space.

On the other hand, it is a Word-full space. The gospel of John says, "The Word became flesh and made his dwelling among us … full of grace and truth" (John 1:14). Prayer is meant to be communion with the Word, who is Jesus, the Logos. In contemplative prayer, we are less interested in quoting scripture or making requests, both of which are perfectly fine in other contexts. We are much more interested in being still in the presence of the Word, allowing ourselves to be captivated by Love, who is the beloved Christ.

ORIGINS OF CENTERING PRAYER

Centering prayer, or contemplative prayer, has its origins in the teachings of Jesus. It is a specific type of praying that is based on a verse in the Sermon on the Mount: "When you pray, go into your room, close the door and pray to your Father, who is unseen. Then your Father, who sees what is done in secret, will reward you" (Matt. 6:6). Centering prayer was developed by the Desert Fathers and Mothers, who were devout God-lovers and ascetics who lived in Egypt around the third century AD. Thomas Keating, a contemporary Trappist monk and priest, popularized the approach and formalized the prayer in an understandable and easy-to-follow format.[2]

In a metaphorical sense, the inner room can be thought of as the deepest place of your heart where you *shut out* every form of distraction and cacophonic sound, while *shutting in* the very presence of God. This inner room is where a mysterious and profound dance takes place between God's Spirit and your spirit, God's heart and your heart. It is a place where the reward, or present, is God's presence.

Centering prayer also has roots in Ephesians 3:14–19:

> For this reason I kneel before the Father, from whom every family in heaven and on earth derives its name. I pray that out of his glorious riches he may strengthen you with power through his Spirit in your inner being, so that Christ may dwell in your hearts through faith. And I pray that you, being rooted and established in love, may have power, together with all the Lord's holy people, to grasp how wide and long and high and deep is the love of Christ, and to know this love that surpasses knowledge—that you may be filled to the measure of all the fullness of God.

God wants to meet you in the deep broken places of your heart and strengthen you. In the quiet place produced by centering prayer, God's desire is to increase your faith in the beauty of Christ and to infuse you with God's vast love. God wants your inner roots to reach down deep to the presence of unconditional love and acceptance. Through centering prayer your inner roots can absorb the necessary nutrients to grow and bear fruit—so you, as well as those with whom you come in contact, can enjoy it. While you may have lost toxic religion, you can certainly have an opportunity to gain a fuller measure of a loving, intimate relationship with God.

CENTERING PRAYER IN A NUTSHELL

Keating recommends practicing centering prayer twice a day for about twenty minutes.[3] It is common for some people to engage in centering prayer when they get up in the morning and before they go to bed. Some, including me, use a timer with a soft bell to signal the end of the twenty minutes. And yes, there is an app for that.

Here's what the practice looks like:

1. Choose a sacred word as a symbol of your intention to consent to God's presence and action within. This could be any word. I personally have used *Jesus, Abba, Love, Peace,* and others. You can ask the Spirit to speak to your heart, or you can search the Scriptures to find a word that resonates with you. Throughout the centering prayer, whichever word you choose will serve to anchor you to your intention when thoughts distract you. When you are thinking about how miserable you feel or that your Christian family member is pond scum, for example, your sacred word will gently refocus your mind on being in the presence of God.

2. Sitting comfortably and with your eyes closed, settle yourself, and silently introduce the sacred word as the symbol of your consent to God's presence and action within. Make sure you are in a comfortable position and have all your

electronic devices turned off. Unless you're using an app, it is preferable to set your devices out of the room to avoid unnecessary distractions. Be relaxed, but not so much that you could easily fall asleep (though if you do, you probably needed to). Close your eyes and say the sacred word to yourself.

3. When engaged with other thoughts, return ever so gently to the sacred word. The word *thoughts*, here, is all-encompassing. It includes feelings, images, bodily experiences, memories, smells, and brilliant new revelations you think you are receiving. Don't judge yourself if they arise; gently bring your attention to your sacred word and let go allowing yourself to come back to God's presence. Picture your thoughts as if they are on clouds that are floating away, or on lily pads floating downstream. You might get lost in thoughts a dozen times, but gently bring yourself back to God's presence.

4. At the end of the prayer period, remain in silence with eyes closed for a couple of minutes. The last guideline is to transition back into your routines peacefully and with reverence. It is an acknowledgment that you have just experienced a special moment with God. Feel free to end this time with one of your favorite verses or the Lord's Prayer.

IT TAKES PRACTICE

Most people avoid such intimacy and vulnerability with God for a reason. Keating writes, "Thoughts are integral, inevitable, and a normal part of centering prayer. They contribute to the unloading of our childhood wounds and help clear the emotional debris of a lifetime."[4]

You may encounter a lot of emotional stuff when you engage God in this way, such as repressed memories, painful sensations, anxiety, and uncomfortable emotions. This is normal.

Being still and silent while spending time with God can also be difficult because you might already be experiencing intense emotions and rampant negative thoughts due to the confusing season you are in. If you try it a few times but are unable to stay seated for the entire twenty minutes, then go easy on yourself. People who begin a running program with a ten-mile goal in mind may be able to run only half a mile at first. It's the same with centering prayer. Developing your silence and solitude muscles takes practice.

MY OWN CENTERING PRAYER JOURNEY

When I started learning how to connect with God through centering prayer, it was really difficult. As I sat silently in prayer, focused on the sacred word and enjoying intimacy with God, painful mom-and-dad memories often rose to the surface. Not my idea of fun, especially when I naively thought the consequences of prayer automatically meant peace, calm, and spiritual bliss. However, it was God's way of helping me heal and freeing me from the extra baggage I had been carrying around for many years.

There were also many times I set my intention and began the prayer, and twenty seconds into it a million thoughts raced through my mind. Sometimes, I was in the God-zone, experiencing the blessedness of solitude, and then moments later I found myself salivating over thoughts of greasy cheeseburgers and a pint of cookies and cream ice cream I had in the freezer.

Initially, sitting still and silent was like climbing Mount Everest in blizzard conditions, wearing worn-out tennis shoes and carrying a one-hundred-pound knapsack. It seemed impossible. With years of practice, I have come to highly value and appreciate that special intimate time with God. Although it can still be hard to sit still, I know that praying is how my heart cries out for home, and it is where God whispers, "Welcome home, my beloved; I missed you."

THIRSTY? THEN DRINK

The psalmist writes, "As the deer pants for the streams of water, so my soul pants for you, my God. My soul thirsts for God, for the living God" (Ps. 42:1–2). Is this the cry of your heart? If not, that is okay. Everyone is in a different spiritual space. God loves you where you are. If you have a deeper hunger to connect with God, then take a risk and "taste and see that the LORD is good" (Ps. 34:8). If you have a deeper thirst to experience the love and tenderness of God, then centering prayer can help you encounter the One who said, "Whoever drinks the water I give them will never thirst. Indeed, the water I give them will become in them a spring of water welling up to eternal life" (John 4:14).

Leanne Payne, a contemporary contemplative author and speaker who recently passed, wrote beautifully concerning prayer. "In God's Presence, we've come before the One who speaks worlds into being, who delights in speaking new worlds of *being* into our very souls, affirming, as He does so, those very parts of ourselves that have (for whatever reason) not been called forth and blessed in our families and earthly relationships."[5]

I am convinced that God's desire is for every person to be able to shout with confidence: "I belong to my beloved, and his desire is for me" (Song 7:10). May you find a deeper place of intimacy with God as you journey, through the practice of centering prayer. May you be strengthened and encouraged. In this difficult season of your spiritual journey, may you experience the new life-giving words God is whispering into your being, fortifying your identity as God's beloved child.

WEEPING AND CRYING OUT

Weeping and crying out are two other uncommon practices of prayer that can help you grieve well. You might already be doing them, but I want you to know what these prayer practices look like in detail so that when you experience them, you are able to acknowledge and embrace them as vital modes of connecting with God.

The reason weeping and crying out are considered practices is that it takes practice to become comfortable with experiencing intense emotions and tears and with using your voice to cry out to God. Engaging in weeping and crying out might feel extremely uncomfortable. It feels chaotic and messy, and for some people, sacrilegious, or at the very least, like it is disappointing to God. These practices are seldom talked about and are considered uncommon, but they are extremely important types of prayer, especially in the midst of traveling in the chaotic wilderness.

Weeping is an act of crying, sobbing, and mourning while typically experiencing tears. Loss and tragedy typically lie beneath weeping, as does deep pain, sadness, and grief.

Crying out is slightly different, although it can go hand in hand with weeping. Crying out is the act of raising your voice in lament, concern, or demand for justice.

Of course, people can weep or cry out because they are happy and filled with joy, but for the most part, when the Bible speaks of weeping or crying out, it's usually in the context of loss.

Let's look at weeping and crying out in more detail.

WEEPING

Weeping is a wonderfully intense physical and emotional process. It's a gift that God has given to us to deal with our various disorientations, although it might not feel like a gift when we are experiencing it. I would much rather experience joy than grief. Nonetheless, weeping allows us to enter into our loss in a profound way, and when shared with God, weeping becomes deeply hallowed prayers. That's right. Weeping and tears are prayers to God. Although weeping is usually done without words, God understands the messages behind them. The psalmist writes, "Record my misery; list my tears on your scroll—are they not in your record?" (Ps. 56:8). God understands the language of tears. God has a sacred scroll with a record of the details of your tender tears of affliction and never forgets them.

Chris Ann Waters writes in her book, *Seasons of Goodbye*, about the importance of tears:

> When we have loved someone or something, love is never over, so neither is our sense of loss. The tears of change that flow down our hearts are tears signifying participation in life. Tears reveal our connection to someone or something else. We chose to love. Tears are not a sign of weakness or embarrassment for men or women. Tears are water, a sign of life, an element necessary for growth. When shared, love changes and brings tears to the eyes, they are but symbols of our involvement in life.[6]

Your tears are not a sign of weakness but a powerful symbol that shows you were courageous; you took a risk on the unpredictable nature of love and loved anyway. Those who have ceased to cry have ceased to love and participate fully in life.

Weeping also has a practical function. Tears are a God-given language we have from birth that communicates distress and loss. Tears are designed to communicate to those most important to us that we need them to come close and offer comfort or sustenance. Science backs this up.

Jaak Panksepp, a renowned neurobiologist, believes there are at least seven different emotional systems in the brain that generate distinct emotions and behaviors when activated.[7] When we are grieving, our panic/grief system is activated. Once it is activated, some people yell out in distress or cry. Some move toward others who love them; others move away to soothe themselves. Crying, like other grieving behaviors, is meant to activate in other people the part of the brain Panksepp calls the "CARE system," or the "Care-Circuit," a system of tending and befriending. When activated, the CARE system moves people around us to offer compassionate care and comfort.

John Bowlby, a famous English psychiatrist, made researching relationships his life's work. He noted that the weeping that takes place when an adult loses a loved one correlates with the weeping that takes place when a child misses an absent parent.[8] The child's tears communicate, "Please, take care of me. Come here. I need you right now." They signal the need for the mother, father, or primary caretaker to return. They cue the parent to give the child food or hugs and cuddles, which make the child feel safe and secure again.

Though you are not crying out for your mother, your tears are an unconscious plea for a reality that you have once known to come back. Perhaps, your tears are saying, whether to people you have loved, or God, "I miss you. I am in so much pain. Please come back. I want to feel safe and secure again." I say this with deep compassion. Thankfully, God sees your tears, hears your weeping, and is always drawn to the inner ache of God's beloveds.

David spoke about God's soft spot for God's weeping children.

I am worn out from groaning.

All night long I flood my bed with weeping
    and drench my couch with tears.

My eyes grow weak with sorrow;
    they fail because of all my foes.

Away from me, all you who do evil,
    for the LORD has heard my weeping.

The LORD has heard my cry for mercy;
    the LORD accepts my prayer.

All my enemies will be overwhelmed with shame and anguish;
    they will turn back and suddenly be put to shame.

(Ps. 6:6–10)

Have you experienced that kind of grief because of events that happened on your D/R journey? Tears that could drench a couch? The kind of crying that leaves your eyes so painful and puffy that you can barely see? David, a warrior and very much a man's man, surely did. He wrote in another psalm, "When my prayers returned to me unanswered, I went about mourning as though for my friend or brother. I bowed my head in grief as though weeping for my mother" (Ps. 35:13–14). He never allowed fear of being thought weak to keep him from expressing himself authentically to God. When David experienced brokenness, he let God know. And God heard his weeping, saw his tears, and accepted them as heartfelt prayer.

CRYING OUT

Have you recently raised a fist at God in protest? Have you yelled, complained, gotten angry, doubted, or questioned God in your excruciatingly confusing season of spiritual disorientation? Such interactions with God are often called prayers of lament.

Maybe going through this seismic spiritual shift has been the best thing that ever happened to you and you have instantly moved to prayers of praise and thanksgiving. If so, that is awesome. On the other hand, maybe you have to wail prayers of lament before you get there. That is okay, too.

Psalm 88 is an example of a prayer of lament, though it is one of the rare laments that do not end with thanksgiving or praise.

I am overwhelmed with troubles
    and my life draws near to death ...

I am confined and cannot escape;
    my eyes are dim with grief ...

Why, LORD, do you reject me
    and hide your face from me? ...

You have taken from me friend and neighbor—
    darkness is my closest friend.

Can you feel the pain and inner torment? There is such a holy haunting and beautiful darkness that surrounds this psalm. It is such a powerful portrayal of honesty and depth that epitomizes what it means to engage in the uncommon, prayerful practice of crying out to God.

Psalm 88 is a vulnerable and, some would consider, slightly dark worship song written by a passionate God-lover, which pushes up against the "I always have to have it all together" mentality so pervasive in our culture and churches. When was the last time you heard a congregation sing this type of song? I have never heard a song quite like that in a worship service. As a former worship leader, if I ended a song with "darkness is my closest friend" in church, I think some of the older folks out of loving concern would immediately start a secret prayer-chain and others might question my salvation.

Sometimes the most faithful thing we can do is that which appears faithless. There are times when singing songs of lament, which appear to hyper-religious folk as faithless, would be far more honest than singing today's all-too-common, upbeat, pop praise songs. Sadly, if there was a church where songs of lament were continually sung, there might be many who would choose to never return to the church, judging the members as unspiritual or worse, unsaved. That judgment couldn't be further from the truth.

HIDDEN RULES

It is healthy to inquire about any irrational rules or unnecessary culturally formed beliefs you have about emotions or their expression, so those beliefs do not keep you from grieving and reconstructing well. Some believe, for example, that so-called negative emotions such as anger, frustration, depression, loneliness, and the like, are not Christian or godly emotions. Some people believe they are not glorifying God if they're not constantly showing the "joy of the Lord." No matter how they feel inside, they believe they have to wear a Sunday smile because "that is how an optimistic God wants me to deal with my negative emotions." They believe showing sadness and hurt ruins their witness.

Jim Palmer, a pioneer in helping those who are deconstructing and reconstructing their faith writes in his book *Divine Nobodies: Shedding Religion to Find God (and the Unlikely People Who Help You)* about a time when he was depressed. He went on to talk about his church's implicit and explicit messages he received about his depression and encouragement from leadership and other Christians to display positive emotional states,

> Though I tried leaving my depression at the door, I failed miserably; and subsequently, once inside, I felt ashamed. You're not supposed to be depressed if you are a Christian. After all, it's "non-Christians" who

are the miserable ones needing to see our ecstatic, smiling, problem-free faces and hear our radical transformation stories if they are ever to find Jesus. You're never going to grow a church with a bunch of despondent people moping around![9]

Pretending is never the way to do authentic community. It is never the way to be fully human mirroring the Divine impulse toward truthfulness. Ironically, authenticity is the best witness in this post-postmodern culture, where everyone is suspicious and weary of the salesperson mentality.

Is crying only for babies? Is it a practice we grow out of as we become adults? Do you worry that if you allow yourself to feel something intensely you will get lost in a sea of emotions? Is lamenting before God part of your worship? Is it even allowed in your worship? Are you free to experience the primary, universal emotions: anger, sadness, surprise, shame/disgust, fear, and joy? Do you think some are godlier than others? Is there an implicit or explicit rule in church to put on the Sunday smile and not be anxious or depressed? Continue to reflect on your hidden rules and revise them as necessary.

A TIME FOR WEEPING AND MOURNING

The wisdom writer in Ecclesiastes reminds us that we will all experience different seasons in our lives.

> There is a time for everything,
> and a season for every activity under the heavens:
> a time to be born and a time to die,
> a time to plant and a time to uproot,
> a time to kill and a time to heal,
> a time to tear down and a time to build,
> *a time to weep* and a time to laugh,
> *a time to mourn* and a time to dance.

(Eccl. 3:1–4, italics mine)

The word *mourn* comes from a root word meaning "to wail or howl" and has come to mean "to beat the breast or lament."[10] Mourning encompasses what we mean by *crying out*. Both weeping and crying out in despair or protest are important practices we should not easily dismiss from our repertoire of spiritual practices. There is a time for both. While you can't always flick a switch and weep or cry out on the spot, I suggest that when such emotions and impulses do spring up like a fountain you embrace them as precious gifts.

GOD HEARS YOU

God listens to your cries of pain and shame in this whirlwind of a season. Exodus 2:23–24 says, "The Israelites groaned in their slavery and cried out, and their cry for help because of their slavery went up to God. *God heard* their groaning and he remembered his covenant with Abraham, with Isaac and with Jacob." (italics mine) And the psalmist confidently declares that God listens, saying, "The righteous cry out, and *the LORD hears* them; he delivers them from all their troubles." (Ps. 34:17 italics mine)

Rest assured that God is certainly a God who acts *and* who listens, so you can run into God's compassionate arms. This is a time, therefore, for you to raise a fist, yell, weep, question, wail, and howl if you need to. Do whatever is honest, whatever is true within your heart. You don't have to fake it. God loves honesty.

It is evident throughout the Bible that God keeps it real with us. So why not keep it real with God? When we set our hearts on grieving well and engaging in authentic spiritual practices, we can be confident that what we "sow in tears" we will eventually "reap with songs of joy." (Ps. 126:5)

IMAGINATIVE MEDITATIVE PRAYER

Another uncommon prayer practice is imaginative prayer. Imaginative prayer takes seriously the command to "Love the Lord your God with all your heart and with all your soul and with all your strength and with all your mind" (Luke 10:27). It is designed to engage all of our senses, including our imagination, in prayer.

I designed a prayer drawing on imaginative prayer of the Ignatian Christian tradition and from lovingkindness meditation. Before I share it let me briefly describe the origins of imaginative prayer and give a description of lovingkindness meditation.

IGNATIUS OF LOYOLA

Ignatius of Loyola was born in 1491 and eventually became an expert in spiritual direction. He believed God could speak to his people through their vivid imaginations and that prayers should be holistic, engaging the mind, heart, and emotions.[11] Ignatius loved immersing himself in the captivating stories of Scripture. He used his imagination to journey into the sacred texts, almost as if he were experiencing a 4-D film. He attempted to live in the story, allowing it to engage all five senses within his imagination.

Although some early Christians opposed the use of the imagination in one's relationship with God, Ignatius did not allow their fears to keep him from using his God-given senses. It appears that as long as his experiences did not contradict the Scriptures, all was fair in prayer.

LOVINGKINDNESS MEDITATION

Lovingkindness meditation is a brain-training exercise where participants repeat loving phrases toward oneself and others as a means to foster an attitude of compassion and goodwill. The lovingkindness exercise fits well within the Christian tradition as we are asked to dwell on "whatever is true, whatever is noble, whatever is right, whatever is pure, whatever is lovely, whatever is admirable" (Phil. 4:8). The exercise repeated over time actually changes the brain, particularly in the area involved with empathy.[12] Research shows that when practiced over time, the lovingkindness exercise increases compassion, self-compassion, and positive emotions—all while decreasing depression.

The prayer below, "God's Lovingkindness," combines a lovingkindness meditation with imaginative prayer. Add this formalized prayer to your repertoire and use it when you feel overwhelmed with emotions such as shame, anger, and fear.

God's Lovingkindness Meditation

Make sure you're seated and comfortable. Become aware of the sacred space and of God's presence. Notice your breath. Feel the air moving into your nostrils and into your body. Breathe in, and breathe out. *Pause for five seconds.*

Take a few moments to attend to your heart. *Pause for five seconds.*

Lovingkindness involves opening and softening the heart. Feel your breath coming and going. Place one or both hands over your heart. Breathe in and out, in and out, thanking God for the breath of life. *Pause for ten seconds.*

This is a sacred space. Allow God to hold you in lovingkindness. As I offer some phrases for you to consider, please feel free to change them to whatever allows you to hold yourself in lovingkindness. If you find yourself distracted by other thoughts or feelings, simply return to your breath—without judgment.

Now imagine yourself enfolded in the arms of a compassionate God. Repeat these phrases to yourself as you breathe in and breathe out: "May I be held in your lovingkindness. May I be well in both body and mind. May I continue to grieve well. May I learn to forgive and be free." *Pause for ten seconds. Slowly repeat these phrases for five minutes.*

Listen to God gently say, "I love holding you in the same way parents love holding their beautiful child. My desire is for you to be well in both body and mind. Do not be afraid, my child, for I will never forsake you. I have come to give you abundant life." *Gently repeat twice.*

Imagine yourself kneeling humbly before Jesus. Imagine his radiance and pleasure in seeing you. Imagine his strength and tenderness. *Pause for ten seconds.*

Imagine yourself putting your pain, shame, anger, and grief in a bowl and presenting them to God. Picture God gently taking the bowl from you.

Listen to God gently say, "Nothing can separate you from my love. I can see how much pain you are in, and because you hurt, I hurt with you. I will not leave you alone on this healing journey. I love you deeply."

What was that like for you? Were you able to get through the exercise in its entirety? Did you find yourself getting distracted with other thoughts? Were you able to encounter God and feel a sense of warmth and love? Was your pain too loud to hear anything else?

If it was a positive experience for you, take note and use this meditation when your thoughts seem dismal and your pain feels overwhelming. If it was not a positive experience, that is okay. There is no judgment. You are no less spiritual. Accept yourself for where you are and extend compassion toward yourself and continue to look for spiritual practices that resonate with you.

QUESTIONS

1. There are many forms of prayer, such as prayers of thanksgiving, intercession, consecration, exaltation, lament, and others. Which ones do you engage in the most and why?

2. Why is it so hard to sit in silence before God?

3. What does it mean when Thomas Merton writes, "The deepest level of communication is not communication, but communion. It is wordless ... beyond speech ... beyond concept."

4. Why have we become so even keeled when it comes to prayer in churches? What keeps us from crying out, weeping, lamenting, and protesting before God?

5. If you could raise a fist before God and protest, what would you lament?

6. If you could mourn before God and share your losses, what would they be?

7. Is it easy for you to experience God's lovingkindness in the midst of your doubts and emotional pain? If not, what makes it difficult?

8. If you could ask God any questions about prayer, what would they be? What are some of your guesses as to the answers to some of those questions?

CHAPTER TWELVE

THE GIFT OF THE "F" WORD

"As I walked out the door toward the gate that would lead to my freedom, I knew if I didn't leave my bitterness and hatred behind, I'd still be in prison."

— NELSON MANDELA

There he is. John is at it again ...

"I hate most Christians."

"Those who read the Bible literally are a bunch of morons!"

"A part of me loves God, but mostly, I think God is a jerk. He doesn't truly care about anyone."

"I am angry at myself for even believing that Christian fundamentalist nonsense!"

"I don't need anyone but myself."

John is in great pain. He is dealing with the profound realization that his conservative and strict Christian parents did more harm to him than good while he was growing up. John has also left the church he was attending because he couldn't stand the rigid rules and hypocrisy any longer. Sadly, he hasn't let anyone know he's hurting. All John does is show his anger. He is like an abused and scared dog who is always snarling at people, letting them know how powerful and ferocious he is; though, underneath the seething anger and pseudo power is intense hurt, heavy sadness, and a profound desire to be listened to and loved.

There are consequences to living with so much resentment and anger. Since leaving his church he doesn't have many friends. To cope with his painful feelings and loneliness, he watches porn two hours a day and drinks heavily on the weekends. He ruminates a lot on his past and can't enjoy and live in the present. John is not living the best life he could be living.

What is a powerful spiritual practice that can help free John and ourselves from bitterness, hatred, and resentment? You guessed it, the infamous F word—Forgiveness! Keep in mind, I am suggesting forgiveness "can help." I am not saying it is a cure-all for every ounce of emotional pain and spiritual suffering we have. Nonetheless, we should not underestimate the radical potential for forgiveness to release the negative emotional energy of unforgiveness.

For some, forgiveness can be an ambiguous word that immediately conjures up religious disgust. They have been preached at and were told that forgiveness is something that they have to do, or else God would be mad at them and choose not to forgive them out of spite. It is no wonder why that they have a bitter taste in their mouth when it comes to the F word.

WHAT IS IT?

Forgiveness. What is it? Forgiveness is not forgetting, not pretending we weren't hurt, and not a fancy word for psychological suppression. Forgiveness is a subversive prayerful process of surrendering to love and making a choice to release the debt we feel the injurer owes us because of how deeply he or she hurt us. Forgiveness is courageously taking the cobwebbed key and unlocking the cumbersome locks on the protective armor surrounding our wounded hearts, allowing our true and expansive self to come out of fearful hiding.

True forgiveness does not deny but accepts the full impact of the injuring person's choices and decides to let go and let God perform God's transformational work in our lives. Forgiveness is also a powerful gift from God that releases us from the poison and bitterness of unforgiveness. Forgiveness is a compassionate gift unto ourselves. We are invited to engage in this ancient sacred practice in order to break free from the past and to reconstruct something more beautiful in our lives.

RESEARCH ON FORGIVENESS AND UNFORGIVENESS

In a recent research study on forgiveness, participants were randomly assigned one of two conditions: either forgiveness or unforgiveness.[1] Those assigned to forgiveness were asked to write about a time when they were seriously offended by someone and chose to forgive them. Those who were assigned the unforgiveness condition wrote about a time when they were seriously offended but chose not to forgive.

Both sets of participants then engaged in two experiments. In the first experiment the participants examined a hill for steepness and gauged the difficulty in climbing it. The researchers observed the difference, if any, in the groups' visual perceptions of the hill's geographical slant. In the second experiment participants jumped five times without bending their knees, and the researchers measured the difference between the heights the groups achieved.

In the first experiment, those participants who had forgiven viewed the hill as less steep than did those who had not forgiven. In the second activity, those who had forgiven jumped higher than those who had not. Here's what researchers concluded: "A state of unforgiveness is like carrying a heavy burden—a burden that victims bring with them when they navigate the physical world. Forgiveness can 'lighten' this burden." They also said, "Forgivers perceive a less daunting world and perform better on challenging physical tasks."

Forgiveness is shown to increase the health of one's heart and over-all cardiovascular system, while anger, which is typically present in the absence of forgiveness, can make the heart weaker.[2] The poison of anger can cause the heart to become less efficient in pumping and circulating blood, which ultimately means the rest of the body gets less oxygen. Less oxygen to the rest of the body can lower a person's immune system and cause fatigue.

In another study, sixty-five hundred people responded to the question, "Would you say this is true or false: I've held grudges against people for years?"[3] Those who reported holding grudges had higher rates of stomach ulcers, back problems, chronic pain, headaches, and higher blood pressure than those who did not. This is why quick-witted Anne Lamott wisely says, "Not forgiving is like drinking rat poison and then waiting for the rat to die."[4] Grudges are toxic to those who harbor them.

Although forgiveness does not require forgetting, research shows that a byproduct of forgiveness is forgetting.[5] In other words, forgiveness allows you to move away from painful events from the past and truly live in the present. Not having pain-laden events at the forefront of your consciousness allows you to focus instead on the beauty and goodness all around you.

No wonder we are encouraged to "Bear with each other and forgive one another if any of you has a grievance against someone. Forgive as the Lord forgave you" (Col. 3:13). God wants us to forgive because it is in the Divine DNA, and God wants us to be like Godself. We are asked to forgive because God knows the emotional, physical, and spiritual consequences of not forgiving. In other words, God wants us to forgive so we can live and be free to love and be loved. If we continue to allow the seeds of anger, bitterness, rage, and resentment to soil our hearts, they will reap disastrous consequences in our lives. God's tenderness and love for us moves God to invite us to forgive.

Jesus said, "For if you forgive other people when they sin against you, your heavenly Father will also forgive you. But if you do not forgive others their sins, your Father will not forgive your sins" (Matt. 6:14-15). When I first read that verse, I couldn't understand how it was possible for the Father not to forgive us. Wasn't a major point of Christianity the fact that we couldn't save ourselves? Isn't it salvation through Jesus, and not salvation through how spiritual we are in flexing our forgiveness muscles? Both statements are true. We are saved moment-by-moment through the grace of God. Period. It is not by works so that any one of us could boast. So, what may be another reading of Jesus's bold declaration?

I think Jesus is saying, "Look, God's love is non-coercive and uncontrolling. If you want to hold on to anger, resentment, and bitterness from past hurts, then you are free to do so. Just know that if you do, since God cannot force God's healing love in your heart, then you will carry around unforgiveness. Since you are holding on to your pain so tightly, God simply will not—or better stated—God *cannot* forgive you. But, if you allow God's love and healing to penetrate your heart, then you can experience God's forgiveness. Though it may be in dribs and drabs, the healing and forgiveness you experience from God will eventually funnel through your heart to others." Remember, forgiveness is for us, not God. While we may be forgiven by God infinitum, we need to experience God's forgiveness, and become aware of that forgiveness, ourselves.

PROCESS OF FORGIVENESS

I don't know about you, but when preachers and teachers tell us to forgive, I always think to myself, "How? How do I forgive someone who has hurt me?" Am I supposed to count "1, 2, 3," and then flick the forgiveness switch and all will be magically okay? Forgiving others always seemed so nebulous. Thankfully, there are really smart people out there who have spent their careers studying the process of forgiveness. Everett Worthington is one of those folks.

Worthington is a Christian psychologist and counselor who has dedicated his life to studying forgiveness after someone raped and murdered his mother. He developed a five-step model of forgiveness, which beautifully portrays what the process of forgiveness looks like.[6] The following is his acronym REACH:

- **R**ecall the hurt

- **E**mpathize with the one who hurt you

- **A**ltruistic gift of forgiveness, offer

- **C**ommitment to forgive, make

- **H**old on to the forgiveness

These steps are not meant to be a cookie-cutter approach to forgiveness, but rather a helpful guide for practicing and increasing our ability to forgive. With anger, resentment, and bitterness out of the way, you can expend more positive energy to your reconstruction process.

The first step is to *recall* the hurt and injury. In other words, fully enter into the details of the event, including the hurt, pain, and sadness. Let's say that a dear Christian friend has rejected you and called you a God-forsaken heretic. Think about what they said, did, or didn't say or do, that caused you pain. You could also try writing the story out, starting when you first met, moving on to how the event unfolded and what they said, and ending with how you presently feel toward them. Really get in touch with the emotions and bodily sensations you feel when thinking about what they said. Do you feel shame, anger, rage, sadness, or fear? Allow yourself to feel whatever arises within you. Additionally, every emotion has an implicit longing. Ask yourself what you needed from that person. Was it to be loved? Protected? Listened to? Valued? Honored? Picture them in a seat across from you. What would you tell them you needed from them instead of what was done to you?

Secondly, *empathize* and meditate upon what the other person might have been going through that would move him or her to hurt you. Going back to the example of the person who rejected you, what do you think was going on in their life, heart, and mind at the time? What dynamics in his or her childhood would cause him or her to act in certain ways in the present? Think about times when you might have hurt someone in a similar way. As hard as it might be, try to place yourself in the other person's shoes and understand what his or her life was like before the hurtful event (or events) happened.

Let's take the example of someone harshly judging and rejecting you. Perhaps, due to their difficult upbringing, Christianity has brought incredible comfort and feelings of safety for them. Your complex questions and doubt concerning cherished Christian doctrines may have caused them to become highly anxious in the moment. Attacking you could have been a way to ease their own anxiety. Maybe they had similar questions but pushed them down deep into their unconscious, so they didn't have to face the questions themselves. It could also be that through diligent study, they truly believed their understanding of the biblical text. So, attacking and demeaning you was not about their anxiety at all. In order to protect God's honor, they felt they had to come on strong to what they considered heresy.

311

Who knows? You are simply trying to be empathetic and understand what may have been going on with them before they hurt you. Keep in mind, empathizing is not excusing, it is seeking to take a wider lens and understand the broader context of their hurtful act.

Thirdly, extend the *altruistic* gift of forgiveness to the other person (and yourself). Let go of the debt you believe they owe you. This usually takes time, and it can be one of the hardest steps to do. It could be an exercise of your will at first, but at some point, your emotions will follow. Keeping the other person in mind, and what they have done, you can silently say to yourself, "With the grace of God, I choose to forgive so and so."

If you need help accomplishing this step, start by remembering a time when you hurt someone else and how it felt when that person forgave you. If you continue to struggle, start praying for them. Or, if you can't pray for them, share with God how hard it is to even consider praying for them. Then, at another point in time, try praying for them again. Don't force it. Be congruent and honest with yourself. With time and grace, you will eventually be able to let go of your resentment and forgive.

The fourth step is to make a *commitment* to the forgiveness you've extended to the injurer and make that decision known to others, whether it is by sharing it with your unholy huddle or, if it is safe enough, with the person who hurt you. If seeing the person is too risky, write a letter to him or her, or write a letter to yourself in your journal. Please keep in mind, forgiveness does not mean reconciliation. You can forgive someone without needing to be in a relationship with them. Whether you decide to be in a relationship with the injurer or not, symbolize your decision to forgive in some tangible way: plant a tree, find a special rock and make it a memorial stone, or make a certificate. Use your imagination.

Lastly, *hold* on to the forgiveness you purposed in your heart, especially when old memories and painful feelings rise to the surface. One day you can go through the steps, find tremendous peace, and believe you have forgiven them. Then, only days later, you may be angered by a memory and believe that your original forgiveness didn't work or was not real. Max Lucado writes, "Forgiveness vacillates like this. It has fits and starts, good days and bad. Anger intermingled with love. Irregular mercy. We make progress only to make a wrong turn. Step forward and fall back. But this is okay. When it comes to forgiveness, all of us are beginners."[7] When you are struggling to forgive, that is a time to hold on to the forgiveness you have initially committed to, trusting yourself to Divine love to help you complete the process in due time.

Just so you know, there are really good reasons for why anger and revenge well up only days after you thought you had forgiven the person who hurt you. Neuroscientists differentiate between the higher region of the brain (neocortex) and the lower regions (reptilian and limbic system). Your feelings resurface not because you haven't forgiven that person but because painful memories deeply encoded within your nervous system and lower regions of the brain have not yet caught up to your will, which is in the higher region. In other words, it takes time for your heart (the seat of your emotions) to catch up with your mind (the logic and rational faculties).

CAVEAT

Life is complicated. There are some who may choose not to forgive right away. Their fear of engaging in forgiveness is that it may gloss over evil or unjust and oppressive systems. Their choice to say, "No," to forgiveness is a way to hold on to their power and God-given right to choose. When there are some in society who may desire people to quickly forgive as a means to hold power over them, or to quickly change the energy and attention from the wrong or evil that was perpetrated, *moral unforgiveness* may be a subversive and sacred act. However, the act of forgiveness in the midst of blatant injustice and evil may also be an equally subversive and sacred act. The point is, people should not be demonized for not forgiving folks right away. And, the choice to do so, or not to do so, should not be what their eternal destinies are hung upon. People should be listened to and respected for where they are on their spiritual journey.

FORGIVE YOURSELF

You may have transgressed an inner vow or value and caused an injury to yourself. In essence, you have become both the victim and the assailant. Because you believe you did something wrong, you are resentful and angry with yourself. You can't let the act go. You continue to beat yourself up for it, making self-forgiveness very important.

From the late 1200s through the 1300s, a Christian sect took self-punishment to the extreme. At certain times, they went on long sacred pilgrimages, shouted out the sins they were struggling with, got down on one knee and lashed themselves using whips tipped with sharp pieces of iron. The more religious of the bunch lashed themselves to the point of tearing their own flesh, causing blood to run down their bodies. This is where we get the term *self-flagellation*, which basically means self-punishment.

The Flagellants loved God but certainly could have used a lesson or two in self-compassion and self-forgiveness. And they definitely needed instruction on what Jesus came to offer them through his life, death, and resurrection.

I have met many Christians who quote dozens of verses on how God loves and forgives them but act as the Flagellants did. They don't use literal whips; rather, they say harsh and critical words to themselves or engage in self-destructive behaviors to punish themselves. They believe an unconscious lie that says if they can make themselves hurt or feel bad enough, that will make up for what they did. Of course, it only causes more damage in the long run.

Lacie, a woman I met in church, loved God but couldn't forgive herself for leaving her husband. She was torn. One part of her believed she did the right thing, but another thought she was still disobeying God. She felt like she had to leave because he was controlling and verbally abusive. He also used the Bible as a weapon and made her think that she deserved what she got. He found out she did not believe in God anymore and hit her. That was the last straw. She took their child and left to go to her parents' house and filed for divorce.

The divorce turned her world upside down. She believed God was angry with her. A tsunami of grief flooded her with self-hatred and shame, so she started taking drugs just to numb the pain. It was also a form of self-harm because a part of her felt like she should be punished.

Of course, none of this made any sense because self-hatred and self-punishment never do. They make things worse. Lacie thought that by hurting herself she could make up for the damage she caused to her family, but her actions only entrenched the shame and propelled her into even more destructive actions. She desperately needed help. Thankfully, through her process in counseling she eventually received God's forgiveness and forgave herself.

There are many who are on the D/R journey and have tremendous guilt due to their use of the Bible as weapon. Drew, a friend who has been deconstructing and reconstructing his faith said, "I look back at my fundamentalist days and I cringe. I can't believe how many people I have hurt with the Bible. When I think about how I shamed people and condemned them to Hell for believing differently than me, I feel terrible. When I think about telling those of the LGBTQ Christian community that God hates them, I feel like a horrible human being." Feelings of remorse for hurting God's children is warranted. Healthy guilt (or godly sorrow) is a good thing as it seeks to make amends for our hurtful acts. It can propel folks to become allies and engage in restitution. Negative feelings, unforgiveness, and even self-hatred is unwarranted. It doesn't serve you or the people that you hurt in beneficial ways.

You are forgiven. You don't have to punish yourself. C. S. Lewis wrote, "I think that if God forgives us we must forgive ourselves. Otherwise, it is almost like setting up ourselves as a higher tribunal than him."[8] Think about it. When you punish yourself, you are declaring that what Jesus declared on the cross, that God has always forgiven all humankind, was not good enough. The faulty equation states, *God's Forgiveness + Punishing Yourself* = Complete Forgiveness. But of course, that is like saying 1+1=5. It is just plain wrong. I don't mean to add to your guilt or shame by correcting your theological math. I'm trying to keep you from harming yourself further.

If you are having a difficult time forgiving yourself, then spend time in the loving presence of others. Let their words of hope, forgiveness, and encouragement bring solace to your thirsty soul. If you are having a difficult time forgiving yourself, then spend time in God's loving presence. According to 1 John 1:9, God is faithful, God will forgive you, and God will make you clean and whole again. The mystic in Psalm 103:11–12 wrote, "For as high as the heavens are above the earth, so great is his love for those who fear him; as far as the east is from the west, so far has he removed our transgressions from us." Let the truth of God's profound love for you and the depth of God's forgiveness dwell deeply in your heart. Then, when God's love fills every nook and cranny of your tender heart, you can drop that devilish whip and treat yourself the way God treats you.

FORGIVING MY GHOSTS

A long time ago, I was at a United Pentecostal Church (UPC) conference. The UPC was the denomination I was connected to for a while. They were strict, no-nonsense, Holy-Ghost–stammering Christian folk who took faith and the Bible extremely seriously. Women couldn't cut their hair because it was a sin. I couldn't have facial hair or long hair because supposedly it said not to in the Bible. According to them, only those who spoke in tongues were saved and non-tongue-talking Trinitarians were going to Hell. At this conference, I had a conversation with a well-known preacher. I thought I was in the presence of royalty, and I was so nervous I could barely speak.

After some small talk, I briefly mentioned that I drank wine at a wedding. Being a fairly new Christian, I didn't think much of it. His eyes began to widen with a fierce sternness, and his cheeks began to flush. He looked at me with his piercing eyes and firmly told me I was in danger of hellfire. I was shocked. My heart began to race wildly, and I immediately began to fear for my life. It was as if God himself spoke to me. The thought of going to Hell terrified me, and I knew at that moment I would never drink wine again. His words affected me for a very long time. Even after eventually leaving that cult, it took me years before I was comfortable drinking wine without thinking God was going to violently punish me.

As I began my journey of deconstruction, I realized that pastors, teachers, and other Christians are just people. They are just like me— imperfect, wounded, searching, pretending, longing, and anxious, with a dose of relational ineptness. After pondering their fragile finitude, I started experiencing empathy for them. I began to look at that well-known preacher with new eyes. Sure, years after the incident I was still angry with him. He had used his power to instill fear in my heart. He made a loving God into a monster and pit that God against me. But what was his backstory? Why did he speak to me that way?

Did someone speak to him that way when he was growing up in the faith?

On the journey of deconstruction, it is vital to look at and tend to our own "stuff," including the wounded, judgmental, and angry parts within us in order to see clearly, forgive, and reconstruct a spirituality that is new and healthy. Alexander Shaia poignantly writes:

> We each have inner voices of Sadducees and Pharisees that roil and breed ceaselessly within us like a nest of "brooding vipers." When we hear them, they often seem to be in a superior or elevated position, yet their true faces are our own wounds, anxieties, and even fear of change. Held in their grip, we are inflexible and incapable of renewal. We know only one answer and are unable to entertain a new question. The poison in their terrible fangs will quickly kill any possibility of the new life we are trying to discover—quickly, silently, and certainly.[9]

Please hear me: I am not condoning or excusing what the pastor said to me. I am not saying it was okay. I am merely trying to withhold harsh judgment and empathize with him. Empathy requires withholding judgment and seeks to enter into the world of the other. That is what I tried to do. I also recognized my own inner Pharisee and lust for power. I reflected on my dysfunctional background and how that negatively (and positively) shaped me into the person I was. I then imagined what he may have gone through to become the person he was.

I wondered what nature/nurture factors contributed to his being an uptight, judgmental, Pharisee-type Christian. While I can only speculate, perhaps he was never shown grace and tenderness by his parents. Perhaps when he was learning to be a disciple, he was not shown love and compassion by other Christians. Perhaps he felt deep shame and had tons of insecurities that led him to pursue a prestigious position traveling the world as a preacher. Perhaps exerting power over others made him feel special. Who knows. But the more I reflected on how he was possibly shaped to portray God like a vindictive monster, the more empathy I felt. I also wondered how terrifying it may be for him to feel like he can go to Hell for not being perfect. I thought about how tragic it is that he cannot feel unconditionally loved and accepted by a compassionate, forgiving, and merciful God.

Forgiveness became a sacred, life-giving discipline for me that came naturally after I began exercising my empathy muscles. There came a point when I didn't want to have a boulder on my shoulder and be bogged down with a negative and judgmental attitude toward the church. I didn't want to have unfinished business, hate, and unforgiveness festering in my heart. I was tired of my attitude—always deconstructing something and never offering something positive and empowering in its place. I decided to research forgiveness and practice it—not for the people who hurt me, but for myself.

Although it has taken years, I have finally forgiven my parents, my stepfather, religious fundamentalists, God, life, myself, and anyone else who has ever hurt me. I realized that if God has forgiven all my sins and continues to do so, then how can I withhold forgiveness from anyone else? Even after all my wanderings and the continually shutting of my spiritual ears to God's loving voice, God always gives me another chance. Moment to moment, God offers me forgiveness and healing graces. While I have not reconciled with and become close companions of all those who have caused me pain, I have made a choice to forgive them and set myself free. And that is the point. It is not about those who have hurt me; it is about loving myself enough to let go of some of the pain and hurt that keeps me from being my true self.

Jesus did not command us to forgive to make life hard but rather to emancipate us from a hard life. Forgiveness propels us toward a future where we easily feel and express love. The author of Hebrews lovingly encourages us to "make every effort to live in peace with everyone" and cautions us to see to it "that no bitter root grows up to cause trouble and defile many" (Heb. 12:14–15). If we choose to harbor the bitter root and negative energy of unforgiveness, then we waste additional energy to keep those destructive elements at bay. What if you forgave? What if you released yourself from the negativity and instead used the freed-up emotional energy in positive ways? You could use that energy to love yourself, God, and others with much greater capacity. You can reconstruct your faith with more clarity and potency. There is no greater joy than to freely love and to be loved!

QUESTIONS

1. What is your gut reaction when you hear the word "forgiveness"?

2. Can you describe forgiveness and unforgiveness in your own words?

3. Who is a person that you have not been able to forgive? What did they do to you? With that person and the hurt they caused in mind, what would it be like to go through Everett Worthington's model of forgiveness?

4. The second step of Worthington's forgiveness model is to *empathize*. Why might empathy for the perpetrator of your pain help you forgive that person?

5. During this D/R journey, what do you need to forgive yourself for?

6. How can unforgiveness affect your relationships?

7. What do you think about applying Worthington's model to God?

8. What does God's forgiveness for ourselves have to do with our forgiveness of others?

CHAPTER THIRTEEN

THE POWER OF LOVE, SERVICE, AND VALUED-LIVING

*"The simple path: silence is prayer, prayer is faith,
faith is love, love is service, the fruit of service is peace."*

— MOTHER THERESA

In Matthew 22:36, an inquisitive expert in religious law asked Jesus, "Which is the greatest commandment in the Law?" Jesus answered boldly and without hesitation, "'Hold fast to those secondary doctrines, arbitrary rules that you draw from my words and those of the Law and the Prophets, and do not neglect endlessly debating them.' And the second is like it, 'Make sure to shove those rules in the face of strangers, who you already suspect are guilty of violating them, and cram them down the throats of others who disagree.'" Isn't that how you remember it? You sure would think so after spending time in some Christian circles I have been around.

Here's how the real conversation went down: "Which is the greatest commandment?" asked a Pharisee, a confident expert in religion. Jesus replied, "'Love the Lord your God with all your heart and with all your soul and with all your mind.' This is the first and greatest commandment. And the second is like it: 'Love your neighbor as yourself'" (Matt. 22:37–39). The greatest of all the commandments (and there are a lot of them) is an invitation to love with all of your being.

Throughout history, particularly through the mystics, the Divine has always whispered through a megaphone that life is all about vibrant and intimate relationships; relationships that will last into eternity. Unfortunately, as Christians, sometimes our priorities can be out of whack. Our interactions with those theologically different than us can devolve into the type of religious debates for which Jesus called out the Pharisees. I think Jesus would remind us that, in spite of our differences, what matters most is whether or not we love God and others. Period.

BACK TO BASICS

Have you ever wondered why we make it so darn complicated? Do we really need to know every piece to every theological puzzle? The alluring hamster wheel of theological reflection is an endless adventure into layers upon layers of brilliant human creativity and constructions about the mysterious known/unknown God. There is no end to imaginative theological speculation. There are only perpetual new beginnings. And, just when you think you have studied a topic and have all of the nuances figured out, another theological rabbit-hole emerges.

For some on this journey, it may be wise to get off of the hamster wheel. It may be time to stop trying to figure it all out and to focus on what truly matters. Our zeal to be heavenly-minded can cost us healthy, earthly relationships.

At some point, our ruminations about an ineffable God who can't be fully figured out simply become a defense mechanism. After all, creating, crafting ideas, and speculating is one of the ego's greatest delights. Wandering these elaborate theological castles in our heads seems to protect us from the painful realities we would otherwise be facing. In those castles, we are shielded from:

- Our pain due to our fractured relationships with parents, spouses, siblings, and friends.

- Our guilt about how we treated others in the past.

- Our shame due to how we treat—or neglect to treat—others in the present.

- Our perpetual feelings of smallness, insecurity, and unworthiness.

- Our incessant pride and feelings of superiority that create ideological and theological barriers between other people.

- Our disappointment with ourselves knowing that we theologize *about* God rather than engage in an intimate relationship *with* God.

- Our existential dread due to living in a world that is both beautiful and chaotic.

- Our internal suffering due to how we criticize and treat our selves.

- Our internal angst due to feeling like we are a cog in a wheel and lack purpose.

- Our guilt knowing that we neglect to work on a healthy relationship with our children.

It is natural to want to get lost amid the countless doctrines and endless theologies mined from over 31,000 Bible verses. It is easier to avoid the painful, harsh, and difficult realities of our lives and neglect to live and love in the present moment. It feels more comfortable reading theological books, and getting our point across to others, than being compassionately present with loved ones or people who need our love. It is much easier to focus on the afterlife than to focus on the task before us after we've been captivated by the life of Christ. Perhaps we should stop habitually theologizing and, instead, focus mainly on what God has called us to—God-love, others-love, and self-love.

Robin Meyers, author of *Saving God from Religion: A Ministers Search for Faith in a Skeptical Age*, writes:

> People often tell me that they wish Christianity were more like Eastern spiritual traditions, which emphasize faith as following a "path" instead of as adherence to doctrines. The irony, of course, is that this is precisely how Christianity started—as a journey, a way of life, not a system of creeds and doctrines demanding intellectual assent to theological propositions. In the beginning, there was no doctrine of Jesus, only the radical ethic of Jesus and, after his death, the unforgettable Jesus. Consider this remarkable fact: In the Sermon on the Mount, there is not a single word about what to believe, only words about what to do and how to be.[1]

I've always wondered why we care so much about completely understanding twenty-five different doctrines, along with commandment number 144, while neglecting to practice commandment number one—a radical, sacred ethic of love. Of course, creeds, doctrines, and propositions can be beneficial. I am not naïve. Obviously, any intentional and articulate ethic of love constitutes those things. But what is our focus and priority?

Why do we obsessively seek to solve the impossible theological puzzle of what happens in the afterlife when no one who is living has been there (unless you have some really cool ghosts for friends we should know about)? Why do we spend time answering such esoteric questions when we have fractured relationships with loved ones, God, creation, and even with ourselves? Instead of prioritizing right doctrines, shouldn't we focus on righting wrong relationships? It's imperative that we work on commandment number one, seeking with all of our heart, mind, and strength to have healthy and loving relationships. Perhaps it would be wise to listen to the Christian mystic who penned these words:

> If I speak in the tongues of men or of angels, but do not have love, I am only a resounding gong or a clanging cymbal. If I have the gift of prophecy and can fathom all mysteries and all knowledge, and if I have a faith that can move mountains, but do not have love, I am nothing. If I give all I possess to the poor and give over my body to hardship that I may boast, but do not have love, I gain nothing.[2]

The call to love is not merely a humanistic endeavor. It is also not a love that is conjured up after a dose of magic mushrooms or taken from the fragile pages of a rare and abstract philosophy book. True love encompasses the biblical qualities found in 1 Corinthians 13:4–7 and it is the fruit described in Galatians 5:22–23. It is the perfect kind of love Jesus talks about in Matthew 5 and the type of love epitomized by Jesus' life. What does perfect love look like? Well, for starters, it is called for whether the respondent receives or cares about you or not. Even if the recipient comes across as entitled and ungrateful, perfect love still prays for them without any hint of arrogance or self-righteousness. Perfect love is inviting your father to Thanksgiving in spite of the fact he wasn't there for you when you were growing up (Matt. 5:44). It is offering a job to a repentant, registered sex-offender (Luke 6:35). It is the kind of love

327

portrayed in Jesus' parable of the gift-giving Father (Luke 15:11–32). When we prioritize love, we make sure we are compassionately present, embodying the gospel for each person we meet. It also means we have the courage to open up our own hearts and allow other compassionate people to be present for us. Love fights alongside the marginalized and oppressed so they can experience deeper levels of shalom; the same type of shalom we may experience ourselves.

The path of love is simple yet can be radically difficult. No wonder we would rather engage in impossible theological jigsaw puzzles and debate with others. It is much easier to ruminate and stay in our heads than to actually let God enthrall our hearts and follow the risky and adventurous way of Jesus. Jesus is moment-to-moment inviting us to ask ourselves, "What does love require of me in this moment?" That is the heart of following The Way—risky business indeed!

LOVE COMPELS US TO SERVE OTHERS

Think about what happens when a loved one knows they are going to die. Maybe you've experienced this with a family member or friend, or you've seen one of the numerous Hollywood death-bed scenes. In most cases, the dying person calls their most loved family members and friends to join them and then opens their heart, making sure they say everything they need to say. It usually boils down to just three things: "I'm sorry for _____;" "know that I love you and want the best for you;" and "Take care of _____ for me." That is exactly what Jesus did (though he had nothing to apologize for).

The night before Jesus was going to die, he not only told his disciples what was most important—he showed them. Jesus "got up from the meal, took off his outer clothing, and wrapped a towel around his waist. After that, he poured water into a basin and began to wash his disciples' feet, drying them with the towel that was wrapped around him" (John 13:4–5). Jesus could have emphasized his disciples' need to understand deep theology by delving into the mysteries of the Trinity, the nuances of pneumatology, or the secrets of eschatology. Instead, Jesus emphasized his love for them through action and demonstrated for his disciples just what it means to be a sacrificial, servant-follower.

The story of Jesus washing the disciples' feet is an incredible example of the humility and life of service he modeled for us. The perfect and holy God of the universe incarnated as a man did the inconceivable. The day before he was to suffer immeasurably, Jesus chose to wash the crusty, smelly feet of those whom he loved dear. By this act, he extended extravagant grace to Peter, who was always rash and impulsive, to Judas, the man who would betray him a day later, and to the rest of his disciples.

This act was also inconceivable from a cultural perspective. In Jewish culture, it was typically the poor slave who stooped down low and washed the feet of the host and his guests. By defying cultural norms and choosing to humbly serve, Jesus gave us an example to follow. Ultimately, Jesus's greatest example of servanthood was prophetically loving all the way to the cross for the sake of the world. If we decide to be a follower of The Way (Acts 9:2), then we are invited to model our lives after the one who paved the way.

THEOLOGY WITHOUT LOVE IS DEAD

Don't get me wrong—Theology matters. There is no question it is a life and death endeavor. In some ways, complex theology is only necessary in practice because toxic theology exists to the extent that it does. The marginalization and domestication of others through dominance and ideological rhetoric, in the garbs of pseudo-liberative religion, has demanded further relationally-saturated theological complexity. Therefore, opposing theologies have always been in a symbiotic relationship with one another. For thousands upon thousands of years, humans have participated in an endless cycle of made-up God-talk needing to counteract made-up God-talk.

Crafting complex theology can be a fun and noble endeavor and is also needed to counteract toxic theologies. However, when we are engaging in theological mastery so that it stays in the head and puffs out like a peacock's feathers to impress or oppress, you know we are missing the point. As important as theology is, theologizing must be done for more than winning arguments. The hope is that we are engaging in theology that liberates and aims to help us all connect and love one another.

What if the point of a healthy, spiritual-based religion—*religion* being the structure, form, and rituals that come from a deep, communal spirituality—was to love? What if our religion was meant to be more like what the ancient Christian mystical writer had in mind when he wrote, "Religion that God our Father accepts as pure and faultless is this: to look after orphans and widows in their distress and to keep oneself from being polluted by the world" (James 1:27).

As you continue to reconstruct your faith, consider this question: What if the healthiest type of reconstruction was one in which you continually practiced and adored the presence of the Divine and where sacrificial and loving service toward your neighbor, yourself, and all of creation was your primary aim?

I know countless people who are stuck on the D/R journey, pressing pause on their lives, because they think they don't have the right answers. They have convinced themselves that the fruits of this new way to live in the world, a life they are continuing to piece together, can't blossom until they have finished building their new theological castles. In their minds, they must spend countless hours deconstructing every theological morsel they remember from their past while critically evaluating each new morsel that presents itself. Unfortunately, analysis can lead to paralysis. A person can have an active mind but live a passive and paralyzed life.

Now, I understand. That makes sense from a trauma and neuro-biological perspective. The brain is a meaning-making machine that needs to make sense of the religious, traumatic upheaval (and anything related to it) so as not to be hurt again. But what if this "pressing pause" manages to send all of the blood to our brains while our hearts dry out and shrivel up? At some point along our journey, the defibrillator, that shocked our heart and began our disquieted quest to find *all* of the answers to *all* of our questions, now serves to stop the same heart it restarted. Our original goal to reconstruct a vibrant faith—a faith that is secure in Divine love and demonstrates itself by a wholistic love that propels us to love and serve others—has been hijacked without our knowing.

As I have matured, I am no longer impressed with people's eloquent theologies or sassy deconstructive diatribes (not even my own). I'm now impressed by different things. Transformative love is where the theological rubber meets the messy, rocky, and swerving roads of everyday life. Nowadays, I experience a sense of awe:

- When I witness the intimate and vulnerable relationship between my friend and his partner as I visit with them.

- From the inspiration I draw from hearing my cousin describe the time of meditative silence he has carved out of his morning to spend with God.

- When I watch a person, who was deeply hurt, do the unthinkable and forgive a family member who selfishly betrayed them.

- From my wonderment at seeing my neighbor's love-saturated and embodied theology flow out of her with each person she encounters.

- When I see a group of people in the freezing cold picketing a company who was going to destroy a beautiful culture and ecosystem.

- From my amazement at the respect and value for life reflected in the young boy delighted to catch the biggest fish of his life only to lovingly put it right back in the water.

- When I see the man walk over, swipe his debit card, and hand the gas pump to a young couple he has overheard debating how they are going to make it home.

If reconstruction is focused solely on finding the right beliefs about God, then we are on the wrong trajectory. I suggest it is primarily about *how* we believe and only partially about *what* we believe. I am not creating a false dichotomy here. I am merely suggesting that theology without love is dead. I am inviting us to avoid using theologizing as a defense mechanism which keeps us from living the life of love God intended for us. Our task is to avoid becoming a theological glutton and intentionally consider how our beliefs are reflected in our actions. To the degree we have right theology is the degree to which we have right relationships.

The Christian life is about *inspiration* that leads to *perspiration* in a context of *conspiration* or there will be *expiration*. It is not enough to merely be inspired by the Bible or provocative books and podcasts from authors and eloquent teachers. It is not enough to be a master of deconstruction. Deconstruction without reconstruction is simply destruction. A static state of destruction is antithetical to God because, as Leonard Sweet says, "God is a God of motion, of movement, of mission. Or, as it is popular nowadays to say, two-thirds of the word 'God' is go."[3] Death and destruction is never the end of the story. God, in each moment, is always on the move, breathing life, love, and hope into all the world and into every creature and situation.

Regardless of our lack of answers to the mysteries of God and life, we are ultimately called to perspire—to undertake a mission, to sweat out and exude the love of Christ utilizing the unique gifts and personalities God has given us. But we are to do this as a conspiration, a joint effort with other religious refugees and love-sick warriors who are also on a mission. If we reach a point where we are no longer inspired, missional members of the body of Christ in God's service to the world, part of our soul will shrivel up and die. The Divine never meant for us to perpetually build theological castles, live purposelessly, or live without mission and movement, isolated and alone.

VALUED-BASED LOVING

Have you ever seen the movie *Castaway*? Put yourself in the place of Tom Hanks' character. After your plane crashes, you find yourself alive on a deserted island. Everyone back home thinks you are dead and, eventually, holds a funeral in your honor. You finally get rescued and fly home, bringing your precious volleyball (who was your only friend on the island), to see your friends and family.

Imagine that once you have settled in, you find a video of your own funeral. And as you watch the ceremony, you see your loved ones go up to the microphone to talk about their memories of you. If this was a real scenario, what would they say about:

- the sort of person you were?

- your greatest strengths and qualities?

- the way you treated them?[4]

Now, what is it you would want them to say? Maybe you would want them to say, among other noble things, something like, "She always lived according to her values." If I'm honest, that's what I would want people to say about me. But what are values?

Values are words that signify our chosen manner in which we want to engage ourselves, others, and those around us. Values are what we want to stand for in the world; they are our inner compass. What we would want to hear our friends and loved ones say about us at our funeral is a good indication of the nature of our values.

Values are not goals. While goals can be attained, values cannot. Values guide us as we work to achieve our goals and experience a meaningful life. They hopefully prevent us from living a life that robs us from the experience of healthy connections and divine success.

For example, getting married was a goal of mine while being a loving, supportive, and faithful husband are values I held long before meeting my wife. Those values are tied up in what I understand a husband to be.

Values propel our actions. Our minds simply won't allow a disconnect between our values and our actions. We can deceive ourselves by thinking we have certain values, but our actions in our everyday lives reveal whether or not those values actually exist. A man who says he values protecting the environment but cannot be bothered to even separate his items for recycling, is just fooling himself and saying what he thinks others want to hear.

Because of the complexity of life, our multiple values can regularly come into conflict with one another. A wealthy woman may value her time, her comfort, and her privacy in addition to caring for the environment. When she books her air travel, she must decide if traveling commercial, to help the environment, is more important than the comfort, privacy, and efficiency of her private jet. A person with lesser means might need to make a similar decision about bicycling or driving to work (and living close enough to work to do so). We each must make our own value-based decisions.

Consider the Amish for a moment. We tend to think of them as a backward community that simply shuns technology, but I believe that is a complete misunderstanding. The Amish value community above almost anything else. They are not afraid of new technology—they are simply very intentional and only adopt technology that supports their values. When a new technology is released, one member of the community will try it out and weigh its benefits and its drawbacks as related to the impact on the community.

The community tried automobiles when they were invented, but decided that it would take community members far away for long stretches of time. They determined that the benefits of transportation did not outweigh the cost to their community. Their value was more important to them than keeping up with the times. You may be thinking, "But what about those Amish guys on tractors?" Amish people's use of tractors, and other farming technology, is the best example of value-based decisions. Farming vehicles, not meant primarily for transportation, bring benefits without adversely affecting the community.

Their decisions on whether or not to use telephones or electricity were made for similar reasons. The point is that the Amish make intentional decisions about their lives and behavior based on their highest values rather than letting the wider society make those decisions for them. Living within bicycle distance of work, which would likely mean living in a smaller home, is always an option; but it reveals that most of us have other values that we consider more important than the environment—and that is OK. You don't have to let society dictate your values.

Have you ever taken the time to name and label your own values? If not, you really should. Below are some examples to jumpstart your own time of reflection:

- **Acceptance/Self-Acceptance:** to be accepting to yourself and others

- **Authenticity:** to be genuine and keep it real with yourself and others

- **Spiritual:** to connect with that which is transcendent

- **Love:** to take actions that put another's interests and desires above your own

- **Gratitude:** to express appreciation for the people and experiences in your life

- **Justice:** to advocate for and support those who are oppressed and marginalized

- **Curiosity:** to ask questions with the intention of discovering answers that provide understanding

- **Adventure:** to take risks and explore new experiences

- **Cooperation:** to partner with others toward common goals

- **Forgiveness:** to acknowledge a wrong done to you by yourself or another, but that you demand no further punishment nor harbor further ill-will related to that offense

- **Courage:** to act to achieve a goal in the face of threat or difficulty[5]

- **Honesty:** to speak truthfully and completely

- **Integrity:** to act in accord with your values in private as well as public

- **Self-Control**: to exercise restraint over desires to act against your values

- **Patience**: to wait for a desired goal without entitlement

- **Persistence**: to continue to act towards a goal in the face of obstacles or fatigue

- **Kindness**: to treat others in a gentle manner that pleases them

- **Humility**: to act without the need or desire for praise or recognition from others

- **Transparency**: to open your actions to the visibility and scrutiny of others

- **Safety**: to provide an environment sheltered from threats to your person or that of others

- **Community**: to belong to a group with similar beliefs, values, behaviors and interests

Did you see some of your own core values on that list? Which ones take precedence in your life? What are your top five? What values do you have that weren't on the list? In the course of the D/R journey, which can be a roller coaster of ups and downs, it is important to know what your values are. Your feelings and moods can change. Your active thought-spitter, otherwise known as your brain, can get stuck in the past or worry about the future. Once you identify and prioritize your values, they become anchors that help you navigate through the stormy emotional and mental seas vying for your attention. Despite your uncertainty about different Christian doctrines, and what exactly happens in the afterlife, they help ensure that you live a life worth living in the present. After all, the present is all that we have. Let's live in it!

WHEN IN DOUBT (OR DISORIENTATION), LOVE

What if you engaged in value-based actions regardless of whether you have all of the answers to life, faith, and God? What if you lived and loved according to your values despite struggling emotionally and spiritually?

What law in the universe says that we must have complete certainty before we love and connect with others or with God? Is that the standard we set for our spouse? Is it the same law we follow when it comes to our children? Would we dare apply this logic to strangers in need of assistance? We don't even fully know ourselves, but it would seem silly to suggest we shouldn't love ourselves until we have everything figured out.

There is a model for this in Alcoholics Anonymous (AA). The third of the 12-steps—for members to give their will and lives over to God—was problematic for the earliest members of AA, many of whom were agnostic (and/or themselves on a D/R journey). They found themselves in a life-or-death predicament, aware that the best psychiatrists, doctors, and religious leaders had tried desperately to help them, and hundreds of others like them, but had failed miserably. However, as time went on, they saw that the hope of members, who had been able to turn their will and lives over to God, was an essential part of their recovery and sobriety process. It was a dilemma that could not wait to be solved.

So, they re-worked the third step to say, "the God of your understanding," recognizing that every person is on a journey to understand the Higher Power of our universe—a journey that will never end in this life. It was not some "new age" drivel that many Christians, who have never belonged to AA, deride it as being. Surrendering to the mystery and higher power that was God was paramount to the healing and reconstruction of their lives. Their lives depended upon action. And that action could not wait until they sorted out their theological questions. They needed to heal their broken relationships with others and help others who were hurting, or they could not recover.

There is no universal law that dictates we must be free from disorientation before we are potent forces of love in the world. Life is full of beauty. Life is full of suffering and loss. There is no way to avoid life's complex combination of chaos and order. When in doubt, and feeling disoriented, engage in value-based living. Love with gusto!

In the reconstruction phase of your spiritual journey, you get to call the shots. You get to figure out what you believe, why you believe it, and how you want to live in the world. Of course, that is no easy task. The dizzying mess of the D/R journey is bound to unhinge any unwelcoming soul. Yet, the D/R journey is invaluable. It is the opportunity to exponentially grow and mature. It is an invitation to know God more intimately. It gives each of us the freedom to untether ourselves from the religious Matrix in which we must adopt a false identity or live in an illusory world. Snipping the umbilical cord to the big Other is the darkened and inevitably enlightened path toward emotional, relational, and spiritual maturity. Engaging in value-based living, regardless of your feelings or circumstances, is an invitation to reconstructing well.

If you have been traveling through the D/R journey, feeling bogged down, and isolating yourself—refusing to tap into your potential as tenderhearted lover—open your heart to the practice and sacred discipline of loving others; especially those you disagree with. You are as unique as the flowers in a field. Romans 12:6 says, "We have different gifts, according to the grace given to each of us." First Peter 4:10 says, "Each of you should use whatever gift you have received to serve others, as faithful stewards of God's grace in its various forms."

You were never meant to sit passively on a couch, bitter and broken, playing armchair theologians. You are not called to live vicariously through characters in the pixel fantasylands of television and movies or through people in their carefully selected, forever-happy photos on social media. You are meant to be an active adventurer in this game called Life even when you don't have all of the answers. Spiritual gifts are in your DNA so that you can accomplish a mission of love, service, and grace to others. The key is not losing that big picture during your D/R journey.

NO REGRETS, BE YOURSELF IN GOD

Bronnie Ware, a palliative caregiver who was able to hear the vulnerable, tragic, and treasured stories of those on their death bed, wrote *The Top Five Regrets of the Dying*.[6] She discovered that one of the top regrets of those coming close to the end of their precious time on earth, was, *"I wish I'd had the courage to live a life true to myself, not the life others expected of me."*

In her book, Bronnie tells the story of a woman named Grace. For over fifty years, Grace remained unhappily married to a cruel and controlling husband. She longed to live apart from his constricting grasp to perhaps travel and live a more adventurous and happier life. When her husband went into a nursing home, she thought she finally had her chance. She thought she could be free. Suddenly, she began to feel terribly ill and, after going into the hospital, was diagnosed with a terminal illness.

The tragedy of Grace's story was that the terminal illness was caused by her husband's habitual smoking. As her strength and vitality slowly drained from her mind and body, filled with feelings of anger and regret, she humbly shared with Bronnie, "Why didn't I just do what I wanted? Why did I let him rule me? Why wasn't I strong enough?" Not long after sharing those words, her life came to an end.

I don't know about you, but I don't want to be like that precious woman, Grace. At the end of my life, I don't want to have regrets because I was afraid of being the unique person God has co-created and co-shaped me to become. I prefer suffering the social consequences of exclusion to pretending and living a lie that conforms to people's religious projections of how I should live and what I should believe. My hope is that the embodied thought that God loves us as we are, and not as others think we should be, will give us bold courage to live a life true to ourselves and according to our unique talents and values.

MIRANDA'S STORY

Miranda had been on the D/R journey for eight months and had been plagued with obsessive thoughts about God and Hell. Fearing where her doubts and questions might lead her, she felt depressed and anxious much of the time. Miranda would constantly try to think her way out of her theological conundrums, but it was to no avail. She tried to distract herself, but like lost puppies, her sadness and anxiety always seemed to follow her. She had three good friends, but she wouldn't confide in them because she had convinced herself she needed to handle her doubts, questions, and emotional pain on her own.

After I helped her explore some of her values, Miranda realized she valued intimacy, encouragement, fairness and justice, courage, physical fitness, and emotional and spiritual health. As a Christian, she relied on her faith, as reflected in the experiences she had with God, and her belief in the inspiration of the Scriptures (although she wrestled a lot with what *inspiration* actually meant), to help her identify her values. Reading books by Brené Brown, Rachel Held Evans, Sarah Bessey, and other literary mentors also served to solidify her core values. Miranda came to realize that despite her confusion about a lot of issues surrounding faith, many of which seemed outside of her control, identifying her own values was immediately within her control. Identifying her core values empowered her since they were intrinsic (coming from the inside of her) and not extrinsic (coming from the outside of her).

Miranda's decision to intentionally identify her core values was instrumental in allowing her to reconstruct her life and her faith. She didn't wait until she was healed (whatever that meant) before beginning to live a life worth living. Since encouragement was one of her core values, Miranda began to encourage herself on a daily basis. She also chose three days a week to intentionally encourage others. Recognizing she had not accorded fitness—another of Miranda's values—its proper place in her value hierarchy, she decided to start running again. She also joined an online group with members who were deconstructing their faith. Instead of being isolated, Miranda reminded herself that she valued courage and intimacy. So, she acquired an unholy huddle, full of Somewheres and Story Catchers, where she found both tremendous support and a place where she was able to support others in their own struggles.

Deconstructing other people's values, that you unknowingly or knowingly adopted as your own, is part of the D/R journey. Slaying the false gods in your life—those powerful figures whose beliefs and values you internalized—is integral to integration. Sometimes gods must die and be given a funeral so that new life can spring forth. Identifying your values, choosing them for yourself and living them out is a part of the reconstruction process. This process can restore authenticity and congruence to your life, propelling you to live the life *you* are meant to live and to lovingly serve others with more of your authentic self. You will be enlivened and empowered when you confidently engage in goals that are driven by your own values and not those of other people.

LOVING OTHERS THROUGH STORY CATCHING

We can't talk about love without talking about story catching, the act of listening and empathizing with people whose values may be different than our own. James 1:19 encourages us to "be quick to listen, slow to speak," instead of being quick to speak and slow to listen (the default for many of us). Truth be told, despite my therapist training, there are times when I am guilty of the latter. There are times when I zone out as a person is sharing his or her heart with me. I catch myself drifting, begin to listen authentically again, only to drift off a short time later.

The truth is we desperately want answers to the mysteries of the universe, but we can't even focus and be present with the person right in front of us. Despite its difficulty, I am convinced that one of the most practical and powerful ways people can love others is by listening to them. Yes, you need your unholy huddle. But I would also encourage you to be a part of someone else's unholy huddle. Serving others, by empathically listening to their hearts and stories, changes us and those we listen to in deep and profound ways.

HANNAH'S GRIEF

In the Hebrew Bible, there's a story of Elkanah and his two wives, Hannah and Peninnah. The author tells us that "Peninnah had children, but Hannah had none" (1 Sam. 1:2). In Hannah's culture, having children—being "fruitful" (Gen. 1:28)—was a sign of blessing and favor from God. But because Hannah was unable to bear a child, the conclusion of most of her friends and family was that she was cursed. To add to Hannah's grief, Peninnah liked to "provoke her in order to irritate her," so much so that Hannah "wept and would not eat." And what is worse, "this went on year after year" (1 Sam. 1:6–7). If Peninnah had done that to some of the women I know, she would have been knocked out cold, but that was not Hannah's style. She silently suffered the shame and disgrace of barrenness.

Hannah, in the middle of her shame and grief, was desperate and needed an empathic story catcher. She needed her husband Elkanah, the most important person in her universe, to validate her experience and to empathize with her suffering, shame, and sorrow. Instead, Elkanah, a man of God, said, "Hannah, why are you weeping? Why don't you eat? Why are you downhearted? Don't I mean more to you than ten sons?" (v. 8). Way to guilt and shame your wife, buddy!

Needless to say, Elkanah could have used a few lessons on relational intelligence and the sacred art of empathic listening. He had spent many years with his wife and still didn't have a clue about the depths of her grief. He might as well have said, "Hey, babe, why are you so upset about what you don't have? Don't feel that way. You've got me, your knight in shining armor!" Epic failure.

He was clueless. But, keep in mind, they didn't have marriage seminars or access to classic books like *Men Are from Mars, Women Are from Venus* back then.

Can you relate to Hannah? Have you experienced something similar to what Hannah endured during your own spiritual makeover? Perhaps you tried to share your story with someone you thought would be empathic and compassionate only to have them shut you down, minimize your pain, or invalidate your feelings. Maybe your friends or family were more subtle in the way they brushed you off, advising you to read your Bible or to get something to eat to relax.

As story catchers, we don't have to conform to our culture. We don't have to let obstacles get in the way of compassionately listening to the stories of others or, in the midst of silence and solitude, of listening to ourselves. It's not easy, but we can choose to embody like-mindedness, sympathy, compassion, and humility wherever we go.

Practically, we can go against the grain by choosing not to shun but to honor our own messy, imperfect emotional and spiritual experiences—and more importantly, that of others. We can intentionally lean in and listen to pain and suffering wherever we find it. Story catchers throw perfect*shun*ism out the window and vow to gracefully encounter both the horrid and the holy, within and without, until the day they breathe their last breath.

We can take our story-catching cues from Jesus, who was the epitome of a fearless story catcher. He did not shun his own difficult emotional experiences but expressed his feelings freely (Mark 14:34; John 11:35), diving deep into the pain and shame of others (John 4:1–26; 8:1–11).

We don't need to bear false witness about our experiences, nor do we need to encourage others to do so. We can give ourselves and others permission to be messy and imperfect because we know that God loves all of us just as we are. Of course, God doesn't leave us where we are. God gently guides us into greater measures of abundant living: code for the degree to which we are able to love and be loved by God, others, and ourselves.

Prioritizing relationships will mean intentionally choosing people over pixels. One practice, if you need help following through on your commitment to be a story catcher, is to leave yourself a note on your refrigerator or your desk at work. You could write, "How many times this week have I been face-to-face with others catching their stories?" or "How many times this week have I been face-to-face with others letting them catch my stories?" Another practice might be to meet a friend for coffee, at the same time and place every Saturday morning, taking a sabbatical from your devices while you're there. Don't just silence your cell phone. Turn it off and keep it out of sight. Forget about your e-mail or texts for an hour or so and focus on each other.

LOVE THOSE WHO ARE DIFFERENT THAN YOU

The Israelites were once an oppressed people in Egypt. And once they became free, they turned around and oppressed, enslaved, and annihilated others (all in the name of God) to steal their land. They were a perfect example of the fact that hurt and traumatized people tend to hurt and traumatize others. There is a sad irony in the oppressed becoming the oppressor, the victim becoming the victimizer, and the former fundamentalist—pretending to be free from the constraints of toxic religion—becoming fundamental-ish.

Fundamental-ish people are those with sacrosanct religious beliefs who take a prideful and exclusivist stance that dehumanizes others. There is a difference between attacking people and attacking ideas. But unfortunately, I have seen far too many religious refugees become free from toxic religion only to attack others for not believing the way they do.

Just the other day, I saw a Facebook post from someone who could be considered a *done*. They have been on the D/R journey for about a year, love Jesus, and are passionate about issues of equality and social justice. On Facebook, they responded to a conservative evangelical, who publicly supported particular public policies, writing, "You call yourself a Christian! You are definitely not following Jesus and you are definitely not Christian. I don't know who you are praying to, but it can't be to the God I believe in."

How can we harshly judge anyone and say that they are not a Christian? How can we say definitively who is in and who is out? The apostle Paul, or Saul of Tarsus as he was known to some, was a well-known terrorist who persecuted Christians for the glory of God. King David, a man after God's own heart, lied, manipulated, murdered, and womanized. Aren't we all hanging out at different stations in life? I can understand calling someone's actions un-Christlike. But to confidently declare that someone is not in relationship with Christ, or God, is more than a bit arrogant. Why do we expect to be treated with love, patience, and respect by those in the church while we treat them the complete opposite way? Aren't we supposedly *woke*? Isn't the conservative evangelical Christian, who holds to inerrancy and voted for a different president than we did, just as loved and valued by God as anyone else? Judgment, hate, and name-calling do not change anyone. All they do is put people on the defensive and sever relationships.

Confession: I have a slight aversion to Facebook. I recently realized that my aversion to Facebook is due to the same reason I wouldn't want to attend some family gatherings. I'm not enticed to mingle with people, who I care about, while they complain, bicker, fight, and slander one another in the name of "Truth."

It is both nauseating and heartbreaking. People are arrogantly adamant that they have a monopoly on capital "T" truth and refuse to slow down and genuinely listen to the other's position. And, that's the other problem—OTHERS. Others are dehumanized and reduced to labels rather than precious human beings with hopes, dreams, fears, longings, and passions. There are no winners in Facebook theological battles. I am all for wrestling through weighty matters, but is it possible we can be so focused on arguments, and proving our points, that we forget about the person behind the keyboard? There must be another way.

We can fight oppressive ideas with our own robust ideas and subversive action. But we can do it while loving those same people whose ideas and actions we find so repulsive. We can be passionate about what we believe, even calling out injustice when we see it, and at the same time view people as created in the image of God. We can have empathy and patience with our spouses, leaders, and friends, who may not be hanging out in the same station as we are, and still live according to our values. We can create bridges through dialogue instead of raising defensive barriers against those with whom we disagree. This is especially important if we are seeking to lovingly change minds and hearts. We can model God's perfect love as we actively love those who are different than us.

MY ENCOURAGEMENT

For a while, you might feel as if you are living in a haunted house. You will go through your days, doing what you need to do to survive and thrive when, suddenly and unexpectedly, the ghosts of intrusive memories, or disturbing, fear-based religious doctrines pop up. And they will bring along ghastly pain, sadness, anger, and misery, throwing you into a tailspin. I invite you to be kind toward yourself. Life is too short to treat yourself like an enemy and an outcast. You deserve better than that. Why should you seek to treat everyone else around you with Christlikeness except yourself? You shouldn't. Practice self-compassion in the midst of your struggles.

I also invite you—even as you are full of doubts, fears, and the rest of the difficult emotions that come with deconstructing your faith—to reconstruct and choose to follow Jesus' example of loving and serving others. I invite you to do this in the midst of the tailspin. As you do, you may find that it truly is more blessed to give than to receive. You may also find that the more you give your love, the more love finds you, and the more you find love.

The topsy-turvy force of love, led by the Spirit and with a trajectory of justice, is knocking on the door of your heart waiting for you to open up and receive your subversive instruction and to engage in your individual mission. Be brave. Be courageous. Be vulnerable. Don't let bitterness, anger, and unforgiveness take up space in your soul. Conspire with God. Become the change you so desperately want to see in the church and in the world.

You are a fierce lover. You can feel it in your bones. Regardless of the labels you have been given by others, you know what you are called to do. Kick shame and fear in the face and do it. Live according to your values. Unleash your gifts and passions into the world and the lives of others.

Love others who are different than you. Become a story catcher for the relationship-starved people around you. There is a world full of people who are longing to be heard and who are craving an opportunity to tell their stories to someone who cares. Remember, the word *ear* is in the word *heart* to remind us that listening well is the fastest way to one's heart.

Love, as I envision it, is considered weakness by those who are violence-prone and who value persuasive theological propositions over people. Nevertheless, that love is fierce. It is strong. It is powerful. It pierces and transforms every part of who we are—if we let it. To some, it may feel like a hot cauldron of liquid-judgment pouring down into their mouth, burning their esophagus and singeing their heart—especially if they are hell-bent on oppressing and marginalizing others. It is the strongest force on this planet. After religion is no more and all of the hay and stubble of humanity's religious creations are burned up, all that will remain is love.

QUESTIONS

1. What are your thoughts about obsessive theological reflection being a defense mechanism to avoid practical and personal matters of life? Can we be so heavenly-minded that our earthly relationships suffer because of it?

2. Why is love the most powerful force on this planet?

3. What are the benefits or pitfalls of reconstructing a faith where service to others is paramount?

4. Why do some people get stuck deconstructing and never engage in reconstructing?

5. What is your answers to the thought exercise about watching a video of your funeral? What would you love to hear your friends saying about: The sort of person you were? Your greatest strengths and qualities? And, the way you treated them?

6. What are your top five values in rank order?

7. What are your thoughts about engaging in value-based actions regardless of how you feel and whether you have all the answers to life, faith, and God?

8. What is your reaction to one of the top regrets of those on their death beds: "I wish I'd had the courage to live a life true to myself, and not the life others expected of me"?

ENDNOTES

INTRODUCTION

1. Rachel Held Evans, *Searching for Sunday: Loving, Leaving, and Finding the Church* (Nashville: Thomas Nelson Inc., 2015), 48–49.

CHAPTER ONE

1. Thom S. Rainer, "Hope for Dying Churches," January 16, 2018, https://factsandtrends.net/2018/01/16/hope-for-dying-churches/.

2. See Allison de Jong, "Protestants Decline, More Have No Religion in a Sharply Shifting Religious Landscape," ABC News poll, May 10, 2018, https://abcnews.go.com/Politics/protestants-decline-religion-sharply-shifting-religious-landscape-poll/story?id=54995663.

3. David Kinnaman and Mark Matlock, *Faith for Exiles: 5 Ways for a New Generation to Follow Jesus in Digital Babylon* (Grand Rapids: Baker Books, 2019), 15.

4. See Barna, "Church Attendance Trends Around the Country," May 26, 2017, https://www.barna.com/research/church-attendance-trends-around-country/.

5. See Phyllis Tickle, *The Great Emergence: How Christianity Is Changing and Why* (Grand Rapids: Baker Books, 2012).

6. Brian D. McLaren, *The Great Spiritual Migration: How the World's Largest Religion is Seeking a Better Way to Be Christian* (New York: Convergent, 2017), xii.

7. Diana Butler Bass, *Grounded: Finding God in the World--a Spiritual Revolution* (New York: HarperOne, 2017), 21.

8. Josh Packard and Ashleigh Hope, *Church Refugees: Sociologists Reveal Why People Are Done with the Church but Not Their Faith* (Loveland, Colorado: Group, 2015), 14.

9. Ibid., 28.

10. Kathy Escobar, *Faith Shift: Finding Your Way Forward When Everything You Believe Is Coming Apart* (New York: Convergent Books, 2014), 20.

11. David Kinnaman and Aly Hawkins, *You Lost Me: Why Young Christians Are Leaving Church . . . and Rethinking Faith* (Grand Rapids: Baker Books, 2016), 64–65.

12. Ibid., 92–93.

13. Josh Packard and Todd W. Ferguson, "Being Done: Why People Leave the Church, But Not Their Faith," *Sociological Perspectives* 62, no. 4 (August 2019), 499–517.

14. https://www.youtube.com/watch?v=NeNKHqpBcgc

15. Packard and Hope, 91.

16. Heinz Streib, Ralph W. Hood, Barbara Keller, Rosina-Martha Csoff, and Christopher F. Silver, *Deconversion: Qualitative and Quantitative Results from Cross-Cultural Research in Germany and the United States of America: Cross-Cultural Research in Germany and the United States of America* (Germany: Vandenhoeck & Ruprecht, 2009), 232.

17. Kinnaman and Matlock, 97.

18. Packard and Hope, 23.

19. Ibid., 100.

20. Packard and Ferguson, 505.

21. Ibid., 509.

22. Nancy L. Eiesland, "Barriers and Bridges: Relating the Disability Rights Movement and Religious Organizations." In *Human Disability and the Service of God: Reassessing Religious Practice*, ed. Nancy Eiesland and Don E. Saliers (Nashville, TN: Abingdon Press, 1998), 218.

23. Evans, 51–52.

24. Lisa Gungor, *The Most Beautiful Thing I've Seen: Opening Your Eyes to Wonder* (Grand Rapids, Michigan: Zondervan, 2018), 104.

25. Philip Salim Francis, *When Art Disrupts Religion: Aesthetic Experience and the Evangelical Mind* (New York: Oxford University Press, 2017), 3.

26. Ibid., 42.

27. Michael Foust. "Hillsong's Marty Sampson: 'I'm Genuinely Losing My Faith'." ChristianHeadlines.com. Salem Web Network, August 13, 2019. https://www.christianheadlines.com/contributors/michael-foust/hillsong-s-marty-sampson-i-m-genuinely-losing-my-faith.html.

28. Packard and Hope, 40.

29. Ibid., 44.

30. Rick Hanson, *Hardwiring Happiness: The New Brain Science of Contentment, Calm, And Confidence* (New York: Harmony Books, 2016), xxvi.

31. Stephen D. Moore, "Mark and Empire: 'Zealot' and 'Postcolonial' Readings," 134–48 in *Postcolonial Theologies: Divinity and Empire*, edited by Catherine Keller, Michael Nausner, and Mayra Rivera (St. Louis: Chalice Press, 2004), 138.

32. Elizabeth Baker, "My Evangelical Church Is Gaslighting Me, But I Refuse to Fall For It Anymore," Huffington Post, November 28, 2018, https://www.huffpost.com/entry/evangelical-christians-trump_n_5bfc326de4b03b230fa57ae9.

33. Paul Matthew Harrison, *Deconversions: My Journey Through Evangelical Christianity* (Galena, IL: Clever Words, 2019), i.

34. See Reba Riley, *Post-Traumatic Church Syndrome: One Woman's Desperate, Funny, and Healing Journey to Explore 30 Religions by Her 30th Birthday* (New York: Howard Books, 2016).

35. Marlene Winell, *Leaving the Fold: A Guide to Former Fundamentalists and Others Leaving Their Religion* (Berkeley, CA: Apocryphile Press, 2007).

36. Valerie Tarico, "Religious Trauma Syndrome: Psychologist reveals how organized religion can lead to mental health problems," September 5, 2019, https://www.rawstory.com/2019/09/religious-trauma-syndrome-psychologist-reveals-how-organized-religion-can-lead-to-mental-health-problems/.

37. Linda Kay Klein, Pure: *Inside the Evangelical Movement That Shamed a Generation of Young Women and How I Broke Free* (New York, NY, Touchstone, An Imprint of Simon & Schuster, Inc, 2018), 8.

CHAPTER TWO

1. Escobar, 20.

2. Winell, 16.

3. *Relevant Magazine*, "Hillsong Songwriter Marty Sampson Says He's Losing His Christian Faith," August 12, 2019, https://relevantmagazine.com/culture/hillsong-songwriter-marty-sampson-says-hes-losing-his-Christian-faith/.

4. Karen Adriana Lee and Peter Madsen Gubi. "Breaking Up with Jesus: A Phenomenological Exploration of the Experience of Deconversion from an Evangelical Christian Faith to Atheism." *Mental Health, Religion & Culture*, vol. 22, no. 2, Feb. 2019, 171–184.

5. Ibid.

6. Riley, 10.

7. Keith Giles, September 20, 2019, "Finding a Firm Foundation for Reconstruction," https://www.patheos.com/blogs/keithgiles/2019/09/finding-a-firm-foundation-for-reconstruction/.

8. Andrew Newberg and Mark Robert Waldman, *Born to Believe: God, Science, and the Origin of Ordinary and Extraordinary Beliefs* (New York: Free Press, 2008), 11.

9. Harrison, 323.

10. Ibid., 118.

11. Ibid., 125.

12. Ibid., 323.

13. Ibid., 320.

14. Ibid., 323.

15. Winell, 19.

16. Packard and Hope, 75.

17. Frank Schaeffer, *Why I Am an Atheist Who Believes in God: How to Give Love, Create Beauty and Find Peace* (North Charleston, South Carolina: Createspace, 2014).

18. I picked up the term a/theist from Peter Rollins, *How (Not) to Speak of God* (Brewster, Massachusetts: Paraclete Press, 2011).

19. Beth Allen Slevcove, *Broken Hallelujahs: Learning to Grieve the Big and Small Losses of Life* (Downers Grove, Illinois: IVP Books, 2016), 64.

20. Alexander J. Shaia, *Heart and Mind: the Four-Gospel Journey for Radical Transformation,* 2nd Edition (Santa Fe, NM, USA: Journey of Quadratos, LLC, 2017), p. 96

CHAPTER THREE

1. Richard Rohr, *The Naked Now: Learning to See as the Mystics See* (New York: Crossroads, 2009), 125.

2. 2 Corinthians 10:5

3. I picked up the term "sub-Christlike" from Gregory A. Boyd, *Crucifixion of the Warrior God: Volumes 1 & 2.* (Minneapolis: Augsburg Fortress, 2017).

4. Yes, I am going back and forth between "Old Testament" and "Hebrew Bible." That is in part because the "Old Testament" is how people have referenced it, as opposed to my preference of "Hebrew Bible," which to me is a much more respectful title (especially to my brothers and sisters in the Jewish faith).

5. 1 Corinthians 3:11.

6. See Randal Rauser, "Four Pitfalls for Apologists Defending Biblical Violence," August 12th, 2019, https://randalrauser.com/2019/08/four-pitfalls-for-apologists-defending-Biblical-violence/?fbclid=IwAR0VIzH6GJPZw_rGc-mzu194qXkOf68N6C2ikqG_Ht94Fm5-CaWSU-Z8VXew.

7. John Howard Yoder, *The Politics of Jesus: Vicit Agnus Noster,* 2nd Ed. (Grand Rapids, Michigan: Eerdman's Publication, 1994), 155.

8. Karl Forehand, *Apparent Faith: What Fatherhood Taught Me About the Father's Heart,* (Orange: California, Quoir, 2019), 55.

9. Peter Enns, *How the Bible Actually Works: In Which I Explain How an Ancient, Ambiguous, and Diverse Book Leads Us to Wisdom Rather than Answers— and Why That's Great News* (New York: HarperOne, 2019), 149.

CHAPTER FOUR

1. Walter Brueggemann, *The Message of The Psalms: A Theological Commentary,* (Minneapolis: Augsburg Fortress, 1984), 51.

2. Joshua A. Wilt., et al. "God's Role in Suffering: Theodicies, Divine Struggle, and Mental Health." *Psychology of Religion and Spirituality*, vol. 8, no. 4, Nov. 2016, pp. 352–362. EBSCOhost, doi:10.1037/rel0000058, 353.

3. C. Nathan DeWall, et al., "Acetaminophen Reduces Social Pain: Behavioral and Neural Evidence," *Psychological Science* 21, no. 7 (2010): 931–37, *Business Source Complete*, EBSCO*host*. 10.1177/0956797610374741.

4. See Louis J. Cozolino, *The Neuroscience of Human Relationships: Attachment and the Developing Social Brain*, (New York: Norton, 2006).

5. Judith Herman, *Trauma and Recovery: The Aftermath of Violence—from Domestic Abuse to Political Terror* (New York: Basic Books, 1977), 52.

6. Tarico.

7. American Psychiatric Association. *Diagnostic and Statistical Manual of Mental Disorders: DSM-5*. (Arlington, VA., 2017), 271.

8. Philip Salim Francis, 127.

9. Slevcove, 88.

10. Evans, 53.

11. Janet Hagberg and Robert A. Guelich, *The Critical Journey: Stages in the Life of Faith* (Winnipeg: Media Production Services Unit, Manitoba Education, 2011), 120.

12. Gungor, 102-103.

13. Francis, 121-122.

14. Winell, 20.

15. Lee and Gubi, 178.

16. Rile, 114.

CHAPTER FIVE

1. J. David Creswell, et al., "Neural Correlates of Dispositional Mindfulness During Affect Labeling," *Psychosomatic Medicine* 69, no. 6 (2007): 560–65, *PsycINFO*, EBSCO*host*. http://0-dx.doi.org.library.alliant.edu/10.1097/PSY.0b013e3180f6171f.

2. Matthew Lieberman., "Diaries: A Healthy Choice," *The New York Times*, December 12, 2012, http://www.nytimes.com/roomfordebate/2012/11/25/will-diaries-be-published-in-2050/diaries-a-healthy-choice/.

3. Jon Frederickson, *Co-creating Change: Effective Dynamic Therapy Techniques* (Kansas City: Seven Leaves Press, 2013), 1.

4. Valerie Tarico, *Trusting Doubt: A Former Evangelical Looks at Old Beliefs in a New Light* (2nd Ed.) (Independence, Virginia: Oracle Institute Press, 2017), 242.

5. Proverbs 29:22.

6. Ephesians 4:26 (NRSV).

7. Packard and Hope, 35.

8. Amy Phillips, "The Resurrection of Self: How Deconversion from Religious Belief to Atheism Healed a History of Rejection, Trauma, and Shame." *Dissertation Abstracts International Section A: Humanities and Social Sciences,* vol. 77, no. 3–A(E), ProQuest Information & Learning, 2016.

9. Brené Brown, *The Gifts of Imperfection: Let Go of Who You Think You're Supposed to Be and Embrace Who You Are* (Center City, MN: Hazelden, 2010), 38.

10. Lewis B. Smedes, *Shame and Grace: Healing the Shame We Don't Deserve* (San Francisco: Harper SanFrancisco, 1993), 1.

11. See Ronda L. Dearing and June Price Tangney, eds., *Shame in the Therapy Hour* (Washington, DC: American Psychological Association, 2011), 6.

12. Curt Thompson, *The Soul of Shame: Retelling the Stories We Believe About Ourselves* (Downers Grove, Il: Intervarsity Press, 2015), 22.

13. Ibid., 31.

CHAPTER SIX

1. Christopher P. Fagundes, "Implicit negative evaluations about ex-partner predicts break-up adjustment: The brighter side of dark cognitions," *Cognition and Emotion*, 25(1), (2011): 164–73. doi:10.1080/09602011003683976.

2. Jerrold M. Post, and Alexander George, *Leaders and Their Followers in a Dangerous World: The Psychology of Political Behavior*, (Ithaca: Cornell University Press, 2004), 191.

3. Ibid., 187

CHAPTER SEVEN

1. Henry Nouwen, (2004). *Out of Solitude: Three Meditations on the Christian Life*. Notre Dame, IN: Ave Maria Press, 238.

2. Bessey, 115.

3. Beth Allen Slevcove, *Broken Hallelujahs: Learning to Grieve the Big and Small Losses of Life* (Downers Grove, IL: InterVarsity Press, 2016), 181.

4. Lisa F. Berkman and S. Leonard Syme, "Social Networks, Host Resistance, and Mortality: A Nine-year Follow-up Study of Alameda County Residents," *American Journal of Epidemiology* 109, no. 2 (1979):186–204.

5. Julianne Holt-Lunstad, Timothy B Smith, and J Bradley Layton, "Social Relationships and Mortality Risk: A Meta-analytic Review," *PLOS Medicine* 7(7) (2010), doi:10.1371/journal.pmed.1000316.

6. Simone Schnall, Kent D. Harber, Jeanine K. Stefanucci, and Dennis R. Proffitt. 2008. "Social Support and the Perception of Geographical Slant." *Journal of Experimental Social Psychology* 44 (5): 1246–55. doi:10.1016/j.jesp.2008.04.011.

7. James S. House, "Social Isolation Kills, but How and Why?" *Psychosomatic Medicine* 63, no. 2 (2001): 273–74.

8. John T. Cacioppo and William Patrick, *Loneliness: Human Nature and the Need for Social Connection* (New York: Norton, 2008), 92.

9. John Bowlby, *Attachment and Loss, vol. 1, Attachment*, 2nd ed. (London: Hogarth, 1982), 176.

10. Brené Brown, *Daring Greatly: How the Courage to Be Vulnerable Transforms the Way We Live, Love, Parent, and Lead* (New York: Gotham Books, 2012), 113.

11. Richard Jacobson, *Unchurching: Christianity without Churchianity* (United States: Unchurching Books, 2016), pp. 169-170.

12. Melba Colgrove, Harold H. Bloomfield, and Peter McWilliams, *How to Survive the Loss of a Love* (Los Angeles: Prelude Press, 1991), 72.

13. Lysa TerKeurst, *Unglued: Making Wise Choices in the Midst of Raw Emotions* (Grand Rapids: Zondervan, 2012), 44.

14. Dietrich Bonhoeffer, *Life Together: Prayerbook of the Bible.* Edited by Geffrey B. Kelly. Minneapolis, MN: Fortress Press, 1996), 110.

CHAPTER EIGHT

1. For a detailed exploration of the concept of Hell, see Keith Giles, *Jesus Undefeated: Condemning the False Doctrine of Eternal Torment* (Quoir, 2019) or J. D. Myers, *What is Hell?: The Truth About Hell and How to Avoid It* (Redeeming Press, 2019).

2. Leonard I. Sweet, *So Beautiful Divine Design for Life and the Church: Missional, Relational, Incarnational* (Colorado Springs: David C. Cook, 2009), 46.

3. I am aware that "the lizard brain" is a term that is going out of style and is a term that oversimplifies very complex cognitive processes.

4. Winell, 1.

5. Philips, 48.

6. Ibid., 49.

7. See Ronda L. Dearing and June Price Tangney, eds., *Shame in the Therapy Hour* (Washington, DC: American Psychological Association, 2011), 4.

8. Jeff Turner, *The Atheistic Theist: Why There is No God and You Should Follow Him*, (Amazon Digital Services, 2016), n.p.

9. Jerry Basel and Denise Basel, *The Missing Commandment: Love Yourself* (Grand Rapids: Heart & Life Publishers, 2013), 18.

10. Tania Bright, *Don't Beat Yourself Up: Learning the Wisdom of Kindsight* (Oxford: Monarch Books, 2015), 79.

11. Kim Fredrickson, *Give Yourself a Break: Turning Your Inner Critic into a Compassionate Friend* (Grand Rapids: Revell, 2015), 16.

12. See Christopher Germer and Kristin Neff, *Teaching the Mindful Self-Compassion Program: A Guide for Professionals* (New York, New York: The Guilford Press, 2019).

13. Henri J. M. Nouwen and Michael J. Christensen, *Spiritual Formation: Following the Movements of the Spirit* (New York: HarperCollins, 2010), 46.

14. Galatians 5:22–23.

15. Annie Maheux and Matthew Price, "The Indirect Effect of Social Support on Post-trauma Psychopathology via Self-compassion," *Personality and Individual Differences*, 88 (2016):102–7, doi:10.1016/j.paid.2015.08.051.

CHAPTER NINE

1. Alan L. Sroufe 2005. "Attachment and Development: A Prospective, Longitudinal Study from Birth to Adulthood." *Attachment & Human Development* 7 (4): 349–67. doi:10.1080/14616730500365928.

2. Hall, Todd W., Annie Fujikawa, Sarah R. Halcrow, Peter C. Hill, and Harold Delane. 2009. "Attachment to God and Implicit Spirituality: Clarifying Correspondence and Compensation Models." Journal of Psychology and Theology 37 (4): 227–42. http://0 search.ebscohost.com.library.alliant. edu/login.aspx?direct=true&db=psyh&AN=2010-00145-001&site=ehost-live&scope=site.

3. prodigal. Dictionary.com. *Dictionary.com Unabridged*. Random House, Inc. http://www.dictionary.com/browse/prodigal (accessed: August 6, 2016).

4. John Dominic Crossan, *The Greatest Prayer: Rediscovering the Revolutionary Message of the Lord's Prayer* (New York: HarperCollins, 2010), 40.

5. Ibid, 22.

6. Tim Desmond, *How to Stay Human in a F*Cked-Up World: Mindfulness Practices for Real Life*. (San Francisco: HarperOne, 2019), 127.

7. Ibid.

CHAPTER 10

1. For a more extensive overview of these topics, I encourage you to read my book, *Divine Echoes* and Thomas Oord's book, *God Can't*.

2. Matthew 5:48

3. For a deeper understanding of the topic of God's uncontrolling love, see Oord, Thomas J. *The Uncontrolling Love of God: An Open and Relational Account of Providence*. Downers Grove, IL: InterVarsity Press, 2016.

4. William Hasker, *God, Time, and Knowledge* (Ithaca, NY: Cornell University Press, 1989), 196, author's italics removed.

5. "Control," *Oxford Dictionary of English*, 3rd ed. (Oxford: Oxford University Press, 2010).

6. Gregory A. Boyd, *Crucifixion of the Warrior God: Volumes 1 & 2* (Minneapolis: Augsburg Fortress, 2017), 491–92.

7. Sarah Bessey, *Miracles and Other Reasonable Things: A Story of Unlearning and Relearning God*. (New York: Howard Books, Atria, 2019).

8. Timothy Keller, *Walking with God through Pain and Suffering* (New York: Penguin Books, 2016), 4.

9. Thomas Jay Oord, *God Can't: How to Believe in God and Love after Tragedy, Abuse, or Other Evils* (SacraSage Press, 2019), 14.

10. Oord, 87.

11. Elliot Aronson, *The Social Animal*. 11th ed. (New York: Worth Publishers, 2012), 51.

12. Fischer, P., J. I. Krueger, T. Greitemeyer, C. Vogrincic, A. Kastenmüller, D. Frey, and M. Kainbacher. "The bystander-effect: A meta-analytic review on bystander intervention in dangerous and non-dangerous emergencies." *Psychological Bulletin* 137, no. 4 (2011): 517–37. doi:10.1037/a0023304.

13. Oord, 200.

CHAPTER ELEVEN

1. Thomas Merton and P. Connell, *Thomas Merton: Selected Essays*, repr. ed. (Maryknoll, NY: Orbis Books, 2014), 238.

2. Thomas Keating, *Open Mind, Open Heart: The Contemplative Dimension of the Gospel* (New York: Amity House, 1986).

3. Thomas Keating, *Centering Prayer: A Training Course for Opening to the Presence of God* (Boulder, CO: Sounds True, 2009), 24.

4. Ibid., 36.

5. Leanne Payne, *The Healing Presence: How God's Grace Can Work in You to Bring Healing in Your Broken Places and the Joy of Living in His Love* (Westchester, IL: Crossway Books, 1989), 61.

6. Chris Ann Waters, *Seasons of Goodbye: Working Your Way Through Loss* (Notre Dame, IN: Sorin Books, 2000), 116–17.

7. See Jaak Panksepp and L. Biven, *The Archaeology of Mind: Neuroevolutionary Origins of Human Emotions* (New York: Norton, 2012).

8. John Bowlby, *Attachment and Loss* Volume 1 Attachment (New: Basic Books, 1969), 66.

9. Jim Palmer, *Divine Nobodies: Shedding Religion to Find God (and the Unlikely People Who Help You)* (Nashville, TN: W Pub. Group, 2006), 71.

10. Geoffrey W. Bromiley, *The International Standard Bible Encyclopedia, vol. 3* (Grand Rapids: Eerdmans, 1988), 64.

11. Kevin F. Brien, *The Ignatian Adventure: Experiencing the Spiritual Exercises of Saint Ignatius in Daily Life* (Chicago: Loyola Press, 2011), 141.

12. Lutz Antoine, Julie Brefczynski-Lewis, Tom Johnstone, Richard J Davidson (2008) Regulation of the Neural Circuitry of Emotion by Compassion Meditation: Effects of Meditative Expertise. PLoS ONE 3(3): e1897. doi:10.1371/journal.pone.0001897.

CHAPTER TWELVE

1. Xue Zheng, Ryan Fehr, Kenneth Tai, Jayanth Narayanan, and Michele J. Gelfand. 2015. "The Unburdening Effects of Forgiveness: Effects on Slant Perception and Jumping Height." Social Psychological and Personality Science 6 (4): 431–38. doi:10.1177/1948550614564222.

2. Ross W. May, Marcos A Sanchez-Gonzalez, Kirsten A Hawkins, Wayne B Batchelor, and Frank D Fincham. 2014. "Effect of Anger and Trait Forgiveness on Cardiovascular Risk in Young Adult Females." *The American Journal of Cardiology* 114 (1): 47–52. doi:10.1016/j.amjcard.2014.04.007.

3. Erick Messias et al., "Bearing Grudges and Physical Health: Relationship to Smoking, Cardiovascular Health and Ulcers," *Social Psychiatry and Psychiatric Epidemiology* 45, no. 2 (2010):183–7. *MEDLINE with Full Text*, EBSCO*host*. http://0-dx.doi.org.library.alliant.edu/10.1007/s00127-009-0054-0.